TEACHING AND ADDRESSES
ON CHRISTIAN SCIENCE

TEACHING AND ADDRESSES ON CHRISTIAN SCIENCE

EDWARD A. KIMBALL

This volume consists largely of notes and reports by various students from extemporaneous addresses and from class teaching by Mr. Kimball, covering a period of fifteen years of his activity, which notes have been extensively copied and widely circulated in typewritten manuscript for a number of years.

COLLECTED, COMPLIED, EDITED,

TOPICALLY ANALYZED AND INDEXED

by

Rev. G. A. Kratzer

ISBN 0-930227-15-8

Published by
The Bookmark
Post Office Box 801143
Santa Clarita, California 91380
United States of America

THIS VOLUME IS DEDICATED TO MARY BAKER EDDY, THE REVELATOR OF CHRISTIAN SCIENCE TO THIS AGE, AND TO STUDENTS OF THIS SCIENCE. THE UTTERANCES OF CONSCIOUS MIND SET FORTH IN THIS BOOK ESTABLISH FOREVER "ON EARTH, AMONG MEN" THE IMMORTALITY OF ONE OF THE WORLD'S FOREMOST METAPHYSICIANS, BELOVED EDWARD A. KIMBALL, C.S.D. FOR A STUDENT TO APPROPRIATE AND PRACTICE THE PURITY OF METAPHYSICAL APPLICATION HEREIN DECLARED, AS LIKEWISE TAUGHT IN "SCIENCE AND HEALTH," IS TO CONSCIOUSLY REALIZE AT-ONE-MENT WITH THE LIVING, IMMORTAL PRESENCE OF EDWARD A. KIMBALL, AND MARY BAKER EDDY, THEREBY BECOMING A LIVING MONUMENT TO TWO OF THE GREATEST EXPONENTS OF ETERNAL TRUTH.

"Whoever in any age expresses most of the spirit of Truth and Love, the Principle of God's idea, has most of the spirit of Christ, of that Mind which was in Christ Jesus."—Mrs. Eddy in "Pulpit and Press," page 75.

TABLE OF CONTENTS

	PAGE
PREFACE	7
INTRODUCTION	9

PART I. SPECIAL ADDRESSES

GOD AND MAN	15
WORDS SPOKEN FROM EXPERIENCE	18
THE CURTAIN LECTURE	27
OPERATIVE CHRISTIAN SCIENCE	40
THE CAUSE OF CHRISTIAN SCIENCE	49
TALK AT FORT WORTH	71
ASSOCIATION ADDRESS, 1908	77
ADDRESS TO WORKERS	98

PART II. MISCELLANEOUS NOTES

These cannot be listed under titles, but occupy pages 133-192

PART III. DESTROYING EVIL

THE GREAT GIFT OF GOD	195
RISE IN THE STRENGTH OF SPIRIT	197
FAITH, INTUITION, SCIENCE	199
TALK ON SUPPLY	201
AN OPEN LETTER	203
LETTER TO A PATIENT	205
TREATMENT OF A TREATMENT	209
ANIMAL MAGNETISM DESCRIBED	211
MALICIOUS ANIMAL MAGNETISM	214

	PAGE
MENTAL WICKEDNESS DEALT WITH	218
SOME WILES OF THE DEVIL	221
QUENCHING THE FIERY DARTS OF THE WICKED	224

PART IV. PUBLIC LECTURES

PROOF OF THE EXISTENCE AND NATURE OF GOD	231
THE ENFORCEMENT OF LAW	234
ACTIVITY IN THE TRUTH	241
SCIENCE OF MIND AND THOUGHT	250
WHAT THINK YE OF CHRIST?	274
HUMANITY'S NORMAL RIGHTS AND POWERS	299
KIMBALL REPLIES TO CHAPMAN	313
VICTORY OVER FEAR	330
THE CAUSE AND SCIENTIFIC CURE OF DISEASE	339

PREFACE

On page 297 of "Miscellany," appears the following declaration by Mary Baker Eddy:
"*My beloved Edward A. Kimball, whose clear, correct teaching of Christian Science has been and is an inspiration to the whole field, is here now as veritably as when he visited me a year ago. If we would awaken to this recognition, we should see him here and realize that he never died; thus demonstrating the fundamental truth of Christian Science.*"
In "Miscellany," page 120, Mrs. Eddy has written:
"*We look for the sainted Revelator in his writings, and there we find him. Those who look for me in person, or elsewhere than in my writings, lose me instead of find me.*"
On May 6th, 1904, Mrs. Eddy caused the following statement to be published in The Christian Science Sentinel, under the heading—

"CHRISTIAN SCIENCE BOARD OF EDUCATION."

"The Magna Charta of Christian Science means much, multum in parvo,—all-in-one and one-in-all. It stands for the inalienable, universal rights of men. Essentially democratic, its government is administered by the common consent of the governed, wherein and whereby man governed by his Creator is self-governed.

"The Church is the mouthpiece of Christian Science,—its law and gospel are according to Christ Jesus; its rules are health, holiness, and immortality,—equal rights and privileges, equality of the sexes, rotation in office.

"*The long term of the incumbent teacher in the Board of Education, Mr. Edward A. Kimball, C. S. D., expires in June next, when he retires crowned with honors—his Teacher and Leader loving him, his students praising him, and the race benefited by his labors. May his successor go and do likewise.*"

INTRODUCTION

In some of the classes of Mr. Edward A. Kimball, C. S. D., notes, shorthand or otherwise, were taken by various students, and considerable material was given by dictation. The present volume contains a set of such notes taken in his last class by one of his most capable students, a full report of the Association Address following, also notes by students in other classes.

Mr. Kimball, at various times, spoke before practitioners and other prominent workers, and gave them special instruction on the needs of the cause and on methods of working in healing the sick. This book contains shorthand reports of some of the addresses so given, and of several other addresses delivered at various times, which have never appeared in print, and reports of some public lectures printed in local newspapers, but never published in form for preservation.

The material above described has been extensively copied and recopied, and widely circulated in manuscript form for a number of years. These notes and reports undoubtedly correctly represent, with reasonable accuracy, the subject-matter and the spirit of Mr. Kimball's teaching, and are very valuable to workers in Christian Science, else they would not have continued to have the wide and increasing circulation in manuscript, to which they were attaining.

That there can be no certainty of Mr. Kimball's exact words in all cases is a matter of no great moment; for this volume doubtless represents his utterances as correctly as the four Gospels represent the teachings of Jesus, and as the Pauline Epistles represent the original text of Paul's letters to the various churches which he had founded.

As is well known, Jesus never wrote anything, and there is no evidence that his disciples took any immediate notes of the instruction which he gave them; but, aferward, they set down what they could remember. No original text of any of the Pauline Epistles is extant, but the Greek manuscripts from which our present New Testament is compiled and translated consist, both in the case of the Gospels and the remaining materials, of copies which had gone through the recopying process a number of times, with all the consequent liability to changes, omissions and additions, in the verbal statement. It is well known that scholars differ as to what the exact wording should be in the Greek text at thousands of points in the New Testament. Nevertheless, there is probably no one who would hold that this would be adequate reason for never having published the New Testament, or for now discarding it. Though there doubtless are some faults and misrepresentations, it is nevertheless regarded by all Christians as distinctly worth while.

The present volume subserves exactly the same purpose for the most practical portion of Mr. Kimball's life work as a teacher of Christian Science, as is served by the New Testament for the teachings of Jesus and his immediate disciples. Neither the Gospels nor the other portions of these Christian records were put into writing primarily with any thought of publication. They were intended for special and personal use, and, without doubt, had, at the start, only a private circulation. The writers of the original texts had no idea of any general publication. At the first, possessors of copies of these texts merely allowed friends to make other copies for personal use; and these friends, in turn, allowed others to make copies; and, finally, through this wider circulation, these texts attracted so much attention on account of their value, that a demand arose that they should be edited and established in permanent form; and this was done, as far as possible, in an age when the printing press had not yet appeared. When the art of printing was invented, as is well known, the manuscripts composing the Bible were among the first to be given to the world in print, as a product of this new art.

So there is abundant precedent, of the highest order, for doing just what has been done with the valuable material now presented to the reading public in this volume, entitled, "Teaching and Addresses," which its editor and publisher believes will meet with the wide demand which its importance and usefulness would naturally indicate.

A claim has been set up in certain quarters that there is doubt as to the authenticity of some of the manuscript material in circulation, and attributed to Mr. Kimball's teaching as a source. Be that as it may, Mr. Kimball's style of speech and writing and the terminology which he used were so strongly characteristic that any of his students, or others who are familiar with his published articles, when they read this volume, will feel absolutely assured that every paragraph which it contains emanated from Mr. Kimball's utterance. The style is unmistakable and inimitable.

Even if it were possible that some of these articles or fragments were not records of Mr. Kimball's speech or writing, there are still some important facts to consider. The consensus of the scholarship of the world is in agreement that no one knows who originally uttered most of the material in the first five books of the Bible, long supposed to have been written by Moses; but it is pretty generally agreed that if Moses was the author of some of the material embodied in them, he never saw the books in anything like their present form, and nobody knows to a certainty who put them in their present form, even as to the Hebrew texts from which our English translations are made. There is grave doubt among many scholars whether Isaiah wrote some portions of the book attributed to him. Many psalms long accredited to David are now regarded as not being of his authorship. Coming to the New Testament, many question whether Paul wrote the Letter to the Hebrews, and if he did not, nobody knows who did. Likewise, there is considerable doubt as to the authorship of the Book of Revelation. Yet who would have these books omitted from our Bible because of the possibility, or even probability, that they were not written by the men whose names are attached to them, or because it is impossible to know to a certainty who did write them? People who might be inclined to be prejudiced against this volume recording Mr. Kimball's utterances should, by parity of reasoning, be prejudiced against their Bibles.

As to the accuracy of statement, Christian Science is an exact science, deducible from a fixed Principle, and it is therefore possible to know, and easy to determine, whether a given sentence is correctly scientific, independently of certainty as to the exact words of the original pronouncement. The present volume is substantially the utterance of Edward A. Kimball, and, with the careful editing which it has been given, it is the exact and unadulterated utterance of Truth, which, after all, is alone of primary importance; for the real Edward A. Kimball expressed and now expresses the exact Truth, and could express nothing else.

THE EDITOR.

PART I
SPECIAL ADDRESSES

GOD AND MAN

Short Address Delivered in 1900

God is absolutely All, at this moment, and God is good; hence it is an absolutely incontrovertible, unchanging fact that there is nothing in the universe but Good and Its perfect effect.

This God is Mind, forever conscious of its own selfhood, and never was and never will be conscious of anything else. Mind is eternally one, and this One is all-inclusive. It is now including all that by any possibility can be needed for perfect Mind.

Mind is self-governed. It is now and forever conscious of its own divine impulsion, Love. It is inspired by, energized by, prompted by and forever moving in accordance with this one and only impulsion, Love.

For this reason, Mind—the only Intelligence—is calm, trustful, tranquil and eternally confident, because it is simply experiencing the potency of its own nature, Love.

Therefore, there is in the limitless realm of Mind no possibility or occasion for fear. There is nothing in Love to engender fear, nothing in Mind to cognize it, nothing in Good to maintain it, no room in the universe of Love for any such thing.

Mind—perfect Self-Consciousness—knowing Itself to be One, and forever governing Itself, forms the basis of Its perfect nature, Love, and is immortal Life. This means that—since everything that Mind holds in consciousness is evidence—expression—of Itself, and Itself is substance, Mind simply now realizes that It is experiencing immortality.

All the ideas in the universe, at this instant, are statements of this one Mind; therefore they are kept, maintained, vitalized, governed and directed by Itself, everlasting Good.

These ideas constitute the Word of God, which—according to His promise—shall accomplish that whereunto they are sent.

This Mind, filling all space, leaves no room for any other mind; containing all that can by any possibility be needed for life, action or power, leaves nothing to compose any other mind; and being conscious of acting as infinite causation, leaves no cause or element of causation for any other mind.

This conscious Mind, being conscious of completeness, of satisfaction, of infinite knowing, makes it an utter impossibility that there can be, ever was or ever will be, another mind.

This one Mind, including all and being All, can never know, meet or have, opposition. There is nothing to oppose, to oppose for, to oppose with, no method of procedure, no medium, and no cause, action, or power for any such thing, because God is All and cannot oppose Himself.

Being All, God is perfectly conscious of His own divine authority, simply knows the perfection of His own government, realizes His own limitless control, has evidence—proof —of His own unopposed supremacy.

He is conscious of doing whatsoever He will, and His will is good. Mind, therefore, is all the government, legislation, law, and operation of law there is, and this law is incontrovertible, infinite in extent and power.

Man is forever enfolded within the perfect consciousness of Good. He cannot get away, for one instant, from the protecting, loving, all-inspiring, all-sustaining, all-seeing, all-controlling purity of Love.

He has no care, no responsibility, nothing to arrange, to plan, to accomplish, to get, to long for, because he simply has all possible good.

There is no future in the eternal now of infinite Mind. Hence, there is no future in which to realize Truth, or to know

God, or to reach perfection, and no demonstration to make, because the only demonstration there is, ever was, or ever will be, is God's, and that is made now, and man is the knowledge of this fact. He simply knows, beyond the shadow of a doubt, the eternal facts of being in Good.

He, man, has spiritual cognition, complete conviction of good, knows Good to be one in government, one in power, one in activity, one eternal presence, one consciousness, one tangible, veritable state of being.

What he eternally is, is the consciousness of Good, the spiritual discernment of Truth, the knowledge of one Mind. He is one state of pure, natural, unclouded consciousness, acting, moving, having his perfect being in the unchanging love of God.

He cannot fall from his high estate. His dominion cannot be taken away. He cannot lose his God-given knowledge. He cannot be misguided, misled, fooled in any way, since all He knows is Mind, God.

WORDS SPOKEN FROM EXPERIENCE

Continuation of Mr. Kimball's answers to questions propounded to him before the Bloomington (Ill.) Chautauqua, November, 1894.

Mr. Kimball's Healing

Seven years ago, after wandering about the earth in the fruitless search for health, I turned in despair, and as a last resort, to Christian Science, and was healed. I have been the beneficiary of its mighty influence in such abundant degree that if I failed, whenever suitable opportunity occurred, to lift my voice in grateful testimony thereof, "the very stones would cry out against me." I make this personal statement because I wish it known that I speak from the standpoint of actual proof and not theory.

Christian Science, Why the Name?

Christian Science! Why is it called Science, and why Christian? It is called Science because it is the statement of an immutable and infinite Principle with an invariable rule, which, when understood, is manifested in absolute demonstration—unmistakable, immortal proof to the demonstrator. It is often said: "I do not like the use of the word Science in connection with religion; it makes it seem cold and cheerless." Ah, dear friend, have you forgotten that nearly every modern creed, including that of your own denomination, expressly declares that God is omniscience—**all science?**

Science, Nature of

Do you not know that if God, who is Love, is all science, then Love is the **Substance** of Science? Love that transcends in warmth and cheer and blessed continuity the most lofty flights of human imagination. Do you not know that humanity has degraded its own sense of science until it means to it little more than study or investigation, and that this low estimate is the man of straw that you condemn?

Science, Meaning of

The term Science, properly understood, refers only to the laws of God and His government, inclusive of man; and the highest definition of the word must be synonymous with Truth. If you were to go to school to study mathematics, you might learn that the science of mathematics is the highest finite sense of truth, but you would also learn that the only possible way for you to learn that science would be to gain a demonstrable understanding of the principle, and then prove it for yourself. This is true of any of the exact sciences, and there is no such thing as an **inexact** science.

Christian Science Defined

But as relates to infinite science—the science of Life, of Being—people are educated to believe that they may think anything they please. God being all Science, we must see that all science is projected by God and not by man, and that God is always manifested scientifically, and that whatever is not scientific is not of God.

Science Called Christian

It is claimed for Christian Science that it is the truth about God and God's laws and their relation to man including the universe. It is called **Christian** because Jesus, who did the will of his Father, manifested the infinite will of infinite Good—he manifested the science and law of God.

Law, Nature of

Mortals have been limiting their idea of the infinite within the radius of their own finite sense; but when we gain a supersensible understanding of God, we get a larger grasp of the vast import of the term "infinite God," and begin to see that God and His will—His laws and power—are eternal, changeless, impartial, universal, unlimited, the same yesterday, today and forever, never spasmodic, intermittent, or local in nature or operation.

Laws of God Infinitely Natural

Does it detract from your estimate or opinion of God, to contemplate the entire action of the divine nature as scientific, when you perceive that it means the manifestation of demonstrable, omnipotent Truth? Are you losing any hold on heaven in seeing that the laws of God are divinely natural, and that only the natural and scientific law of God is real or true, and that God is manifested in no other way than naturally?

Christianity Scientific

Jesus the Christ, the founder of the true worship of God, said of himself, "I came to do the will of my Father," and if we admit that he manifested God and reflected His infinite will, then there is no other conclusion than that the Messianic mission, and all that it includes, was scientific; and that the proper understanding of that mission, as disclosed by the words and works of Jesus, constitutes scientific religion or Christian Science, which is a religion with "signs following."

Proof by Works

The signs that followed as proof or demonstration of Christianity in Jesus' time were manifested in the destruction of evil, the reformation of the sinner, the healing of the sick, the raising of the dead, the casting out of devils, and the preaching of the gospel of salvation, all in obedience to the universal law of God. And the universality of this law was recognized and disclosed by Jesus when he said: "These signs shall follow them that believe."

Law Invariable

Does it lessen your esteem for Jesus' work, for you to know that it was the manifestation of infinite will rather than a special supernatural or miraculous law, the very enactment of which would necessitate a departure from the infinite, which is impossible? Did the Infinite ever become less than infinite? Was eternal law ever fluctuated for special effect outside of the universal purpose and order established by Him whose work as the Principle of the universe was all done before Abraham was?

Principle Unchangeable

Finally, it is called **Science,** because the declaration of Principle which it includes cannot be changed. If it could be changed, altered, amended or revised, the entire structure would collapse. Demonstrable Truth cannot be changed, for it is eternal and infinite. Error alone is changeable, and any statement of dogma or doctrine that needs alteration must be error.

Changeless Ethics

Plato gave to the world a code of ethics that seemed to serve the needs of humanity for hundreds of years. The same is true of the ecclesiasticism of Judah. But not until we get the words of Jesus, do we realize that they alone will provide perpetually for the human necessity, and that they need no alteration; for they are in accord with the omniscience of God.

Christian Science Misunderstood

I do not think of any subject now before the world that is so little understood, or so thoroughly misunderstood, as is Christian Science. A celebrated Frenchman once said: "My history is being written by mine enemies." I will not apply this statement in full to Christian Science, but it is a fact that almost the entire bulk of opinion concerning it proceeds from those who have not one atom of understanding of what it really is, and whose opinion refers solely to their false concept of it. There is a general impression, however, that it presents to the public two particular phases. One is as a religion, and the other is as a remedial or healing agency.

Science, Religious Aspect of

Let us consider its religious aspect. What is religion? True theology must pertain to God, Truth. False theology is a false conception and does not pertain to God, but is error. True theology pertains to the infinite and immutable and **must itself** be changeless and universal, otherwise it would be contrary to God.

Theology, True and False

Instead of there being a universal religion, reflecting the nature of divinity, there are thousands of beliefs—all different. Only one of many contradictory statements of God can possibly be right. Which one is it? Because God is infinite, it does not follow as a possibility that he can be outlined and declared by an infinite variety of diverse and conflicting opinions.

Good Intentions Not Sufficient

It has come to be a habit of thought with us, to assume that, if a man subscribes to some religious belief and endeavors to live up to his highest sense of God and God's law, it is enough; but this amiable though fatal compromise must be seen as a most desolating error, and we must learn that to **know God aright** is "life eternal." An erroneous, limited, finite human conception of Deity does not mean the consciousness of eternal life. Nor have we any assurance that we are obeying the laws of God if we do not **know** what they are.

Understanding versus Belief

It is not sufficient that a man should obey his own opinion of what they are. True religion must include the understanding of the universal truth of God, and true worship must include the obedience to the universal will or law of God. Only in this way can we "know God," and in this way alone will the image and likeness of God appear.

Sectarianism and Its Fruits

What is your conclusion when you survey the bewildering array of belief about God, who can only be known as He is? Do they indicate to your mind that the world at large understands God, and that religion at large really pertains to the **one** only true God? The Christian will admit that the Confucian does not know God, and the Mohammedan is certain that the Christian does not; but it is a matter of history that the differences between the Christian sects themselves have most disturbed the current of modern events.

What Is Christianity

Continuing our definition of religion, let us inquire what is Christianity? Shall we not say that it is the knowledge of God as taught by Jesus Christ, whom we are accustomed to describe as "God manifested in the flesh"? If he manifested the unity of the infinite, must we not see that the Truth he revealed is universal Truth; and if we say that he taught a religion, it must have been a universal religion; and if he established a church, it was a universal church. If we as Christians are not manifesting this universal understanding, is it not palpable that we do not understand the teachings of him who was the manifestation of divine unity? At this point it is usually suggested that in all the fundamental and vital particulars the Christian religions are essentially the same.

Denominational Beliefs

Let us see if this is really so, and without making any extensive comparison of the different dogmas, we can test our thought on this subject by a few questions. Is it essentially the same to you whether you have been predestined and elected by God to be damned or not? If you are a heathen or an infant, is it in that event essentially the same to you whether, for that fact alone, you are to be damned or not? Is it essentially the same to you whether human destiny is to be wrought out in universal salvation or eternal hell? Is it the same thing to you whether Christ is divine or not? Whether there is a personal devil or not; whether infants are regenerated by baptism or not; whether there is probationary opportuntiy after death or not; whether the Scripture record is unerring or not; or whether forgiveness of sin through the human process known as absolution is valid and efficacious or not? These few of many questions will serve to direct our thought and judgment to some of the denominational beliefs which are flatly denied and rejected by others.

False Doctrine, Effect of

Instead of being essentially the same and essentially Christlike in effect, many of these beliefs have manifested themselves in the most desolating wars, murders, persecutions, torture, oppression, and other forms of violence and hatred that deface the pages of history. Shall we ignore the current status of belief, thought and events, and try to allure ourselves to the mischievous conclusion that these contentions have ceased, that the Christian sects are now in harmony and accord with the Mind that was also in Christ Jesus, and that the theology of today is in a state of permanent composure?

Christian Science Demonstrably True

Upon this scene of conflicting dogmas and sectarian turmoil appears Christian Science as a new statement of the understanding of God as revealed by the words and works of Jesus. It heralds itself, not as a new religious belief, but as a demonstrable declaration of God, including or revealing a demonstrable understanding of the words and works of Jesus. It is a statement of Truth which all men can prove to be truth. In other words, it appears as a religion in the highest sense which is demonstrably true and universal. In this respect it is unique in history. There is no other religion claiming to rest on a demonstrable principle, or proof rather than profession, on understanding and signs following, instead of belief and conjecture.

Affirmations of Christian Science

What does it declare? It affirms that God is the supreme Being, Infinite, omnipotent, omniscient, omnipresent, the Life of man, Cause of the universe, the allness of Truth, Love, Intelligence, and Substance, whom to know aright is life eternal. It affirms the immortality of Life, the divinity of Christ, and the actuality of his resurrection and ascension. It acknowledges him as the way and the only way of salvation. It demands absolute obedience to the ten commandments and the sermon on the mount. It demands the annihilation of sin and shows mankind how to resist and destroy it. It demands the elimination of disease, and shows humanity how this is to be accomplished. Its legitimate action is to reform the sinner, reclaim the infidel, to heal the sick and cast out evil of every kind, to establish a better citizenship, a grander manhood, a higher morality, a purer individual and social status, an expanded love for God and the neighbor, and the manifestation of the universal brotherhood of man in God, who is Love.

Needs of Humanity

Unless human conduct is progressing in accord with this, it is not obedient to Christian Science; it is not in obedience to him who is the way of salvation. What is that way, and how is it applicable to the needs of humanity? Let us first see what are the needs of humanity. Look down the vistas of human experience and behold men in the fitful, though vain pursuit of satisfaction. You behold the inveterate anguish of their lot, their poverty, their sin, their beds of pain and disease, the jails and asylums, the broken hearts, the hideous fear, the open graves, and "man's inhumanity to man."

Salvation, Where Found?

Now ask yourself, Is humantiy in need of salvation? If so, where shall salvation be found? Is it to be found in mystery and conjecture, in the mere promise of future felicity, or is it to be found in the speedy and actual destruction of evil? The Bible says of our Saviour that he came to bear witness to the Truth, and that his mission was to destroy the works of the devil. This, then, is the real work of salvation—to destroy evil. And how did he bear witness to the Truth or Science, and manifest it, and how did he destroy the works of the devil? By reforming the sinner, healing the sick, casting out devils, raising the dead and preaching the gospel of salvation, and he said that all that believed on him (understood his teachings) should do these things, and greater things than these, and that there was no other way under heaven whereby men should be saved. Obedience to this demand upon the followers of Christ manifested itself for three centuries in the healing of the sick as a natural phenomenon of Christianity. Christian Science in its applicability to humanity is the declaration that there is a divine remedy available to men, and sets forth the rediscovery of the healing Principle of Christianity and the rule of demonstration whereby men may acquaint themselves with God and be at peace.

THE CURTAIN LECTURE
Address Delivered July 1st, 1899

In speaking to Christian Scientists it is not a part of my work to sugar-coat with soft speeches. I am here to join you in mutual congratulations, because the most wonderful thing that ever happened to any being on this planet has happened to us, in that we have become Christian Scientists.

Significance of Christian Science

What does it mean? It means that an ordinary human being, absolutely immersed in ignorance, sin, superstition, pain, death—everything that is miserable and disagreeable—has had bestowed upon him an understanding of the facts of Being which operates in his behalf, rescues him from his would-be destroyer, puts his feet upon the rock of Life, opens unto him the doorway of heaven, establishes in him the sure confidence that his Redeemer lives and is redeeming him.

Fidelity of Great Religious Leaders

You remember Jesus said, "Your fathers would have rejoiced to see my day." Do you not know that all of the intelligent religious worthies, the very beacon lights in religious history, held with sublime fidelity and uncompromising allegiance to their understanding of God, rather than to become recreant to duty, and rather than to become posthumous in the sight of God?

A Demonstrable Understanding Bestowed Upon You

Do you not suppose that they, every one of them, would have rejoiced, could they have seen your day,—a demonstrable knowledge of that of which they never had more than an undefinable intuitional sense? They never understood the real Science of their own inspiration. But how about you? There has been bestowed upon you this demonstrable understanding, so that you need wander no longer in the mazes of speculation and perplexity to find yourself ultimately shipwrecked upon the rock of despair, doubt and dismay?

Christian Scientists Not Getting What They Should

I am persuaded, in this day of Christian Science, that the Christian Scientists themselves do not get one hundredth part of the good out of Christian Science that they should, not one hundredth part of the benefit that they should be getting, and it is to inquire as to the reason, rather than to cry "Hallelujah," upon the supposition that we are getting it, that I come to speak to you tonight.

Shortcomings of Scientists

I do not think that what I am about to say should be dignified by the name of a lecture, unless we were to call it a "Curtain Lecture." I shall talk as much to myself as I do to you, and I hope to derive benefit from what I shall say. See that you do not have any sense of displeasure, if I call attention to some of your shortcomings in the hope that we may mend our ways, that we may lay hold upon larger possibilities, and that we may soon be able to say that we are approaching the goal of results and the goal of fruition.

The Command to "Heal the Sick"

Now, this gospel salvation bestows upon you certain privileges. We are apt to call them "duties"; and one of them comes in the way of a command. It is really a misnomer to call it a command, but let it be so. "Heal the sick." Now, are Christian Scientists healing the sick? No. Are we taking God at His word? No; not as a class. A very large portion of the Christian Scientists are not taking God at His word at all, or at least very little. Why is it?

Scientists Begin to Make Excuses

How often we hear such words as these: "I cannot heal the sick; I have not enough understanding; Mrs. So-and-so, she has a lovely understanding. I wish I had; and if I had such an understanding, I would move mountains; I would so delight to heal the sick and help those people." Or perhaps the suggestion comes thus: "I am not good enough. I am not worthy to heal the sick. I wish I were good enough;" and so on; a lot of beautiful reasons of this kind. Where do they come from? Are they from God, too? Is that part of the saving program? Do you not think, if God in His infinite wisdom presented to you a way of salvation and told you what you must do in order to follow in it, and then told you that you could not do it, that it would be a most exasperating mockery?

God Commissions You to Heal

When God tells you to heal the sick, it means that you can do it. He says that you can. "Satan came also and stood in the midst of them," and there are a great many Christian Scientists who are mesmerized up to their very eyes by the suggestion that they cannot heal the sick, and that they cannot do this, that and the other thing, in the way of demonstration. Why is it that we are so easily swayed by error in this particular? It is because we do not have the correct understanding of what it is that heals the sick.

False Sense of What Heals

Now, if I get the belief that I as a person, or that I as a Christian Scientist, am a healer; that it is because of some virtue of mine, or something that is worthy in me, or anything that I can possibly wield, that the sick are healed, then that sense of healing is so defective that it is liable to be swayed at any time. It is just as likely to wake up in the morning and think that it cannot heal as to think that it can.

Should a Person Under a Claim Treat Others?

A man said to me one day: "Do you know, I think that I had better not take any more patients. I have a claim of rheumatism that I have not entirely overcome, and I think I had better not take any more patients until I have overcome it. What do you think about it?" I replied: "I do not think your rheumatism will heal the sick. Indeed, I do not think your body, sick or well, will heal the sick; and until you find out that, when the sick are healed, it is in spite of, and regardless of, your body—until you learn that, perhaps you had better not take any more patients, because you do not understand how the sick are healed."

God the Only Healer

Now, how many healers are there? Just one healer of the sick. And what one is that? God. God is the only healer of the sick. Just one. Is He good enough to heal? Is He worthy? Has He enough understanding to heal the sick? Now, when we come to learn what it is that heals the sick, we will stop denying that the healer can heal. Just to the extent that you can find Christian Scientists who say they cannot heal the sick, they do not understand what it is that heals, and as soon as you find a Christian Scientist who understands that God is the only healer, then you find one who stops saying that He cannot do it.

Christ Is Your Consciousness which Heals

How does God heal the sick? Through His son, Christ. Let us see what is happening. We talk about our realizing the Truth, and my declaring the Truth, and my holding somebody in the Truth, my holding the Truth for some one else, and a lot of statements of that kind. Do you know what they are? What do they mean? What is really happening? It is the Truth, or God, good, or divine Intelligence, or wisdom—whatever you choose to give as the name for that which is infinite—this very Truth itself is your consciousness.

"I Am God," Who Heals

God is All, the only doer, the only actor, the only Saviour, the only governor of man. Man does not govern himself by his own wisdom at all. God does it all, and it is God manifesting Himself that constitutes itself as the Christian Scientist. It is "God with us," Life with us, Intelligence with us, wisdom with us. It is power, action, strength with us. It is the allness of Being, manifesting itself as Immanuel. It is the divine Presence; it is the image and likeness of God. It is the son of God. It means the Christ-man; it means the Christ-Saviour; it means the Mighty Counselor; it means the Prince of Peace; it means the healing influence of the Christ-mind. "Let this Mind be in you." What Mind is it? Why, it is the Mind which is Good. The first thing that this Mind does, this healer of the sick, is to declare itself as the healer of the sick, and not to declare you as the healer. It declares that the impersonal Truth, the impersonal Christ, is the healer; and the first thing it does is to get rid of a personal healer.

Not Healing a Person, but Destroying a Belief

How does this Mind, the impersonal Truth, heal the sick? Does it heal a man of sickness? Is your patient a man who believes he is sick, or is it a belief which calls itself a sick man? Is man sick? Is the likeness of God sick? No. Then the healer of the sick does not heal man. It does not accomplish what we call healing by healing man, but what does it do? It heals what we call the sick by uncovering the falsity of all claims that are involved in the supposed sickness; by uncovering the unreality thereof; by uncovering the utter unreality of the claim of law that is supposed to operate it, the law, so-called, of continuity and occupancy. It obliterates the belief and detaches it from the personality of the patient. Christian Science healing is purely metaphysical, purely so. There is no personal healing and no personal patient.

Correct Attitude for the Practitioner

Now, when we come to see that this **active, conscious knowing, understanding** of the Science of Being, is the healer of the sick, and there is none beside, will there be any place for a sense of fear? Will there be any place for a sense of responsibility, of anxiety, about patients? Suppose you have two healers, one living on one side of the street and one on the other. Some one rushes down to one healer and says, "Come over to our house at once; some one is very sick. Hurry up!" Some one else goes down to the other healer and says substantially the same thing. One grabs his hat and goes off almost without his coat and in great haste. The other one takes it leisurely. Which is the one most likely to heal his patient? What condition of thought is it that gets results? A belief in the reality of the claim rushes off to heal it; but the complacent condition of the other one, the one who knows the thing is unreal, is the healing thought that heals without going; and he knows that he does not have to go, for that matter.

The Practitioner Lays Off Responsibility and Fear

Now, all of this so-called fear or sense of responsibility means that there is the belief that the government is upon my shoulders, and that I am, or am not, the healer of the case. Let us agree with that adversary quickly. My supposed self, as a mortal, cannot heal, but God can; and it is "God with us," the **active, conscious knowing, understanding** of the Science of Being, that "I Am," that is the healer of the sick. This power is your power if you know it; but if you go forth simply depending upon your human sense of power, as a practitioner, no wonder that before you get there, there is a lot of fear on board, and responsibility and despair.

There Should Be No Personal Sense of Power to Heal

One reason that we are uttering and muttering the statement that we cannot heal and that we have not enough understanding, is that, as a class, we encourage each other more or less in that direction. We go to some one who has an understanding "as big as a house," we say, and every one is compared with that one; and we sit around encouraging the thought that all cases must be sent to this or that particular one. We say, "Just as soon as you get more understanding you will see how it is," and, "Ever so many things will happen just as soon as you get more understanding." And so, as a class, we encourage each other in the wrong direction.

"My Grace Is Sufficient for Thee"

Now, in the Bible there is a promise that Christian Scientists need to learn more, I believe, than any other. That promise is this: "My grace is sufficient for thee." What does it mean? It used to mean a sort of sentiment or emotion. We used to say it and read it, but whenever we ran short of grace and wanted more, there was not enough forthcoming, because we did not know how to get it, and in fact were in a state of constant denial of it. We did not believe that God's grace was sufficient. Now what does it mean in Christian Science?

Understanding Plus Confidence Equals Mastery

It means that when the new birth takes place, when you have a transformed and reformed state of consciousness, when physical sense is replaced by spiritual **understanding**—then you have a Christian Scientist. Now to that Christian Scientist this may be said with authority: "Your understanding of Christian Science is always equal to the mastery of every error that presents itself to you, every one. But if you can be mesmerized to declare that it is not, that settles the whole business, so far as you are concerned."

Do Not Deny Your Saviour

Now what we want to do is to awaken to an understanding of what is going on. The very Master of this universe has decreed your immortality and is conducting the affairs of this universe, even to your salvation. I used to think that it was a sort of accident or mistake in my case, that I became a Christian Scientist, but I can now see that I was the very one who needed to be a Christian Scientist. I have stopped wondering now. I can see it is divine order. Do you suppose that when the time comes for you to be saved, there will be some mistake about the machinery? Do you suppose there is a defect in the plan? Not at all; and yet, all the time, you are saying that this saving understanding is not enough by which to accomplish your salvation.

The Growth of a Scientist

Now, if you have only a wee bit of this understanding, if you know it, it is enough. But you say, "It is a little bit of a saviour; I will have to wait until it gets a little larger before I will have anything that is worthy of attention." You are denying your very salvation; you are denying your Saviour. The growth of a Christian Scientist is a great deal like the growth of a little baby. It begins to kick and squirm from the day of its birth, and we say that it thus develops. Suppose a little baby should say, "I won't kick a solitary kick until I become a man." How much of a man would he become? Just so it is with Christian Scientists. We must learn that the thing for the Christian Scientist to do is to use his infant understanding. It decays if it is not used, and it can be opened, and opened, if properly applied. All our growth comes by what you might call spiritual volition, spiritual development, bringing to light, by reason of the expansive nature of the spiritual idea, the facts of Being.

Put in Practice What You Have

I became a Christian Scientist at a time when everybody was chasing around to acquire a great knowledge of the letter. Why, we walked the streets nights to find some one who would give us some "high thoughts," as we called them. Now we do not want high thoughts until we have demonstrated some of the little ones. It is a good deal like eating three hundred and sixty-five meals before digesting one of them.

"Let No Man Despise Thy Youth" in Science

The beginner in Christian Science should begin with the same confidence as a person who has been twenty-five years in the work. Why? Because his **understanding** is enough for him, if he knows it; and it is nothing but the crucifier of the Saviour that says it is not enough for him—nothing but that. Let us stop crucifying our Saviour, the **understanding** of Christian Science. This knowledge of Christian Science is the knowledge of God, the knowledge of Good. This **understanding** is your immortal individuality. It is the undying man. It is the only man you are. Our leader once said, "Always remember what you are." The **understanding** of Christian Science is what you are.

Your Consciousness of God Is Your Only Self

Now how many are there of you? Just one. There is not a mortal man and an immortal man; there is one immortal man, and that man is the **understanding** of God. Now is it right for us to wait around for this understanding of God to become good enough to heal the sick? Is it any use for a man to sit around until his rheumatism becomes spiritual? That which calls itself unworthy will never be worthy; but if you will get it out of the way, you will go to work and heal the sick in spite of it.

False Views of the Problem

Another reason why we are so easily turned away from the healing is that we as beginners—and I know it used to be so with almost every one—have too personal and too material a sense of the healing. The healing is being done too much along the plan of supposing that there is a man to treat, or a patient to treat, or that there is something to be done to a body, or something to be done or changed in matter. We are too prone to treat disease, to treat matter, to treat somebody, to treat what we call material cause, to treat a material man or a patient. Too often our work is as material as the matter physician's. He recognizes that he is treating matter and administers matter as a remedy, and we too largely delineate thought as though we were treating matter with Mind. We would be surprised to know to what extent we are treating matter.

Occasion of Doubt in the Efficacy of Treatment

Now let the metaphysician once get the belief that he is treating matter, disease, or a man, and he will not have faith in his metaphysical treatment. Just to the extent that he holds to such notions and to the extent that his thought is directed to matter, just to that extent, instinctively, involuntarily, he will doubt the efficacy of his own treatment. Often, one will go to work as though he were treating a boil, and after he gets through with the treatment be tempted to look at the boil to see if it is a little smaller as a result. Or if he is treating a patient with fever, will want to inquire if the temperature is a little lower. It is a prevalent condition of faulty, unscientific application.

The Whole Problem of Healing Is Mental

What we want to do is to learn this—that all healing is metaphysical; there is no man to be healed; no material body to be healed; no patient to be healed; no matter to be healed; no sickness to be healed; no disease to be healed; no one to be healed; no substance to operate upon; no person, place nor thing. That is the first thing we have to do; we want to understand that, instead of this being a matter proposition, it is wholly a mental presentation. Sickness is always wholly mental, wholly a mental picture, mental illusion and hallucination, a defective depicting of thought. When you have healing to do, have you got to heal a body? No. The whole thing is mental, every bit of it. It has no relation whatever to time, place, matter, person, or man, but is altogether a picture in mind.

Practitioner Must Be Conscious of Perfection Only

Now, in whose mind? I will say, in the mind, so-called, of the practitioner. The very first person to be healed is the practitioner himself. In other words, he must first understand, when he has what he calls a patient, that the patient is purely a mental image, that the disease is purely a mental image, that the only thing to do is to meet it mentally. Then when he clears his own mentality, to know he will have nothing else to do and that he never can do anything else. All the healer can possibly do is to reflect the right thought or the Truth; and that reflection, or realization, or declaration, that uttered Word, denies the claim. It denounces it and denies it, and the healer must understand that, when he has done that mentally, he has met the case. He has nothing to do with matter, nothing to do with his patient, so far as that is concerned. The only thing for him to do is to sit still and watch the glory of God manifest itself in his own consciousness, declaring the utter unreality, the fabulous nature of the supposition of error.

When Your Mentality Is Satisfied, the Patient Is Healed

Then the healing of the sick is simply the action of Truth, or Truth uttering itself in your consciousness, denying and repudiating the claim; and when you have a satisfied healer, when you have a healer in whose thought the healing has taken place as a mental treatment, then you will find that you have a patient who will say that he is well.

Spiritual Conception of Man Heals Mankind's Ailments

But you will say, "Yes, I can understand this, but we must bring this out in the patient." What is God going to do while you are bringing this out? Is He going to sit around and see you do something? God has done all things well. He has left nothing for you to bring out. Now all this supposition that the healer has to do such wonderful things just harasses and impedes his growth. Why, our teacher used to tell us in class that students pile up an endless amount of work for themselves that they do not have to do. We want to learn that the government is upon His shoulder. I think it would be well to say that the Christian Science practitioner is one who stops lying and stops believing a lie.

Method of Treatment Illustrated

If we understand that disease, instead of being material, is purely of a mental nature, then we will have faith in a mental treatment. Suppose some one should come and sit in your chair and say, "I want to be treated." "Well, what for?" He replies, "Two times two are five." What would you do but deny that at once, and state the truth, "Two times two are four"; and that would settle it, would it not? You would understand that there was nothing but a defective mental picture which you would correct by declaring the truth.

Instant Denial and Affirmation

Still, the next man comes in and says, "I want to be treated." "What for?" "For a headache." What do you do? You begin treating for a headache, nine cases out of ten, instead of knowing that this is just as much of a mental falsity as "two times two are five." Exactly so; and the reason we do not get better demonstrations is that we are treating a headache as something that is material, instead of treating it as simply an image of false belief—a mere image.

Error Appears, But to Disappear

When a claim presents itself, we pine, and sometimes we get a little huffy and irritated because this thing has come upon us, and we do not understand it. "I never had anything of this kind before I came into Christian Science." What we want to know is this—that, with the Christian Scientist, error always appears to disappear. Now when we begin to grumble, it is upon the supposition that it comes to stay.

Rejoice in Your Understanding

Where is the healer in this sort of case? We want to know that just so long as we accept any phase of error, error will play upon us as we would play upon the keys of a piano. When such conditions are presented to you, they come to disappear, if you only know it. The proper thing to do is to begin rejoicing instead of getting angry and irritated, not because you have a claim to meet, but rejoice because you have the **understanding** and might of God wherewith to meet it. And if you will turn from it and rejoice, you will find that it will be worth more than fifty or sixty treatments that do not work. Remember this,—to the degree that you manifest any understanding of divine Principle, to that degree you have the identical understanding which Jesus manifested. Therefore, since your Christ, your understanding, when manifested by Jesus, walked upon the water, healed the sick and raised the dead, what have you to be afraid of? Trust your understanding, and rejoice!

"Thy Will Be Done," Interpreted

Suppose that Jesus, on the night of Calvary, had begun to grumble. Suppose he had said: "I never was crucified before I came into Christian Science, and do not see why I should have this claim to meet." Would there have been any resurrection? No. Yet he was tempted in all points like as we are. He was tempted to ask that the cup pass from him, and he said, "Why hast Thou forsaken me?" Then came the Christ-Saviour and declared: "Thy will be done." The world has interpreted that to mean that it was God's will that he should be killed. It did not mean anything of the sort. It meant that the will of God, Life, should be done. It was a declaration of the understanding of the immortality of man and the might of Intelligence to overcome evil. "Thy will be done" was demonstrated, not on the cross, but when Jesus rose from the dead, at the resurrection.

OPERATIVE CHRISTIAN SCIENCE

Christian Science Is the Christ-Salvation

Now, what is it that comes by way of revelation? We call it Christian Science; but how shall we designate it to make it understood? Do the Christian Scientists make a new Saviour? Not at all; Christ is still the same Saviour. Is there any other way by which mankind can be saved? No; there is no other way than through Christ. What was Christ two thousand years ago? The anointed, or "God with us." Christian Science means the Christ-salvation. It is the Mind that was in Christ Jesus. What Mind? We learn it is the one infinite Mind which includes all intelligence, all Truth, all Science. That Mind is enough; it includes all. Then it is the Mind of Christ which is Saviour, which always was and always shall be.

The One Mind Is the Saviour

Paul says, "Let this Mind be in you." Why? Because it is the one Mind which corrects, which exalts, which counteracts fear or evil. It is the Comforter. That is the reason we should have the Mind which was in Christ Jesus. What does it do? It begins to assert the Science of Life, the Science of God and man; to assert the possibilities of man; revealing everything which goes to make up the facts of reality, the scope of existence. This Mind is comforting and governing man, it is sustaining man. This is what the son of God, the image and likeness of God, means. This, according to Christian Science, is "God with us." This is the only God we have.

The Spiritual Idea

Christian Science declares that we can only know God by knowing what expresses God—this Mind with us, this Intelligence with us, Christ with us, God with us as a Redeemer, our well-being, "God with us." "Science and Health" teaches us that this is Christ. This Christ-intelligence, this Christ-enlightenment, is the spiritual idea. What is that? It is the spiritual sense of all things, the true mental idea and scientific concept which means Mind instead of mortality, Spirit instead of matter, good instead of evil. It means "God with us," Intelligence with us; it means the Mind which was in Christ Jesus, Life manifested. When it is active with you, it reveals God aright.

Spiritual Understanding Must Be Active

Just as you, knowing the Truth and knowing God, are the image and likeness of God, so are you like Life, the reality of existence, like Truth, like Intelligence, like Substance, like the power of good. Our mental power is the Messiah. But although you declare that Christ, this spiritual **understanding**, is your Saviour, you must know that only as this Saviour is active can it be a Saviour at all. We are argued with by evil to be dilatory, but let us listen to the Word of God. You must let this Mind be in you. This Mind must sway; it must be accepted as counsellor and healer.

Humans Are Not Originators of Either Truth or Error

The individual is always knowing or believing something which is anterior to himself. If he knows anything that is true, it belongs to the realm of eternal Truth; if not true, instead of being the originator of the evil, he has simply been believing a lie that was a lie from the beginning. So each one of us is either believing the mental falsities termed sickness, hatred, evil, or knowing health, love, good, all the time. We are either traveling in the way of health and holiness, or evil, every minute, every hour.

The False Argument of Being Too Busy

We say we are too busy—to do what? To be decided. Too busy to give attention to Christian Science; too busy to love;

too busy to establish the kingdom of heaven within; too busy for the Mind, which means Truth and Life; too busy with sin, sickness and death, with that which means sin and sorrow. But Christian Scientists are either being saved or not being saved. Christian Science, if it means anything, means salvation already achieved.

The Law of God Is the Law of Your Good

I used to think the hardest thing to do was to obey the will of God. Now what is the will of God? What is the law of God? It is the law of health. Whose? Yours. It is the law of Life. Whose? Yours. It is the law of prosperity, perfection, dominion over evil. Whose? Yours. It is the law of all that means gladness and satisfactory existence. Whose? Yours. Obey God. What does that mean? It means to favor your true self, to add to your own prosperity and happiness. How? Through obedience to Christ, the understanding of God, Good, as the only Presence, Cause and Law.

Christian Science Discovers Truth and Uncovers Error

What does this Saviour, Christian Science, do? It declares the facts of being. It is the basis of all true knowing. It declares everything correctly, everything good. It declares the perfectibility of man. It discovers to men what is right, what is scientific, and uncovers what is false. It uncovers, denies and destroys the claim of error.

Seeing Evil as Animal Magnetism Enables Us to Cope With It

Christian Science shows how to cope with error. As an entity no one ever coped with it. We have a term for evil; namely, animal magnetism. A great many people think that Mrs. Eddy is originating a new devil. It is the best term the English language affords to describe evil; it is the generic term for evil. When you understand what animal magnetism means, you can get rid of it. To be afraid of it is to utterly misunderstand it. Christian Science indicates evil to be what? It declares that it is a false sense of the real, a perverted sense of the actual, a falsity that is not a falsity, nothing. Therefore, all error must be resolved into a false sense. The *modus operandi* of Christian Science is the transformation of thought. It comes to substitute the true idea for the erroneous concept. Instead of having something terrible to wrestle with, all you have to do is to destroy the wrong mental sense of existence.

Christian Science Practice

This brings us to Christian Science practice, which is denying the lie, denying each form of error. This is the place where a person stopped short and said, "If all is good, I do not have to pay any attention to the error." Now, if that is so, you wouldn't have to eat three meals a day. You must not only declare that good is all, but deny the error. The only possible way to be saved is to declare that which is true and deny all error. I know of no way to wholesale a treatment, but it must handle specifically each form of error which presents itself as audible or inaudible suggestion for adoption. To handle specifically each form of error, declare what is true and deny that which is false. An intelligent affirmation about anything necessarily implies the thought that you must deny the false.

Christian Science Shows Things Apparently Material to Be False Material Concepts of Spiritual Ideas

Christian Science resolves things into thoughts. That is the one thing essential. It is not the power of good over sickness. It is not the power of Christian Science over any disordered condition. It shows the sickness to be a wrong conception of that which is fundamentally all right. The physical manifestation of disease is merely a mental falsity objectified; and the supposed law operating the disease is but a belief.

The practice of Christian Science reduces the whole thing to the realm of belief; and the healing process has nothing to do with material structure.

Vivid Sense of Reality, and Perception That Disease Is But Belief, Essential to Good Work

What is the reason Christian Scientists are not more effective in their work? It is because they do not so vividly assert the reality that they do not see the patient, and because they do not know that they do not have to do anything to the disease. To the extent that you are treating a man's body, just to that extent is he held. A Christian Scientist can do nothing else than to bring the whole healing process into the mental realm and not submit to the belief that there is something to cure. It is not a material body, but a belief in it. It is like a rubber ball which has been squeezed out of shape. As soon as you let go of it, spontaneously, according to the law of redundancy, it comes back into shape. Just as soon as you break down the belief, the body will recover.

One Perfect Body

God has a lot to do with the body, the only body and all the body there is; and God is the law of health and perfection to all the body there is, the body of right ideas. Understanding of this is the law of perfection to the human body, because you have gotten rid of a lot of beliefs, and just as soon as you get rid of the beliefs, the law of God operates. What the practitioner must do is to drop the belief that **he** must do something. He needs to break down the belief that holds the patient. Stop treating him as person; stop treating a sick man. It is only a belief that calls itself a sick man. Stop treating disease or the body, and believing you have to bring out something.

What is your treatment? A lot of them sound all right, but there is no good in them. They lack force. Now, your treatment has just as much power as you know enough to know there is Truth in it. Don't stand around and say a few things, and trust to God to do the rest. He has done all. Declare the metaphysical facts of Being and deny the error. You have got to do it. You sit around and say it is your business to bring out. You must manifest that which is, by reflecting God. You have to do this and have faith in it. If it is a good treatment, it will have faith in its acts.

Your Treatment Entitled to the Power of God

What is Christian Science? It is God manifested, "God with us." And the treatment is entitled to the power of God, because it is the spiritual idea which manifests God. The spiritual idea of Life will abolish the false belief termed death; the spiritual idea which manifests action will abolish the false belief termed breaking down, paralysis, inaction. This is why your treatment is entitled to the power of all good. What is treatment? Where does a Christian Scientist turn in every instance? To God, our God. What are you going to break with the patient? Break fear. What breaks it? What will break a claim of evil power? It is the understanding of the omnipotence of God, all-good. So what we want to do is to know that every treatment is the very Word of God. It is the power of Good that destroys the fear of evil.

Disease and Sin Not, Fundamentally, Personal Beliefs

Reflecting the law of God is the annihilation of the law, so-called, of mortal mind. Your treatment has to be big enough to know that it is the operation of the divine law, breaking the so-called law of false belief. When you have a patient with measles, it is not a personal belief; it is a claim of spurious law. He has no fear. You cannot treat a patient with the thought or belief that he has any fear. You must know that he has no fear. If you treat a patient as though he had a belief, you will make him have it. Error is no part of man, you or your patient. You destroy it by knowing it is no part of man. You have nothing to do but break the supposition of fear or belief which Mr. Patient has been victimized into accepting as being his own sense or feeling.

Confidence Versus Discouragement

What we are seemingly lacking in is intelligence, faith and confidence. Error will come up and declare that you do not realize the Truth. What are you going to do about it? Are you going to say, "I don't realize it?" It is easy to wind Christian Scientists up, unless they wake up. What is your Saviour? Is it, "I am discouraged; I cannot realize the Truth"? Is it, "I haven't enough confidence in my treatment"? What is the one who is being saved going to do? He will declare, "I do realize the Truth. It shall not return void. It is the Word of God, and I cannot be mesmerized to believe I have not confidence in it." That is what one who is being saved will know.

Mesmerism Uncovered and Handled

If some one told you that he was going to mesmerize you with the belief that you are discouraged, you would say that he could not do it; but if he mesmerized you without telling you about it, you would say, "I am so discouraged." You must declare what is true about yourself if you want to be saved in Christian Science. If the suggestion comes which says that you cannot do it, declare that you can do it. Whenever error asserts itself, you have to declare your rights. If it declares that you cannot lift your arms, declare that you can. God governs; and in the name of Science and in the name of law you have the right to declare the perfection of everything about you, and only as you do it will you be governed by good. I would therefore say that your Saviour is the right idea about everything. This is Christ with us, the affirming of the power of the right idea.

Operative Christian Science Is the Thought and Feeling of Christian Scientists

We are involved in the cause of Christian Science. The only cause of Christian Science is in the consciousness of Christian Scientists. The thoughts of Christian Scientists constitute the cause of Christian Science, which is just as good as our thought is and that which the thought produces. Christian Science has just as much permanence as there is value to Christian Scientists' thought, as there is Love and Truth, and fidelity to Truth and Love in our thoughts. We felicitate ourselves because Christian Science has come to stay. This is a matter of demonstration. It depends upon whether Christian Scientists can learn to love enough to save themselves.

Love Versus Hatred

History is being made very rapidly. The word of Christian Science is thrusting itself upon the world very rapidly. It is bringing to the front all the resources of evil, and this evil is showing itself virulently. The student says, "I know; but it will come out all right." If the Christian Scientists would be saved, they must love. If there is any health in Love, any life in Love, you must stop hating. Stop saying hateful things; stop doing hateful things. Simply get to work at number one and make a lover of him as speedily as possible. Do not think you ought to find fault with some one else; let him alone. Don't think you ought to say something about somebody. There is more abominable cruelty going on about the things you have got to tell somebody about some one else than you could put in books.

Love and Uncovering Error

Who is it that sits in judgment on his brother? Who declares that all sorts of evil will befall him because he does not do as I say? Is the cause of Christian Science dear to him? Yes, it is dear enough to sit up nights and love, to apply the

Golden Rule. Get right up in the corner and say "Would I like to have some one do just what I am doing?" Ask that question. You have to analyze thought, that which is about you; but you do not have to damn people. Let your efforts to get people into the church or to get subscriptions go, but do not stop loving. We have to do, it and we must. He who loves not, lives not, for Love is Life.

THE CAUSE OF CHRISTIAN SCIENCE
Address Delivered Jan. 18, 1902

What is the cause of Christian Science? Where would you go to locate it? Is it a thing, a place, or object? Has it bounds, form or any material shape? No. The cause of Christian Science is simply the activity of Truth in the consciousness of the Christian Scientists.

The Duty of Christian Scientists

If we do the most we can for the cause, how shall it be done? It is to see to it that we manifest the most Truth, righteousness, intelligence, Love and humility, the earnestness of honest, humble endeavor. Until then you are not a fit subject to feel at ease.

Now, what is the cause of Christian Science? It is the honest, humble endeavor, the loving, tender, charitable nature of the individual. It is the purity of consciousness, the purity of truth within. When that becomes contaminated and fails to progress higher and higher, Godward, it becomes a menace to the cause, and such a condition is harmful to Christian Science, and if it ever fails as a cause, it will be because of the mental condition, attitude and conduct of its so-called Christian Scientists.

Christian Science as a Movement

Now, what shall we do in order to do the best we possibly can for it? Let each one of us pray that he may act as though he thought the entire cause of Christian Science—all its sweet and glorious import—depended upon him; and not congratulate ourselves upon the supposition that it will stand and endure unless we stand and endure temptation and resist transgressions, and grow daily and hourly in the manifestations of that which is altogether lovely, and which is like God.

Instructive Religion

People have been religious instinctively, and they have sought after God, until the day of Christian Science; have looked for Him as if He were an isolated being, remote, separate from man. Everybody has sought for God as though He were an objectified being—something which you could put your hands on if you were there, something that you would expect to look upon, to find after you had gone to heaven—something of that nature.

Nature of God

Christian Science, in declaring the Science of God, declares that God is not a thing, nor a bodily person, nor any presence that the physical eyes can behold, nothing that comes within the range of the finite senses whatever. It declares that the finite education of man has never added anything to God at all. As the Scriptures say, God must be spiritually discerned.

How God Is Known

We know God by knowing that which expresses or manifests God, good. Any good with us is God with us. God is Intelligence; then Intelligence with us is God with us, because it is God manifest with us. God is power and action; therefore, the right understanding of power, action and presence is Good, God, with us.

Idea Manifests God

The right idea of Being always manifests God, and therefore the right idea always means and is, practically, "God with us." The Christian Scientist is the one who is gaining the right sense of all things, gaining the true, scientific spiritual sense of things, instead of the erroneous mortal concept or impression of all things.

What Constitutes a Christian Scientist?

What constitutes a Christian Scientist? A Christian Scientist is one in whose thought, or consciousness of Truth or divine Intelligence, the Mind of God is defining itself, expressing itself, delineating itself; and when the Christ-idea transforms our consciousness, it becomes operative and active, becomes the governor and law of our existence, becomes reality to us.

Self Not Dual

Then, is nothing, or mortal mind, appearing as your mind? How many individuals are you? Are you an immortal man and a mortal man? No! there is but one of you, and that one is God's man, immortal man, the right man; and what you know about Truth, what you understand of Christian Science, what you know about God, constitutes your true selfhood. All the fear, sin, sickness and death is a lie about you, and is not man at all.

What Is the Savior? Emmanuel

Now, in Christian Science we call this appearing, this spiritual or right sense of being, Emmanuel or "God with us," and it corresponds to the Mind which was also in Christ Jesus. This true sense of existence is the saving sense. Savior from what? From all forms of evil, sinful, vicious, erroneous beliefs, misconceptions, illusions, wrong mental tendencies. Jesus said, "Ye shall know the truth, and the truth shall make you free."

The Practice of Christian Science Defined

The process of knowing and declaring the truth, and denying, rejecting, resisting error, is what we call the practice of Christian Science.

Spurious Christian Science

Now, one difference between true and spurious Christian Science is to be found at this point. There are some who believe that they are Christian Scientists who are saying, "All you have to do is to declare that everything is good. 'All is God, all is Good,' etc. Keep on saying that, and you can bring it out in your life."

Affirmation Not Sufficient; Denial Necessary

But Christian Science exposes the fallacy of that practice, and says that, so long as there is a human being on earth, there is but one way by which we may work out our salvation, and that way is to declare specifically the truth, and to deny specifically the error. And you can make no progress in Christian Science unless you do that. The specific denial of specific claims of error, as well as affirming or declaring the truth specifically, is the only way that it can be done.

Recognition of Error

Don't imagine that you can bound upon some fleecy cloud with a silver lining, and simply declare yourself into heaven by saying "Everything is good." A human being must get down into the mud just far enough to see that the mud **claims to** be something, and to have some claim upon us, and then straightway destroy or demolish the claim.

Suppose there were a blackboard here and "2 plus 2 equals 5" were written upon it. I insist that 2 plus 2 is 4. I refuse to pay any attention to the error. I refuse to recognize it, and you would say, "Well, there it is just the same; your refusing or ignoring it does not change it any." Now what have I got to do? I have got to rub it out by or with my understanding of truth, and in its place establish the real fact; then the demonstration is made. So it is with us as Christian Scientists. We have got to rub the error out, and it is no use trying to demonstrate Christian Science on any other basis.

Ignorance Must Be Corrected

An ignorant, unintelligent sense of what is going on is not sufficient. Ignorance must be seen and corrected before we can attain harmony. "A knowledge of error and its operation must precede that understanding of Truth which destroys error. Ignorance of the error to be eradicated oftentimes subjects you to its abuse." (See S. & H., pp. 251, 252 and 446.)

Handling Error, Treatment Defined

This process is sometimes called handling error, meaning thereby that we take up the claims or beliefs, or the seeming nature of evil, and analytically handle it, and break down this action or belief, and its laws, fear, etc.; and we resist and stop their action; and this we call treatment. Then what is Christian Science treatment? **Knowing** is treatment, knowing positively what is true, because truth always turns itself to the destruction of error.

Faith Necessary

Then, if knowing is treatment, a treatment ought to **know enough to know** that it is a good one, and unless your treatment knows this much, failure is probable. There must be absolutely no lack of faith in your treatment. FAITH is the impulsion, the propulsion, of the Christian Science treatment. It does not make so very much difference about the framing of words; the words may be right, the phrasing correct, the syllogisms natural and logical, but what enforces them, connects them to man. FAITH, the faith begotten of understanding. The confidence, the assurance, the voluntary truth—that is the impulsion of Christian Science.

Necessary Elements of Treatment

Now, what has the treatment got to know in order to be a good one. It has got to know that it is true in statement, to stand on. It has got to know enough to know that there is only one Mind, and that Mind is good; therefore, that every form of evil mind is fictitious. It has got to know that there is only one Mind and that Mind is not only the Mind of God, but it is the Mind of man. One infinite Mind is enough for everybody, for all, and that Mind is good, and only in this Mind is the reality of being. It must know that there is one Intelligence only, one Truth, and that Truth is God. It must know that there is one Life, and that Life is our Life, and that Life is the Life of man, and it is immortal and undying. It must know that the only Life there is is the immortal, undying Life—such is man's life. Man has only one Life, and that is immortal.

Reality of Spiritual Power

What else has it got to know? It has got to know, among other things, the reality of power. How little people know about power! How little do they know about the **omnipotence** of God. Suppose you visited a sick person and would say, "Why, don't you know that God is omnipotent?" The sick person might say, "Well, what if He is, how is that going to help me, how is that going to connect with me and make me well?" Just telling him that God is All, and God is omnipotent, would not heal him in a thousand years. Well, how is it in Christian Science? We say that God is omnipotent, Good is Power, Truth is Power, Intelligence is Power, Love is Power. Whose good? Whose Love? **Ours,** because God is ours.

God's Power Ours

You don't have to go to a supposititious heaven to find God on a white throne, in order to find the omnipotence of God. Omnipotence is Good, is yours, just as much as anybody's. Now, how much of it is yours? Turn to the science of numbers. Get the simple idea, "2 plus 2 equals 4." You know all of it, every one knows it. Each person has got the whole of it. Every one has just as much of it as though he made it, and owned it all. Each individual has got the whole thing, and yet there is only one "2 plus 2 equals 4." One is enough, and it is yours, all yours.

Treatment Should Be All-Power

Now there is one Mind; and how much of it is yours? The whole of it. There is one Life. How much is yours? All of it—you reflect the one Life. Now, there is one Power. How much of it is yours? All. How much is your Christian Science treatment entitled to? All; that is, a Christian Science treatment is the manifestation of the all-power of God—omnipotent God. And you have got to get it right down to that. It must not be away off somewhere, trusting in a God away off, far from you. But your right idea of Life is the power of God, and you must know it.

How Doubt Is Dispelled

And when the claim of evil declares that you don't know this, then you say and contend that you do know it. Just declare that this treatment is every word good and true. It is Truth's son sent to us, and it does mean life, is does mean harmony; it does mean a sublime existence, and it is power; and as the power of good, it is the annihilation of any and all claims that evil has power, or can influence, control or govern men.

Government by Law

What else has it got to do in order to have a good opinion of itself? This treatment has got to know another very important thing. We speak of the law of God. What is it? We know enough to know that in the realm of Mind or Spirit, Principle or God governs everything, governs its offspring or phenomena. In other words, God is supreme, and sole governor of all that exists, and governs everything according to Law.

"Chance" a Misnomer

On the other hand, in the realm of mortal mind, as we call it, or of the carnal mind, or the evil sense of existence, mortal mind governs everything according to its spurious laws. Not one slightest thing happens but what happens according to law.

Treatment Is Law

Now your treatment has got to know enough to know that **it is not,** is the law of Divinity, the only real Law, the law of God, Good, Life, and that, as such, it is the law of annihilation to the so-called law of mortal mind. This knowing is particularly important to one who is at work in this cause. In other words, a practitioner in Christian Science has got to know that in every treatment he has got to smash a law of mortal mind.

Disease Not Personal Belief

Now, suppose you are a practitioner. When you have an ordinary case of disease, or suppose you have an hereditary case of disease, we will hear the practitioner say, "Well, I handled the patient's belief," as though that were enough. **It is not,** strictly speaking, the patient's belief. The patient is sick according to spurious law, and according to the law of heredity, a law of prenatal mesmerism or influence. Would you treat for his belief? No. You have got to know the truth about God and man, thereby enforcing the divine law and annulling spurious law.

Belief General, Not Personal

And this is where a Christian Scientist must have the understanding of the necessity of having every treatment he gives expand itself and reach out its quarters so as to abolish the law that is afflicting the patient, or any one that is in the hands of some evil influence.

Treatment Law of Destruction to Evil

Now, when this sense of a Christian Science treatment is a law in itself, it will be power, and as such it will be a law of destruction to every claim of so-called mortal law.

The Elements of a Claim of Sickness

When you have a case of sickness, you have three special features: First, that there is a claim that there is substance to be sick. Second, that there is a cause for sickness. Third, that there is a law to cause that sickness; and unless you break that law, you are not reaching the case. So then, a Christian Science treatment, in order to know that it is good, has got to know these things, or rather has got to know the truth about them.

How the Mystery of Existence Is Solved

Well, what hinders, what prevents? Christian Science declares that, in order to solve the mystery of existence, things must be resolved into thoughts.

Evil in Realm of False Belief, Not in Matter

We must learn that evil is in the realm of universal false belief, instead of in matter, that evil is a subjective state of erroneous mind—a mortal concept, universal and collective, as well as seeming to be personal. In the realm of mind, we must establish the origin of evil, and its influence. We must know that evil exists, not as a reality or entity, but that it is a form of false belief.

What Occasions Doubt in Treatment

Now if, instead of this, the practitioner treats disease as though it were a body, as though it were matter, as though it were natural, then you see he would doubt the power of his treatment, because he would doubt the power of mind over matter, and such treatment is not the Christian Science method at all.

Practice of Christian Science Defined

Christian Science practice is the practice of the power of Truth over error, Life over death, Good over evil, harmony over discord; and it effects the transformation of thought; that is the aim, that is the rule of operation. And just as soon as you rise high enough to see disease as belief, then you will have the understanding that your treatment is good enough.

Nature of Error

Now we say in Christian Science that truth uncovers error. As what? Always as delusion, illusion, nothing; and in your treatment, if you have something that you are not positive of, you may know that you have omitted something, and you have got to go over it all again; or, if you are not confident that your treatment will prevail, you have got to go over it again and again, until you have nothing to be afraid of.

The Most Important Point in Treatment

Now I profess to say that the most effective agency in the healing of the sick is the expectation, first of all, on the part of the practitioner that his reflection of Mind can do it. The practitioner who knows this, goes to his patient with an expectation of healing, and knowing that right thought can do it, he accomplishes the work.

The Devil, How Regarded

To him who is a Christian Scientist or a beginner or a student, understand this—that Christian Scientists do not believe in a personal devil.

We do not believe that evil has an entity at all, do not believe that there are any fallen angels, or any satan. But we do acknowledge this—that there is what is called evil, which calls itself good and real; and we do recognize the fact that something has got to be done to it. We have got to name it in order to understand it. We have got to destroy it. Now, while there is no devil, evil is of such a nature that it amounts apparently to the same thing. So in order to get at it handily, let us suppose it to be a devil, and let us suppose you are trying to get rid of it. You remember, Jesus said, "I am come to destroy the works of the devil."

Evil Acts as Though Intelligent

Again, let us suppose that the devil knows you are trying to destroy him, **because evil is of such a nature that its attitude** is equivalent to knowledge that you are trying to "do it up." It might just as well be a devil that knew you were trying to destroy it. **It acts just the same, though it has been proved to be unreal.**

Wiles of the Devil

We know it would be a poor devil that would not try to kill those who wanted to kill him, "thereby to prolong his existence if he could." Evil would do you up, so that you could not do a solitary thing to it—just take you off in a corner and mesmerize you with the belief that you have not enough understanding; or get you to say that you are discouraged, and that you are in doubt; or that you are afraid. If I were the devil, I would not ask to do anything more than that. I could guarantee that I would prosper, if I could only do that to Christian Scientists. Did he ever do it to you? If anyone had been reading your thoughts, could he have heard you say, "I have not enough understanding. I wish I had. I would so love to heal, but I haven't enough power. I can't heal," etc., etc.?

Source of Discouragement

You say, "O, I am so discouraged." Where did it come from, dear friends? From God? Were there a legion of angels hovering around you to tell you how discouraged you were; that you did not have any understanding, etc.? No, it was all the devil, mortal mind, if you please. What did you do—you who said, "O, I am so discouraged"?

How an Alert Scientist Meets Arguments

What would a wide-awake Christian Scientist say—one who is alert, who detects the action of error, and also knows the truth which will destroy it? When that argument comes—"I haven't enough understanding"—he says, **"I have."** That is what he says. He says, "Get thee behind me," and it will "get." It is bound to "get" under such circumstances. He says, "I know the truth." "I do understand Christian Science—I have proved it many a time, and I cannot be fooled or mesmerized to say that I do not, or to think that I do not."

Resistance of Evil Important

Now the reason there are so many half-awake Christian Scientists is right here—they don't resist. At the first breath of the tempter, he catches them by saying, "You are not good enough to heal the sick; you are not worthy to heal the sick, etc." The teacher of Christian Science is assiduously and forever iterating to the student the need of recognizing just those suggestions, and to use just those condemnations.

Mental Attack on Scientists

It was once said of a man who practiced a mental "ism" of some kind, that he always visited a Christian Science church when he wished to rid himself of a headache or other ills. His explanation of the reason was, because they believe in the power of mind. He would pick out some healthy person, and begin a mental telepathy of, "You have got my headache," and do it over and over again; and unless a Scientist is alert and resisting all error on the first indication or thought, it is easier to reach him than anyone else one can find.

How to Meet a Mental Attack

So, for instance, you are seated in church and suddenly exclaim, "O, I have a headache." This is what you say when you don't resist; what you should say is, "I know what this is—you false argument—get out." And that knowledge and that recognition and that force takes it off.

Human Thought Not Original

How long are you going to wait before you decide and separate between evil and good, and declare the right thing about yourself instead of the wrong thing? Now, a human being is not an original thinker; he never originated any thought whatever.

Error Cosmic, General, Not Personal

A human manifests thought which is exterior to himself, always. In other words, you and I reflect or manifest or express that which is true, universally true, or that which is universally false, one or the other. Humanity has known little of the reality of good, and has manifested mortality, sin, sickness, death and disaster. Now comes Christian Science to enlighten you and to divide between good and evil. Which is it you are expressing, willingly, voluntarily, in your thoughts, and giving voice to, as if it were true? Which is it? Error or truth? Sickness or health? Life or death? It is one or the other.

"Choose Ye, This Day"

Christian Science comes to tell you which is which, and the text-book says to admit only that which you would have true, and ought to be true, and deny and resist everything else. Especially remember this—that each one of us today is surrounded by the universal atmosphere of mortal mind. All men, women and children on earth (the aggregation of mortals) hold a collective influence on the individual and we are touched by that contagion; and you must recognize the contagion and resist it.

"Instant in Season, Out of Season"

So then, the refrain and the urgency of the hour is to be on the alert; be smart enough to know when the enemy is at hand, and begin the process of resisting.

Animal Magnetism Defined and Explained

Now a great many Scientists throughout the field are very sadly awry concerning error, and particularly concerning the scientific term for error, which is "animal magnetism." Some of them will go all to pieces when it is uttered, and more foolish things are said of it, and more unnecessary things, than can be put into a book. The truth of it is, it is simply a scientific term for evil or error and its doings. The world had never evinced an adequate capacity to resist evil, and only when Christian Science solved the mystery of evil, and showed its nature to be as described in the chapter of "Science and Health" on "Animal Magnetism" did we grasp it in such a way that we can destroy it. "Animal magnetism" means error and the operation thereof.

What to Handle

Suppose your boy ran away from home—what ought you to handle? Suppose you fall down and hurt your toe, what ought you to handle? Suppose you have a pain in your back, what ought you to handle? Suppose your house is burned down, what should you handle? Handle "animal magnetism." No matter what the lie is, the solution lies in handling animal magnetism, roughly analyzed as the seven devils, envy, sensuality, jealousy, malice, hate, revenge, anger, all emanating from fear. Now, what is there to be afraid of?

The Great Discovery

Christian Science reduces error, under the term animal magnetism, to its native nothingness; reduces it to such a sense of things that you can destroy it. It is the one great discovery of all the centuries; the mystery of evil solved.

Business Problem Solved

An example: I had two students, a man and his wife. The man was a business man, and he had lost some money in speculation, and his business was dull. He was a manufacturer and retailer. He was not making expenses, and had been blue for a long time and I knew it. He and his wife came to me, one day. The corners of his mouth were down, and both looked blue. The wife was distressed because the husband was so fearful. They told me the story of all their seeming troubles and fears. I said, "I want you to go home and make a demonstration, just for today—get happy today. We have had this same phase of error to meet at our house. For example, my wife and I will stay in the house for some days, and there will be a procession of people come and they will pour into our ears, from morning till night, more tales of woe than we can count. We will go out to dinner with a feeling of depression ourselves; and then we recognize it and we will declare to the contrary, and begin to say certain truths to each other; and we keep at it until presently we do get to be happy, overcoming the claim. Now Mr. Retailer and Manufacturer, you have a good home, plenty to eat and plenty of good clothes to wear. Your business won't fail tonight, or before tomorrow. You go home, and get happy today, and say all the pleasant things you possibly can to your children and to every living creature around you. I want you to declare, 'I am not afraid, and I am happy,' and stick to it."

Mesmerizing One's Business

I said to the man, "You are mesmerizing your business clear up to the eyes. What is your trade? Your trade is thought, before it is trade. Somebody has got to think about trading at your store before you get any trade at all. Your trade is thought. Now if you are exercising fear for your trade, and directing fear to your trade, don't you see that you are mesmerizing it? How can you get trade on such terms? How could you expect to heal your patient if you did not do anything else but be afraid that you could not heal him all the time? He could get nothing but fear from you. Now do let the poor trade alone, and let it get well. Go home and resist this fear, just for today. Do as I tell you, just 24 hours." In about a month's time I saw this same man and asked him how everything was. He said, "Business is immense; shows an increase of 40 percent." Now can you see that that man mesmerized his own trade, his own business? He was doing the very worst thing he could have done, until I corrected him. He was simply reflecting error, reflecting mortal mind, all the time.

Mesmerism Lifted

To a teacher of Christian Science his students will come and say, "I am depressed and I am disheartened. I have been working three months, etc., on it." They stay with their teacher for a while and, as they go away, they say, "I am so glad I came here; the whole thing is gone." Of course it is gone, because I have lifted the mesmerism from you. "Well, why couldn't I do it?" says the student. The reason why you **couldn't** do it was because **you insisted on calling it** yourself all the time; that is, "**I** am depressed. I am disheartened. I am afraid, etc."

Do Not Claim Evil As Yours

Well, if you are afraid, etc., whatever has got it, had better keep it. Christian Science says, "You haven't any claim to evil, and it is not your claim, and fear is not your fear, and depression is not your depression,—the whole thing is a fraud, an imposition, and never was yours." You can never get rid of a claim, a belief, or anything else by calling it yours. And yet you say to me, "I am this, and I am that, and I have got this and I have got that, and I can't do this and I can't do that." You have seen the toy, a monkey-on-a-string, and every time you pull the string the monkey dances. Now this is just the way we do when the devil pulls the string, until we wake up and know enough not to wiggle when that string is pulled, but to smash the whole business.

What Is Your Saviour?

Christian Science teaches the power of Mind, and **shows** that the right idea is that which will save a man from the wrong belief specifically,—there is your saviour. The book says that, to break down any error, the contrary or opposite truth must be declared. In order to illustrate, I am going to speak of another instance, which is well worth the attention of all. Indeed, the significance of it should stir the whole generation to its depths.

Dying Student Healed

I had a student, a young traveling man. Not long after he studied under me, he went out west and fell under a claim of anemia and came back home and was treated for a few days. Later on I took the case and there was no improvement. There was no apparent change whatever, and I suppose we were satisfied to let well enough alone. I went there one afternoon about two o'clock, and the man was dying,—he was in the extremity of belief, eyes closed and sunken, face pallid, etc. He could not utter a sound, he could not even open his eyes. The body was manifesting an extraordinary condition. His wife was crying. She left the room when I came in. I knew that something had to be done for that man right away. I said to him, "I want you to repeat what I say, and if you cannot utter the words aloud, make your lips go so that I shall know you are thinking it. Now you say, 'There is one infinite Life,' —now make your lips go. He made them go. 'And that Life is eternal Life,—and that Life is my life' "; and I kept him saying that over and over again, and after a while he began to make a little noise. Then the words would come faintly. Then he began to open his eyes, and finally he got so he could speak plainly enough to ask me to let up on him. "No," I said, "I will not let up on you; you say it," and I went after him again. I kept after him until he could say it as plainly as I could.

No Fear of Overtaxing Strength

His body resumed its natural condition; his eyes were wide open, and that work healed that man, and all he had to do was to manifest the evidence of convalescence. That healed him; in other words, that was Life's idea. You will see the connection.

Claim Life as Yours

Very likely, if I had told him, God is Life, he would not have lived; because there would not have been any marked relationship between God and him. What I said was, "There is one

Life, and that Life is eternal Life,'' and that broke the sense of a dying life. ''And that Life is **my** Life,'' was bringing that Life down into his own experience as an idea, and that conscious idea broke the mesmerism of death. That is just exactly what the *modus operandi* was.

Do Not Listen to Pleas of Error

What was it which asked me to let up on it? It was death, and if I had not been smart enough to know that it was death, I might have said, ''Yes, I'll let up on you; I'll let up on the poor, dear man.'' Don't you see, now? There is the power of an idea, which equals just the difference between a live man and a dead one. That gives a clear indication to us. Declare the truth, and that the error is a lie. Insist upon it. Understand it. Stand by it. When we do this, we are on the side with God; on the side with Truth; on the side with Power, Life and being; on the side of man, his life and immortality.

Receptivity the Condition of Power

Now, again, what hinders a Christian Scientist? We are dependent, confessedly dependent, upon that which we call right knowledge, the inflow of truth. Everyone will admit that. Through what does it come? Through what does the very voice of God and the power of God and the sufficiency of Science reach humanity? Through a state of receptivity. The open door, the open window, the transparency of thought, the consciousness of man in a state of receptivity. There must be a natural channel, something with which it can operate, as it were.

Evil in Ourselves Closes the Door

Now how many times we are shut out from that which heals, from that which comforts, restores, redeems and equips,—how often we are shut out from it by an evil condition of mentality within ourselves.

Hindrance to Healing

A few days before I came away, I heard my wife talking with somebody, and she said: "Look here, you are being treated, and you say you are not getting any better, and I know you are in a state of chronic resentment about something in your family. You are irritated, you are put out, petulant, angry almost constantly; you have been in this condition for two or three weeks. Something has been going contrary to your wishes, to your desires, and you have just allowed it to corrode and inflame you until it amounts to a stone wall around your consciousness. Now do you suppose that a treatment is going to get through that? It is no use for you to be treated in this condition. It cannot get into you. You can't get it."

The Chief Work of Christian Scientists

What are we Christian Scientists admonished to do? To keep the consciousness clean, to keep out that which is impure; to subdue the human will; to subdue the petulant, frantic self-will; to subdue all the tendencies to hate, everything that disturbs and mars and disfigures and debauches the mentality. That is oftentimes what hinders us; because it shuts out from us that which, if it could only come in, would refresh and restore us. Indeed, what is it that holds men from heaven, more than anything else? It is hatred in its many forms.

The Necessity of Watching

Suppose that each one of us should keep watch for twelve hours and see how many times we admit error, or declare error, or declare for something that is against ourselves. You would be amazed to see how much you do this. If you would keep account of it for twelve hours, it is very likely you would watch yourself forever. Again, what do you suppose you would find if you kept account of every thought that is unlike Love? Here is humanity, and we see it oppressed with hatred in its different forms. People hate, and yet expect to learn to love. The divine demand is to learn to love your neighbor as yourself; to learn to do unto others as you would be done by.

Golden Rule

How far do you have to go before getting at the fault, if you put that rule into **practice?** Put it to the test,—Would I like to have my neighbor do this thing to me, **be thinking this thing about me?** Before the evil words come, before the evil feelings, before the evil actions, if we would stop and say, "Would I like to have him do this to me?" How many times would you say, "No"?

Price of Help from God

Until we stand at the door of thought, with the most intense earnestness, and put the Golden Rule up as the test of our thought and feeling and action, and learn to be governed accordingly, we hope in vain for satisfying help, in vain for heaven, for the healthy or whole idea of Life, because Love is substance, the animus, the Principle of Life. We must get the attitude of Love, and do unto others as we would have them do unto us.

Don't Practice Condemnation

Learn to forgive, utterly to forgive. Cast out the terrible cruelty that defaces mankind. Take off the burden that you lay upon your brother man,—I mean the condemnation. What a pitiful weight do we cast upon a man when we enter upon a campaign of condemnation! How often do we practice idle criticism, which does him no good and hinders us? How long shall we be in forgiving? Never will we realize health and be happy in the brotherhood of man until we learn to forgive; to be merciful, forbearing and loving.

Encourage and Stimulate Good in Others

Practically, we are all sinners, every last one of us. We look upon a person who is sixty per cent bad and forty per cent good, and condemn the bad. Mrs. Eddy knew enough to use the forty per cent that was good. Now that is what we must do: make the most of the forty per cent that is good in our brother man, and wait for it to be fifty and sixty per cent, etc.

A Great Human Problem

The great problem is how to get along with each other. We become detectives, as it were, experts in mind, and we become very critical because of it, and let that criticism sometimes reach the point of cruelty of judgment, unrighteous judgment.

Repress Criticism

Then what we want to do is to repress the exaggerated condition of the human mind. The fact of the matter is that if my brother can get along with me, I prefer to get along with him, as a general thing.

Learn to Love

It is a very easy thing for one to jump upon a pedestal and to say, "Thus saith the Lord." It is with much reluctance that I do it. But I have learned this much. I have made the demonstration of learning to love. I have not one atom of malice toward any person on earth, and there is no one whom I would not forgive; and I have been just as resentful at times as anybody you ever saw. It is more comforting to love; vastly more pleasurable, a great deal more satisfying. It is astonishing that a man can be fooled by such an outrageous lot of stuff as hatred. It is mental gangrene. It absolutely consumes; it produces unhappiness and disease.

What Christian Science Is Doing

Now let us in Christian Science recognize this Cause as being that which is rescuing the race, and all who are to come hereafter, from the bondage of disease. And let us remember that that which will establish the kingdom of heaven within, and open the doors of the millennium—this Cause depends on us. Think of it; weigh it in the balance of your judgment; take it home with you, and contemplate this. Remembering that "Our Church is built on the divine Principle, Love," we may well ponder which is the power for me, love or hate? Which is the power for me, charity or unmercifulness? Which will serve my welfare, my health, my peace, my tranquility, my joy, the more? And then, which will serve my brother, which will serve the world, which will open the door of heaven, and usher me in, love or hate? Which is God? Which is my heritage?

No Life Without Love

Then remember the judgment will be upon us, and if we have not love, then we live not, for Love is Life. As a whole, you see, as a procession, we move on toward this achievement, and all that it depends on is the expansion, the exaltation of our thoughts; keeping our thought reaching out; taking on a larger dimension all the time, having more of Love. Have it do all you can; and declare the right things; declare for that which you would have come to pass.

TALK AT FORT WORTH, TEXAS

March, 1902

Mr. Kimball began by saying that Mrs. Eddy was deeply concerned on account of the slight knowledge that Christian Science practitioners had of the practice of Christian Science, and had requested him to talk to the Scientists on the subject.

The Practical Christ

He said that the truth we declare for our patients is all the Christ there is or ever will be.

Desire for a Personal God

Some Christian Scientists have said that they wished there were a personal God, who knew of their material ills and needs. The effect, when we do our mental work, is exactly the same as if He did; for God acts just as though He knew of them; that is, the result is the same. Furthermore, the devil, or error, acts just as though he were a personality.

Sickness Regarded as Real

Some Christian Scientists treat patients as though they were really sick. Now is it a sick man you treat, or a belief of sickness manifesting itself through a mortal, that you treat?

The Woman with a Belief of Feathers

A woman who believed herself covered with feathers, and thought it so strange that no one could see her feathers (she was crazy, to mortal sense), would ask everyone she saw to look at her feathers. Now, if you had been called on to treat that woman, would you have treated her for feathers, or for the belief of feathers manifesting itself through a false sense entertained by her? Most Christian Scientists, so-called, would treat feathers.

False Sense of Treatment

A patient, for instance, comes to a Christian Scientist with a belief of a boil. The patient walks in and says, "I have got a boil." The practitioner says, "A boil, where is it?" (as though a belief could really be localized!) Patient says, "On my right arm." Practitioner asks, "How long have you had it?" Patient answers, "Two or three days." (Treatment should have begun at once, against belief, not against a boil.) Then the practitioner says, "Well, sit down and let me treat you." Now, what do you treat, a boil?

Another patient comes in and says that his child has a fever, and asks the practitioner to treat it. The practitioner does so, and then rings up the patient's residence to know if the pulse is not a little slower. What now does the practitioner treat? A fever?

Belief in Matter Hinders Treatment

That which is holding most of us is belief in matter. It is like a man trying to swim while hanging to a plank in the water. Another man comes along and says, "Let go the plank and you will learn to swim, but never so long as you hold on to it." This is the way with some Christian Scientists. As long as they cling to matter, they will never learn to treat scientifically, but as soon as they let matter go, by seeing that it is only belief, and so is mental, they will learn.

Scientists Hinder Their Work

Mrs. Eddy says that Scientists pile up mountains for themselves, in this way. When a patient comes to them with a headache, they hunt around and try to find a cause for it, and treat the cause, when there are many causes that could produce headache, such as heredity, constipation, indigestion, cold, and innumerable other beliefs of causes, and the practitioner does not know what caused it.

Do Not Impute Sin

"Handle only the claim the patient brings to you, and Truth will disclose to you whatever else is necessary to handle, if the claim does not yield." In this connection, do not make a man out a sinner, before you find him to be one (to mortal sense). For instance, if the headache does not yield to treatment, and you find the person hates, take up the thought of hatred, and the claim will yield, not because hatred produced the claim, but because it prevents his recovery. Thus sin and other conditions operate to prevent the recovery of patients, but are not always the immediate cause of physical disorders.

God the Healer

God is Truth, and God is Good; therefore we declare the Truth. TRUTH IS PRESENT WITH US; or God, Power, is present with us, and does the healing. There are not enough Christian Scientists in the world to heal a boil, but Christ does the work; the spiritual understanding of divine Law is the enforcement of divine Law to the abolishment of a spurious sense of law called disease.

Needful Power in Treatment

Often a Christian Scientist treats a case and makes a thoroughly scientific treatment, but it is "no good," and why? Because it lacks impulsion or propulsion. It is from the fact that there is no power behind it.

Divine Love Is the Only Power

We must realize that God is omnipotent,—that is, the only power,—and therefore the Truth we have declared (which is God) is the only power, and that God is conscious Mind, and this gives our treatment needful force.

Impersonal Handling of Malpractice

We must not treat against personality in treating against malpractice, for, in bringing a person into our treatment, we bring a fighter, and the only way to handle mental malpractice is without a fighter, that is, impersonally. Suppose a case of A and B. A says, "I have a headache, and I know just where it comes from," and he proceeds to handle B, and B in turn feels A's thought and feels some physical manifestation (such a method often causes one) and he detects the source of the thought and begins to fight back, and thus the fight would continue. Mrs. Eddy says that so-called Scientists sometimes fight like beasts.

Separate Error from Person

A practitioner should never acknowledge power in fear. For instance, some will say, in cases where they fail to heal right away, "Well, I guess it's my fear," or, "It's the patient's fear." A practitioner can never heal in this way, and he should never admit that he or any other person has fear. He has no fear, neither has any person. It is "it" which has fear, is fear, and the only way to handle "it" (animal magnetism) is as "it."

Mortal Law, Not Personal Belief, Must Be Destroyed

We must not say in treating that our patient has a belief. It is all right in speaking to others to speak of a patient's belief, but we must not treat against a personal belief, as it might be a child who is not old enough to have a belief about its afflictions. We must BREAK THE MORTAL SO-CALLED LAW. Every mortal mind effect is produced by a mortal mind law, and we must destroy that so-called law.

Mortal Law of Relapse Must Be Handled

Students must destroy the law of mental malpractice, which operates to cause a recurrence of old beliefs. A patient who was dying was healed by denying the law of recurrence of old beliefs.

Wiles of the Devil

Mr. Kimball said that if he were the devil he would, of course, resist those who were trying to destroy him, namely, Christian Scientists, and would pursue one of three or four courses, according to the particular weakness of each person whom he had to deal with. He would mesmerize some into the belief that they were not worthy to heal the sick; others, into the belief that they did not have the requisite understanding; and others, into the belief of discouragement. He would not be afraid of any such so-called Scientists who could be mesmerized into accepting such beliefs about themselves.

Persistent Effort Commended

Mr. Kimball said, that, once, when he was lecturing in a certain place, a man came to him and said that his healer had told him to read "Science and Health," and he had done so. He spoke very condescendingly of the fact, and said that he could get nothing out of it. Mr. Kimball said to the man, "If you were in hell, the good old-fashioned hell you read about, and you had been there for some time, and had gotten tired of the pleasures of hell, and a rope were let down which provided the means of escape, wouldn't you run after that rope until you got it, no matter if you had to stumble over others, and endure all kinds of hardships, to get it?" The man said that he would. Mr. Kimball replied, "Well, you are in the only kind of hell you will ever experience, and Christian Science is the rope that will pull you out, after you get thoroughly tired of hell, and if you will run after Science just as persistently as you would after a rope let down to you in the old-fashioned hell, if there were one, you will experience healing."

Self-righteousness Exposed

Some Christian Scientists are absolutely cruel in trying to force their views upon others, and make others see as they do.

SELF-LOVE HAS TO BE OVERCOME IN US ALL. It often blinds our understanding. As long as we are ruled by our own will, we forfeit the divine guidance, and are not led by the divine will. There is a great belief in the world of everybody having a will of his own.

Advising Others Discouraged

Mrs. Eddy is the hardest person in the world to get any advice from. She is too wise to give advice, knowing that if students trust to the divine guidance, they will be led, and not until God prepares them can they receive the light, and she is afraid of her own human will and "belief of mind" controlling others. There is but one Mind, and the sooner we destroy the belief of an individual mind and self-will, the sooner we will gain the divine Mind and guidance.

We Must Keep Our Reflection of God Unclouded

We are just like a window-pane. If we keep our spiritual light unclouded, we will get more light all the time, but if we allow malice, hatred, self-will, envy, lust, etc., to becloud our understanding, we will be just like the window-pane covered with dust and mud from the inside, no matter how bright the light without. If the window-pane is not in a translucent condition, the light will not penetrate it.

Individual Demonstration to Be Respected

Each will receive all the light for which he is prepared, and we must not try to force our superior understanding upon another. We are trying to do God's work. We must not judge. Often when we are condemning another, that poor brother is sitting within the closed doors of his or her own consciousness, weeping because he or she is not better.

ASSOCIATION ADDRESS, YEAR OF 1908

The Progressive Practitioner

Mrs. Eddy clearly indicates that Christian Science practice should be improved, not only in the way of results, but also in the way of application or modus operandi. The progressive practitioner will naturally learn to give treatments on a higher plane; and he himself will be in a higher altitude of appreciation and discernment. He will more clearly perceive the nature of error and be more correctly discriminating in his estimate of it and of its claims, and particularly concerning its claims of good, or its claims to be in some respects relatively good.

Impersonal Sense Gained

He will learn to be less personal in his estimate of error, and will gradually grow in the perception that he does not have to deal with persons, but with belief, which is always without a believer—without person. As he gains a better sense of pure metaphysics, the entire trend of his thought changes, and all the aspects of his work, and of the work to be done, take on different form. He finds that he must work differently, that he must move higher or further along, that he must graduate from former methods which will appear to be inadequate.

Mrs. Eddy Expected Progress in Understanding and Discovery

Mrs. Eddy covers the ground specifically in a recent admonition to pay more attention to her teachings of today than to that of twenty-five years ago. Her changes in the text-book show that she is trying to advance the thought of Scientists, that they may keep pace with the progress she is making, and that the public mind may accustom itself to more correct theology. She has been obliged to make many concessions to current religious thought, rather than to upheave it too violently, but it cannot be doubted that she hopes we will push forward to the appreciation of higher statements.

Relative Statements in "Science and Health"

She attempts to reach many different stages of thought through "Science and Health," but it seems to be sensible to assume that we will do well not to cling to the lower plane of statement, or appreciation, that has in many instances been presented for the beginner.

Science Reverses Old Methods

It has long been recognized that Science reverses old methods. It discloses the fact that the way of salvation is different from that prescribed by old theology. I shall refer to some of the important differences, and thereby show why some of them fail to procure the desired results through our practice.

"Renunciation," the Demand of Old Theology

The old theological plan of salvation included the continuous refrain that we must "give up all for Christ," and that our lives should be a process of renunciation and of giving up everything in sight. The result of this kind of inducement has been that people have begun a prodigious onslaught of the human will against everything included in the environment of human life; but this sort of struggle generally results in a destructive career.

Education, Gain, the Demand of Science

It seems clear that the advanced Scientist needs to change his standpoint of application. He needs to stop the many declarations about "giving up," and to cease the effort to progress by means of a "giving up" process. The actual service which Christian Science exerts in our behalf is a purely educational one. Our deliverance from the old belief of evil is to be accomplished, not by "giving up," but by gaining.

Work More for Truth and Good

The statement, "Seek ye first the kingdom of God," is scientifically and literally correct; that is to say, the one to whom Christian Science is becoming substantive needs to seek or desire the right idea about everything, because the right idea silences the false concept of belief. I am convinced that many Scientists procrastinate their own deliverance by working at the wrong end of the problem.

Error Cannot Give Itself Up

The Bible says, "The government shall be upon his shoulder," meaning that the right idea does the work—asserts itself and conversely disposes of false belief. It is certain that an erring belief does not know enough to give itself up. It is certain that an erring state of so-called human consciousness does not know enough to give itself up. It follows, therefore, that a purely human "giving up" endeavor does not give up, but does involve the Scientist in a sense of greater fear. Evil is never disposed of as if it were something. It cannot be given up as though it were something. It can only be disposed of by the activity of right ideas, which resolve the evil claim of temptation as though it were nothing.

Affirmative Condition of Thought

I suggest to you, at this point, the great value of an affirmative condition of thought. Try to realize that, through Christian Science, you are constantly gaining that which will do everything for you, and that you will succeed according to the gaining process. This will open your mentality and make it more receptive of the right idea; whereas a contrary policy of thought, which is ever contemplating a process of "giving up," narrows its own scope and curtails the capacity to acquire the true idea of salvation.

Truth Overcomes Error

It is, of course, true that all forms of erring belief are to disappear, and that the so-called human consciousness is to be divested of all that which, as error or sin, claims to be something, but all this is to be accomplished by the influx of pure knowledge or a correct estimate or appreciation of being.

Suffering Unnecessary

There is another incorrect thought in this same line. It is the declaration that mortals must suffer out of the flesh. Now inasmuch as there is no flesh and man is not in flesh, and never was in flesh, it follows that the thought that we must suffer out of the flesh would admit all that is claimed for the flesh. If we are really in the flesh, we would better stay there; because, if we are actually in it, we cannot get out by suffering or otherwise. If we are not in the flesh, we do not have to suffer out of it. The supposition that we are in the flesh is merely a belief.

Suffering Not a Remedy or a Saviour

We are not to get rid of the flesh, but of the **belief** that we are in the flesh, and that life and body are material. The poorest way to get rid of that belief is to suppose that there is any virtue in applying suffering as a remedy, or to suppose that belief can be corrected by another equally erroneous belief called suffering. It is plain that the thought which is proceeding with the expectation of suffering out of the flesh is being greatly hindered and arrested. Such an expectation is wholly irrational and destructive.

Healing—Not in but from the Flesh

As to those who come to us for Christian Science treatment, let us know enough to know that they righteously desire to be healed, not in the flesh but rather from the flesh,—such application of treatment inspires spiritual healing.

The Knowledge that Body Is Spiritual Overcomes Flesh

The only way out of the flesh is the way which dispels the belief that substance and man are material. The only thing that will do this is the understanding that body is spiritual. Suffering cannot do it and is not the way to do it. All this suffering is absolutely incorrect, notwithstanding the claim that a material and erring sense of life seems to punish itself; but suffering—which seems to be the only way whereby to get into trouble—is not the way out of it.

Penalty and Punishment Not of God's Ordering

Another bad fault has grown out of our old theological belief of condemnation and penalty, and the belief that God devises and institutes and bestows the punishment that is incidental to condemnation. The fact is that the divine Mind knows no evil and does not know that anybody is perpetrating any evil. The supposition that God condemns and punishes sin and other forms of error would, if it were possible, involve God in evil, and would confirm every claim concerning the reality of evil. Such assertions as these are frequently met by the averment that God is not evil but that He knows enough about it to punish it, and the result has been that the ordinary religious belief has been to the effect that penalty and punishment are of divine bestowal and are therefore indispensable concomitants of the divine plan.

The Mortal Ordinance of Condemnation Must Be Met

By thus making a connection between God and penalty and suffering, mankind has involved itself in terror and fear of a revengeful and wrathful God. This fear constitutes a continuing belief of causation and induces the belief of diseases and other evils. Science discloses the fact that, in belief, mortal mind creates mortal man for the purpose of killing him. Before killing him, it condemns and sentences him. It is this condemnation of mortal man that I want you to recognize, and

I want you to know the necessity of canceling it and of adequately protecting yourself and your patients from it. It is more important than we have been in the habit of thinking it to be. In order to show the extent to which false theology has involved itself in the condemnation of mortal man, I quote one statement, namely, "The wages of sin is death." Christian Science proves that the wages of so-called sin is human education—education in spirituality and right living.

Sin, Matter, Manifestations of Mortal Mind

We know that everything that is called sin is a manifestation of mortal mind. We know that everything that is called matter is a manifestation of mortal mind. Indeed, we know that every kind of materiality or corporeality belongs to the unit or unification called mortal mind.

The Legitimate Wage of Sin Is Not Death

For a man to breathe, steal, sleep, lie, or eat food, or to believe that two times two is five—all these are manifestations of the one error. God knows nothing of any of it. All that is included in it is error; all the laws and decrees and penalties and threats and predictions have been devised and put forth by mortal mind. If it is true that the only legitimate wage of the one error is death, then it would be a fact that Christian Science practice is illegitimate. It would mean that the man who breathes and eats food is entitled to death, and that the only proper thing to do to him would be to procure his death.

Our Need Is Salvation, Not Punishment

If you will analyze this subject thoroughly, you will find that what is called theology, physical science, and philosophy, instead of uncovering the error that is involved, have formulated the condemnation, not of error, including breathing, but the condemnation of the man who breathes. **Throughout the ages of religious belief you may find that it is the man who must be punished and who must die. You may discover that every** man and woman is under the rule of a supposedly divine, universal, theological, philosophical, scientific condemnation. This condemnation is one of the most important things for you to recognize and annul in every claim or patient you have. It must be clear that there is no God in it at all, and that—as a rule and law of mortal mind—it is always wrong. The only thing that God does for humanity, or ever needs to do, is to bless mankind; and it is blessing, or correction, or enlightenment and salvation, that we really need, not punishment.

The Sinner Entitled, Not to Death, but to Enlightenment

First of all, then, remember always that suffering is never procured by God as a penalty, or as a consequence, or as an educational process, for any purpose whatever. Then remember that the entire network of materiality, sin, sickness, pleasure, or death, is the output of mortal mind, which is always wrong. Then know that the supreme need of humanity is not of suffering, but of enlightenment, and that it is entitled to enlightenment, because men are not original sinners. ["The sinner created neither himself nor sin, but sin created the sinner; that is, error made its man mortal."—Retrospection and Introspection, by Mary Baker Eddy.]

Never Declare the Necessity for Suffering, Not Even for Sin

Then cease forever declarations like this: "Well, I suppose I must suffer out of it," or, "The patient must suffer out of it." Is there any curative efficacy in a treatment which includes the mental provision that the patient must suffer for any reason? (See note on page 97.—The Editor.)

Declare the Necessity and Presence of Salvation

The mission of Christian Science is to deliver, to save, to redeem. It has no punishment and no condemnation for a mortal man. Inasmuch as mortals are defrauded and imposed upon by mortal mind, it follows that the worst sinner is the greatest victim, and that what he needs and is entitled to is instant salvation instead of eternal punishment. Many Scientists have a bad habit of holding their patients under the ban of condemnation, and thereby frustrating a cure, whereas nothing but righteous judgment will heal the sick.

The Proper Sequence of Sin Is Salvation, not Condemnation

The wages of sin or materiality is not the death of a mortal; that is to say, the natural and inevitable consequence of being, imposed upon us, is not death. Such a provision would not be even ethical. The only proper sequence of sin or error is salvation or deliverance through the activity of real knowledge. Watch carefully against the disposition to join in the universal condemnation of mortals.

The Devil Condemns; God Saves. Don't Imitate the Devil

Christian Science operates wholly to release the victim, not to condemn him; and this is done by condemning the error, but not the man; and error must always be condemned as nothing, not as something. You need to beware of the Bible references which are made to appear as though they condemned man instead of error; no such condemnation is intended. You are never warranted in condemning a mortal, never warranted in condemning yourself. Truth uncovers error as nothing, but it does not condemn the man or require the suffering which error alone bestows on mortals.

Illegitimacy of Penalty Demonstrated

Some time ago I rescued a patient, a Scientist, who had had much treatment, by knowing that she was not under a penalty by reason of a belief in matter, or a belief that she was a woman with a material body, or that she was a mother; that she was not under penalty for the infraction of any law of error, or for anything that she ever did or did not do; that she was not under penalty according to any rule of belief of mortal mind; and that there was no penalty, consequences, or suffering in mortal mind. This treatment, which knew enough to know that the penalty was unreal, knew enough to make an unreality of suffering, and she recovered.

Belief in Limited Opportunity Exposed

One of the worst phases of human philosophy is in its limited sense of opportunity. Christian Science practice is greatly obstructed by the belief of limited opportunity. The patient is very apt to think that his chance of recovery is passed, and that it is too late to win. All kinds of people give up because of the claim of limited opportunity. The practitioner very frequently voices the claim and fails to expect results because of the feeling that there is a lack of opportunity.

The Door of Opportunity Never Closed

Opportunity is infinite and ever present. As a matter of fact, men exist at the standpoint of opportunity. Man is simply a condition of receptivity. It is **his business** to receive constantly and perpetually. He is to show forth the abundance of infinity. This being the case, the opportunity to manifest perfection is not only ever-present, but it is really a part of himself. It would not be very far-fetched to say that man and opportunity are one. The law of opportunity enforces its continuance and availability; and conversely it breaks down and arrests the supposed mortal law which claims to limit opportunity. I know you ought to handle this in every case.

Declare Opportunity Specifically. Never Too Late

It is not sufficient merely to declare that Mind is unlimited and therefore there is no limitation. You must take up this claim specifically, and declare for opportunity frequently, until your own thought is familiar with the expectation of opportunity. Remember that there is nothing in a treatment other than that which is in it as specific thought, and that your patient has no more opportunity to recover than mortal mind concedes, unless your treatment provides infinite opportunity —opportunity to recover. It is never too late for opportunity.

Right Idea of Opportunity Makes for Receptivity

As soon as you grasp this, you will see how deficient your treatments have been in the way of expectation or true faith, and you will see why you have sometimes failed; and you will realize that you have made a great gain, and improved your work, by getting the true idea of opportunity. Principle, law, power, and opportunity are all that is needed in order to move mountains. Do not forget to make the most of this idea in behalf of the sick, or in matters of business and employment, and all the details of daily experience and activity. You will see that the right idea of opportunity is the open door of receptivity.

Human Body a False Belief About Body

What is called "the body" is a false belief about body and not a reality. This disclosure does not warrant us in hating it, or condemning it, or denouncing it, as though it were a monster to be abhorred. There is neither wisdom nor humility in calling it "this vile body," or a "base body," or in making any other disagreeable or libelous remarks about it. True, it represents a misconception, but there is no use in damning or reviling it, or in uttering any disrespectful remarks about it. It being a belief, the thing to do is to improve the belief.

Body Not to Be Condemned, but Improved

Christian Science healing would not be sanctioned by, or attested by, facts, if it were not that such healing indicated itself in improved beliefs concerning the body. There is no body that is to be destroyed, mutilated or decapitated by Christian Science practice. Because Christian Science practice brings into evidence an improved bodily condition or estate, that fact ought to carry the assurance that we need not condemn the body. As a step in progress we are to show forth a better bodily condition, and this will not be accomplished by mentally excoriating that which now seems to be the body.

The Spiritual Body

There is one perfect, spiritual body. An erroneous belief of body must be corrected, or, rather, displaced by the right sense of body. There is no place where suffering may not be dispensed with, because it does not enlighten or re-inforce the idea which is already correct, and which alone can efface, with its calm assertiveness, every and any claim of error. This analysis leads to the conclusion that, as the Scientist progresses, he will find that humanity, and even what is called the human body, will appear with ever-growing kindliness of aspect.

The Body as Sacred as Mind

It is a scientific statement to declare that man exists at the standpoint of body. It follows that body is as sacred as Mind. It also follows that there can be no legitimate denunciation of body. Nothing is legitimate but to supersede a wrong sense of it. Many Scientists seem afraid to declare properly concerning body. Some will do nothing but declare the facts about God, and religiously refuse to declare the truth about man and body. This perhaps grows out of the failure to realize that the truth about God is man, is body. Man, body, constitutes the evidence that there is God. Man shows forth and is an exhibition of God, and man is body.

Learn and Declare the Truth About Body

This being the case, there is the utmost propriety in declaring the truth about man as body, and becoming most familiar with the facts as to man and God. I do not hesitate to urge you to declare constantly—or perhaps I should say frequently—the truth about body, in order that the spiritual idea about body may silence and displace the material concept. Disease is an error about body, and a specific idea of Mind is necessary to correct or dispel it.

Body Consists of Right Ideas. Treatment

One infinite Mind and Its ideas constitute the whole of Being. One infinite consciousness, wherein the infinite aggregation of Mind's ideas manifest activity, constitute the one body, or the embodiment, of Mind. Hence, there is one infinite Mind, and that Mind is our Mind. There is one infinity of body, and that body is our body. Body is the infinite manifestation of Mind, the compound idea of Mind. All the things of body are eternal, complete, perfect and perpetually active as ideas. The law of Mind to body is the law of perpetual, harmonious action. Body will always be body: it cannot fail, be sick, or change. It is the manifestation of vigor, vitality, strength, power, force, and perfect impulsion; and the divine law unto it is the law of strength and normal action.

Only One Body. Malpractice Met

In your treatment, if the only sense of body is the right one, then there is no body that is sick, or can be sick. Moreover, the right sense of body enables you to put out the belief that body is the private body of a man or a woman, and is one that can be sick, or contains place or substance that can be sick. Still further, it may be seen that, if you were in belief of sickness because of mental malpractice, the mere knowing of one body would be sufficient to break the claim, because malpractice could not act where there was no belief of a material, private body.

Do Not Hate or Deny Any Part of Your Body

I have many times heard such remarks as this: "I wish I could, or I will be glad when I can, get rid of this body"; but that line of thought will never solve the problem. I have known of people who had mesmerized themselves into a state of hatred of their bodies, and who seemed to think that they might hate their bodies sufficiently to get rid of them and become clad in spirituality. I do not think that there is any likelihood that you will imagine I am pleading with you to make any sort of admission that the material concept, called body, is real or eternal; but I do want to impress you with the necessity of not mentally sand-bagging or abusing or slandering what seems to be your body, or any part of it.

Overcome Material Sense of Body by Living, Not Dying

As against the statement frequently made by Scientists—"Well, I suppose we must all pass through the belief of death in order to get rid of this material body," we are warranted in this statement: There is no "this material body" to get rid of. The very statement itself, so often made by Scientists, is a death sentence in itself. Moreover, a mortal cannot die out of the belief that body is material. He has to live out of it. There is no way out of the belief of death but to live. Life is Love, Spirit, and if we would overcome the false material sense of life in matter, we must love our way out. He who loves not, lives not, for Love is Life. In order to get the body that manifests life, we must begin to declare for it, and gradually, or rapidly, come into our own—namely, eternal body.

Human Sense of Body Should Endure Until Transcended

In your treatment of the sick, be sure to declare the facts about body. Some of the physicians show a more correct sense of body than do some Christian Scientists. Dr. W. A. Hammond, former Surgeon-General of the United States, has recently said that there is no physiological reason why the body of a human being should die. He refers to the capacity of the body to renew its tissues and to continue its functions, and says that this would go on indefinitely if it were not that the eliminating process becomes defective.

Proper Elimination the Secret of Health

That which most disturbs the integrity of elimination is anger, fear, and other similar improprieties. If a human being were so poised spiritually as to have the dominion which even a human being should show, he might govern elimination in perfect equipoise. Very many of the so-called physical disorders are because of the belief of deficient elimination, and this is what Dr. Hammond acknowledges in his statement; and this in a way confirms the contention made by Christian Scientists to the effect that disease is an impropriety or disorder, and the proper healing process is one of elimination—the expulsion of false belief.

Treatment for Elimination

In the case of the human body, elimination goes on through the skin, bowels, kidneys and breathing. The claim is, that when this process is not complete or perfect, there is a retention of impurities. Hence, the necessity of handling this claim for every patient. A treatment to cover this claim must declare that Mind is the law of elimination to the belief of deficient elimination, to the belief of abnormal retention or secretion, and to the belief of morbific secretions or animal poison. This claim of deficient elimination is an avenue for the claim of malpractice, operating through the so-called law of *materia medica*.

Bodily Activity Normal and Necessary

It has been declared by medical thought that Christian Scientists disdain all care of the body, and all exercise and hygienic precautions and measures, and will therefore show the consequence of bodily inactivity by means of incomplete elimination. This leads me to say something which I hope you will not misunderstand or misconstrue. We are yet in what I call a transitional stage, but there never will be a time when bodily activity will not be proper. Scientifically considered, the body is manifested through action or inaction. A natural freedom and dominion on the human plane may well manifest itself in a normal bodily activity.

Do Not Force What You Have Not Demonstrated

The Scientist is liable, through misapprehension, to try to take a position through force which has not been gained through demonstration. I suggest to you, not a recourse to the ordinary forms of exercise that are indulged in for the cure of sickness, but that you remember that there is no advantage in an unsymmetrical growth whereby a person becomes physically one-sided. We are not yet where we should not use some care to breathe what is called pure air, and drink pure water, and eat what is regarded as wholesome food; to be temperate and moderate; and to realize that it is more temperate to manifest a reasonable amount of physical activity than it is to sit around in a house all the time in a condition of bodily inactivity or stagnation. I do not think that a practitioner is doing the best that can be done who sits in a house all the time treating the sick, without fresh air or free activity, unless he can demonstrate perfect nutrition and elimination according to the law of Mind.

Wiser to Refrain from Inactivity

In the same sense that Mary did well to protect Jesus by taking him into Egypt, it may be needful for the Scientist to get out of the storm. In the same sense that some people avoid the use of tea and coffee because they do not want to be constantly handling the mortal mind law which pertains to the use of tea and coffee, so may a Scientist refrain from inactivity rather than contend against the law which is incidental thereto. I conceive it to be in the line of progress to show forth by demonstration a constantly improving human situation, rather than by any form of human deterioration.

Spiritual Activity Not Manifest in Physical Stagnation

I once heard a Scientist say that the orchid is the most spiritual flower, because it feeds on air. Now there is no spiritual food other than Spirit. Air is no more spiritual than potatoes, and it is in the line of progress for a human being who cannot digest his food because of error to gain the spiritual insight which enables him to digest his food. We are not under the stress or necessity of disdaining nature and the normal things of what is called nature. What we need is not disdain, but dominion. Spiritual activity will not at this stage manifest itself in physical stagnation.

"Replace Objects of Sense with Spiritual Ideas"

I find it desirable to remind you frequently of one thing which you will do well to impress upon yourselves indelibly and at once. It is this: The basis of our practice is the infinite verity that all that is real is already complete and perfect. The universe and all therein contained—man, body, law, power, everything—is finished and is already immortal. There is no need that God should do more, and no Christian Scientist is called upon to do anything to any of the things that exist. He does not need to do anything to man, body. What then may he do? What must he do in order to do the best he can do? He needs only to deny a lie about God, man, body, universe. The practice of Christian Science is the mental activity which resolves so-called material things into thoughts, and discovers that these are simply erring beliefs about that which is true.

Treatment Deals with False Beliefs, Not Persons

There is great, very great objection to your giving treatments as though your patients were men and women who are sick, or believe they are sick. Metaphysical healing has to do with erring beliefs, not with persons. If you have a man or woman as a patient, you are dealing with a corporeality; and if your treatment has a physical person in it, then it has a body that can be sick. The only treatment that is safe and that is entitled to heal is the one that has no thought or admission except the one infinite body. You should never continue a treatment that does not satisfy reason that you have been handling error, or doing something to error, rather than to a man or woman.

There Is No Personal Patient

A treatment is representative of the character, scope, and correctness of your general understanding. How important then to declare that the patient is neither person, place, nor thing, but is simply a suggestion or claim that man is material and is sick. Do not be afraid to leave the belief of a personal patient out of your treatment. In the same way and for the same reason that you would leave out of your treatment the belief of a mental practitioner who could fight back, you must leave out of the treatment the belief of a man or woman who can be sick.

What a Treatment Is

Do not get the notion that you have some wonderful thing to do which you feel you cannot do. A Christian Science treatment has nothing to do with the mortal self, because it is simply the utterance by the spiritual self of truth concerning God, Life, man, body, substance, presence, law, power, and action, and a calm and peaceful announcement that error is unreal and without substance, law, power, or presence. The simpler a treatment, the better; there is no need of a labored treatment.

Calm Dominion

I have heard the statement: "She handles error without gloves," or, 'She goes for it hammer and tongs." If error could talk about it, it would probably say: "I do not care a particle for that kind of a treatment; that kind of a treatment means that I am real and must be hammered, and that is all

I pretend to be. The only treatment that I am afraid of is the one that makes nothing of me—not enough to hammer. I am afraid of the destructive calm of the one who knows I am nothing.''

Self-Depreciation Bad.   False Humility

A bad habit is that of self-depreciation. It does no good, and assumes that it is worth while to waylay and denounce one's self. It poses as a virtue or as humility. Now, Christian Science shows that the right man is just as good as the right God. You are gradually showing forth this man. This man is the man you are. He is entitled to esteem because he is the son of God. So far as he goes, he is good and worthy. This is the man you must stand up for. For this man—which is yourself—you must declare every good thing, every good capacity, unlimited opportunity and ability.

Your Right Thought Is Law and Power

I want to say something concerning law that we need very much to learn; namely—that, in the sense that we are entitled to dominion over all the earth, we are to be a law unto ourselves. Only as we enforce this law in our behalf will it be enforced. We must gain and utter, or define, the right idea of law. Divine law is included in the Godhead. It is a part of the infinity that we are to reflect. Law exists as idea. It is man's business to show forth ideas, to show forth law, to be the utterance and mandate of law. In a certain sense man and law are one. You are to know that your right thought is not only thought, it is law.

Treatment Must Be Law

Your treatment must know enough to know that it is the law, is the law unto the case, is the law unto yourself. The idea that your treatment invokes law, and that law is aloof from you and apart from you, is a mistake; it deprives your treatment of the enforcement of law. You should declare in your treatment: This treatment is the enforcement of the law of harmony and life and perfection. This treatment is the law of extinction to the law of malpractice, etc. The sick are made sick through the enforcement of a spurious law. Your treatment, which is the true idea of law, does annul the spurious law; and it anuls it by **knowing** that it annuls it. You must be very particular to include this in your treatment, because all healing occurs through the operation of law when expressed in or through your treatment.

Treatment Is the Manifestation of God

Get on the highest pinnacle of respect for Christian Science treatment—for your treatment. It is the manifestation of God, it is "God with us," it is the manifestation of Mind which comes to the human mind to redeem and exalt. Regard it as being the Word and might of God, rather than as being your treatment. Declare that the only place to meet error is in the realm of thought, and that right thought is always victor. Error does not continue itself, and cannot. There is no law of a return of old beliefs, and no law of reversal. The divine law is the law of perfection, reconstruction and recovery to what is called the human body. All you need to do is to mentally break all pretence of a contrary rule or mandate.

Error Uncovered

In educating a Christian Scientist, one of the first things to do is to get him to comprehend that evil is not a thing, but a belief. Next, that the belief is mesmeric in its activity, namely —that it is a belief of mortal mind that thought transfers itself from one mortal mind to another. Next, that this claim of thought transference asserts for itself influence and power, and in its worst phases has the sting and mischief of malice.

The Fear of Malpractice Exposed

Generally so much effort is required to get the student to see the claim of error that, when he does see it, he at first is afraid of it. The effort to have him see it as a false claim, to be obliterated as nothing, ultimates, at first, in a belief that it is something and is something to be afraid of. After that comes the long-drawn-out process of persuading him that malpractice, which is nothing more than the belief of a mortal, is utterly unreal and valueless, and then he will see how obvious a lie about anything is in the presence of the truth about it. A treatment against malpractice is just as good as the knowledge that the lie in belief, when side by side with the truth, is nothing, and has no presence, power, or action, and has nothing that it can act upon.

Treatment for Malpractice

I am inclined to think that a treatment against malpractice should more thoroughly include a treatment against the fear of it. This is the important thing I ask you to notice, namely —that the first thing to break in connection with any claim is the fear of it. You have just as much to consider in the item of fear of malpractice as you have in its own supposed activity, and I feel confident that to **be unscared about** it is the best kind of a treatment. **There is no malpractice, and never was any. There is no mortal mind to induce it. It is without law, power, or action. It never did anything to anyone. Therefore, be not afraid of that which never was anything.**

Do Not Malpractice on Yourself

The continuous study of "Science and Health" exalts our appreciation of Science. The book means millions of times more than the mere text implies upon the surface. I need scarcely remind you that it is that which leadeth unto all Truth, and that it will perpetually carry us to greater heights of understanding. This book implores you not to declare things concerning yourself that ought not to be and that you really do not want to have brought out in experience. I ask you to watch yourselves for one day, and see how many times you declare contrary to your welfare and future prosperity and declare falsely concerning your rights or lack of rights.

Right Declaration Is Christ, Your Redeemer

Get on the right side of the situation with your declaration. Then you will be entitled to win, because all things are possible to the right idea. The right idea is the redeemer, the consciousness of the Christ which destroys the belief of evil. At last this redeemer has come to the thought of the human being and declares his absolute redemption. This Christ is with you.

NOTE REFERRING TO PAGE 83

Never declare for the necessity of suffering for sin, in treatment or in your thought of mortals. Only mortal mind can or does try to inflict suffering, for any reason whatever. Yet, to eliminate sin is the only reliable and scientific way to escape suffering and death. Any other expectation or practice is both dangerous and delusive.

On page 385 of "Science and Health," Mrs. Eddy advises: "Let us remember that the eternal law of right, though it can never annul the law which makes sin its own executioner, exempts man from all penalties but those due to wrong-doing." Mr. Kimball does not teach contrary to this. He does teach that Scientists should not try to mentally enforce penalty for sin, but should work to abrogate both sin and penalty.

THE EDITOR.

AN ADDRESS TO WORKERS

Caution with Truth

For the reason that you know much, I advise you to be careful how you let it be known. It is an astounding depravity of mortal mind that shows itself in envy and jealousy concerning those who really know something that is worth while to know about Science, particularly about anything that seems novel or extraordinary. The one who does not instantly understand you is liable to fret or chemicalize, and to make you trouble. Remember that not one in a thousand is ready for an advanced idea, notwithstanding that the idea will sometime deliver them. I advise you to be almost stingy about this.

Not Overzealous in Instructing Others

I can see better than ever before why our Leader has said, in my presence, that there were things about which she could not tell us. I think that all of us bring upon ourselves a lot of mental "sizzling" by reason of our zeal in instructing others. I am glad that, in my lazy way, I am getting out of that rut somewhat.

Practitioners Deserve Compensation

I think you have demonstrated that you are in line with a normal course of events while engaged as a practitioner. I feel certain that thus you can do as much for yourself and others as in any other way. I feel that, while you are not after money in the ordinary sense of the word, there is every reason to know that you are entitled to adequate provision.

Supply Not Limited to One Channel

Everything that is involved in that which people call supply, maintenance, etc., is a thing of thought. What we need to do is to reach out toward unlimited thought in this respect. Humanly thinking, it would be natural for you to think that, while you are in the practice, your supply should come through your practice; but just see what a limited thought that is! Inasmuch as supply belongs to infinity, and is really a manifestation of infinity, how woefully scant is the thought that ignores infinity and limits supply to one narrow channel.

Treatment for Supply

Now then, think thus: Supply is omnipresent and unlimited, and is always where you are and what you want. It is liable to show itself to you through millions of channels; therefore, open up all of the channels and let it come in. Keep yourself in a state of non-surprise; gain a mental attitude in which nothing in the way of supply will surprise you, not even if you found pieces of silver in the mouth of a fish. You are not the victim of any circumstances; you are the child of God. You have an infinite income commensurate with the grandeur of your thought expressing the infinity of being. No sense of man or woman or any belief of occasion, event or inexplicable fatality, or any other belief, can stand any longer before your treatment, which is the very presence and power of the only God there is.

Every Good Is Yours Now

Infinity is wholly accomplished. Life is, and all law and power are established. Reality or the Divine Mind includes nothing but perfection. All the possibilities of being are yours now; there will never be any more. You need not wait for deliverance; today it is yours. You may as well express dominion now as to wait. Declare everything good for yourself; expect everything good now. Insist that no supposition of error can affect or move you.

Treatment for Realization of Good

Declare that there is one Mind, and that Mind is my Mind; that there is one spiritual body, and that body is my body. Our one body is eternal, indestructible, changeless, spiritual, aloof from belief, suggestion, discord, or abnormities, subject only to the law of Life, harmony, perfection, sustained in eternal completeness and activity. That body is spiritual and is one. There are no laws of sin or disease that pertain to it, or can govern it; and there is no law of malpractice that can possibly assert itself or produce any impact. The one body, the one man, is in a state of perpetual equipoise. Man is the perpetual intake of supply.

Treatment for Protection

No matter what the mortal point of view may be, you cannot be seen or known or even thought of mortally. Your right to rebel is just; but rebel with the superb conviction that your freedom is not only assured, but manifested. You are finding your natural, normal expression in so doing. We must all attain our independence, for only thus can we best help others whom we love.

Dwell in Highest Thought and Feeling

Ascend constantly to your highest altitude of equanimity, self-reliance and mental culture, above the plane of concept, where the ordinary human belief cannot move you and substitute itself for your poise. Refuse to descend into the mire of cheap human rubbish, and know that your composure cannot be upset by envy or by any mortal. You have a fundamental ability to do everything that is right to do. Avoid self-depreciation.

Handling Malpractice

The belief of mesmerism, thought transference, mental malpractice, is nothing but a dream; the whole thing is in the realm of seeming thought. You obstruct its activity by declaring: There is no such thing as mortal mind; no mind or body on which it can act or impress itself. If you are in belief suffering because of mental malpractice, the mere knowledge that there is but one Mind and body would be sufficient to break the claim, because malpractice could not act where there was no belief in a material, private body.

Fully Persuaded in Your Own Integrity and Rights

Let not error torment you. What it argues is always false in every way. We must know that we cannot be prevented from doing and being what is right by any argument of environment, false human opinion, judgment or inclination. Our trust in God and our **understanding** is capable of extricating us from all predicaments. When you are under a claim of argument that you are out of joint or confused, do you not see that it is an imposed belief, and is not you? Yet how prone you are to say that the thing that is wrong is yourself.

No Limit to Your Success or Dominion

Who shall limit the possibility of divine law? Who shall declare a limit to your dominion? What shall hinder you being a law of absolute control to your environment and daily existence, expressing, as you do, the infinity of Being? You are dependent upon no one for peace, poise, success. Get on the right side of the situation with your declarations; then you will win, because all things are possible to the right idea. The right idea is the redeemer of consciousness, the Christ which destroys the belief in evil.

No Good Effort Is Lost

Every treatment we give, every effort we make to overcome error, is cumulative and helpful. No good thoughts are lost. All good is eternal and ever present. We have all the life there is now. All of joy, perfection, supply, peace, are now at hand.

Spiritual Identity

We do know the Science of Being. Nothing can dim our perception of it, nor disqualify us from demonstrating it, for man is the understanding of divine Mind, and the unfolding of God's idea is eternal and perpetual. What I know about God is all there is to my spiritual identity.

Success, Culture, Education and Salvation

When we turn for power from matter to Spirit, we can move mountains, surmount all obstacles, achieve every success, and overcome fear and sin. The claiming of our rightful heritage as God's children is the true mental culture and spiritual education, and the only way to be saved.

Supply for Every Legitimate Need or Want Already Exists

In the reality of being is all we need or want or can possibly have; in fact, perfect satisfaction. It includes more than we can possibly now discern or desire, in the measure of happiness and the completion of every wish or prayer that is wholesome or right for us to have. All other longings and desires are destroyed through this realization.

Self-Treatment

I must know that the definition in "Science and Health" applies to me: I am God's image and likeness, reflecting infinity, the perfect image of Life, health, harmony, not under material laws or limitation.

No Death, No "Passing Out"

There is no material plane; we live, move and have our being in Life; we cannot pass out of that. It is just as wrong to believe in "passing out" as it is to believe in death. Break the law that says all must die, knowing it is not God's law. His law is life-giving and life-sustaining eternally. Knowing Good and doing good sustains life.

God With Us

Love is the very nearest thing to us at all times. We can always bring God to us instantly by **declaring** that He is with us. We never reach out for Him in vain. He is always available. He never delays. Everything for man's good is provided and present. God has ordained for us all good, and the continuation thereof is eternality.

Treatment for Malpractice

Malpractice can never blind us to evil, or make us believe we are safe when in danger. It can never argue that we would be happier or better satisfied to admit these erroneous beliefs; our safety and happiness is to cast them out. Hold steadfastly the thought of yourself as the consciousness of Good only, spiritual, perfect. The belief that there are two of me is where all the trouble comes from.

Requisites for Treatment

Every treatment must include the understanding that it is the law of God; that it cannot return void and it is **not** reversed by any so-called law of malpractice or human beliefs. **Error** says we are sick or discouraged; **we** do not say it; it is **error** talking about **itself**. Truth says: "I have perfect eyes, perfect heart. All there is of the 'I' that I am is God manifested, is perfection."

Directions for Mental Work

There is never a moment when we cannot find God by declaring what is true and holding fast to the Truth. We should discard mortal mind judgment and pray for the Christ-Mind. It is human will and judgment that argues why we cannot do so and so. There is no reason why we cannot always demonstrate Truth and be well and happy. We must break the general claim of fear, knowing it has no effect or purpose, no power, control or action. Malpractice cannot act as such a claim. Fear is senseless and sinful, and obedience to God breaks the claim and casts it out. Fear itself is without foundation or reason, therefore no part of my consciousness.

Treatment for Business Success

Our business is always good when God governs it, and there are no reversals or failures. There are no obstacles in our way, no temperamental qualities or disposition that can disqualify us from demonstrating the Truth. Our trust in God and our understanding is sufficient to extricate us from any inharmonious condition or predicament or disease in which we may seem to be.

Demonstration of Health

Health is the law of God, unchangeable and perfect, the result of perpetual, harmonious action. Christian Science works from the standpoint of a well man. The understanding of man's perfection is the true medicine and meets every case.

Directions for Treatment

There is no material body which is sick or needs healing. I am the man that knows health, harmony, prosperity, peace, immortality. A treatment is knowing the Truth and claiming it. The letter of it must be concise and to the point; do not waste words. The knowing what is true is the right mental action and is the Saviour, the source of all wealth and all good. It is necessary to dwell on the facts of existence, the statement of Life, health, being, and to know the facts of Omnipotence and what He has ordained for man.

Declarations of Truth

There is but one infinity and that includes all—man, business, relations, law, perfection, substance. The action, force, power of Truth is self-evident, self-acting and self-sustaining. Nothing can interfere with Truth; it is perfection and Life.

Infinity includes only man that is well, that is perfect and harmonious, and that has dominion and the continuance of all these things, without relapse from or return to harmony.

A Good Treatment Described

All things are possible to Mind and the right idea. A Christian Scientist's thought is accumulative; the work goes on to bless all mankind. A Christian Science treatment is no treatment unless it is accompanied with the knowledge that it is a good one and cannot be lost, reversed or destroyed.

Progression. Universality

We must keep abreast of the times and handle the new and aggressive forms of error as untrue, harmless, lawless, actionless, powerless. We must not confine our treatments or declarations to ourselves or our patients, but declare the Truth for all mankind. Break every yoke by honest, correct endeavor.

Argument Against Relapse

We must break the yoke of mortal belief which argues the return of old beliefs. There is no law of relapse. There is no belief in the law of reversal, no mind to put forth or conceive such a law. Love governs all. All mortal mind can do is to believe these so-called laws; and with the knowledge of "God with us" we can unknow them, annul them, and they are proven nothing at all.

Enforcement and Protection of Treatment

Error is not scientific. Scientific or true knowing is all that is needed to destroy it. A treatment must include the realization that it goes forth with power and Truth, and cannot be reversed by any law of malicious animal magnetism, of nature or materia medica. There is no law of malicious animal magnetism that can make a Christian Science treatment produce the opposite effect, nor can it be made to overlook or forget anything that is necessary for its certain accomplishment of good.

Keep Ahead of Error

We must go ahead of error and keep ahead of it all the way. We never have to and never must give in to error or go down before it. It is nothing but erroneous belief and we know it. The law of God includes a law that annuls every false claim of law, and we know it and must use it.

Practical Directions for Scientists

The return of old beliefs is broken forever by the knowledge that it has no law by which to stand, now and forever. Evil suggestions have no past, present or future. Never did they do anything in the past, nor can they do anything in the future. We must not be apathetic and think we have nothing to do. If well and happy, it is just the time to work, so that we are protected and protecting all, and helping mankind. We must incite each other to more earnest, systematic work, to be instant in season and out of season, and keep in advance of the enemy all the time and not be found napping.

Malicious Animal Magnetism Annulled

We must feel and know that neither we nor our patients can ever be under the law of malicious animal magnetism, for God is the only law-maker. Say: "I do not have to yield to temptation; I will not have such a belief; I will not believe it, for I do not have to, and I know it."

No Continuity to Evil

There is no law of continuity of evil; it is only a belief that said it had a beginning and continuity or actuality. The right idea does destroy these beliefs. Whatever we need to know about a case Mind will uncover if we are working right.

No Transference of Suffering

With the knowledge of Truth we must break the false law which would seem to make it possible for us to suffer because we are Christian Scientists working for the cause. We cannot be made to suffer for anyone else, nor can anyone else be made to suffer for us. There is no law of rebound. We must meet all these lies now by knowing that they are false and never can be true, never can injure us or anyone else.

Peace of God Needed in Treatment

It is the peace of God that is needed in our treatment—the "Peace be still" that does the work. We must not fight. The work of Christian Science is not a fight of beasts, of the human mind or will; it is the omnipotent Good that is never vanquished.

Treatment for Poison

Know there is no material or mental poison; no substance or mind to contain or manifest poison, irritation or inflammation. There is no organism or substance that can be made to give forth impurities, no impeded circulation, no imperfect action.

Treatment Against Ignorance, Apathy and Forgetfulness

Declare always that you will be made to know what to handle, and cannot be made apathetic or forgetful, for Mind is our guide and instructor.

No Reversal of Work or Undertakings

Know that your treatments or affairs cannot be reversed or interfered with. No family or relations, friendships or associations can dispossess us of the Truth or interfere with our success. Christian Science is doing what it promises. The promise and fulfilment are one.

No Vain Repetitions

After we have thoroughly made nothing of the errors, we need not go over them again and again, but know our work is done. Know that your treatments are good ones and have no fear they are not. Fear cannot abide with you. A Christian Science treatment brings with it a consciousness of its sure and immediate effect. We do have faith in God, and know the spiritual facts are established. Every true thought means dominion and redemption.

No Renunciation or Suffering Required

You do not have to give up anything. The idea of renunciation is false theology. Man exists at the standpoint of gain. You do not have to suffer out of the flesh, for you are not in the flesh. The belief of suffering is old theology. Eliminate the beliefs of renunciation, suffering, condemnation. Not one is from God. Until you do eliminate these beliefs, you are under the penalty.

Gain, Unfoldment, Improvement, Are Your Right

You do not have to give up anything, but have everything to gain, because men exist at the standpoint of unfoldment. You are to get out through better beliefs, through getting a better appreciation of Being. All is by way of better beliefs. Realize the grandeur of man.

No Penalty Is Ordained by God

God has ordained no penalty for you. He has ordained no penalty even for evil, for he does not know it. **The wages of sin is spiritual education.**

Declarations Are the Enforcement of Law

Declare concerning yourself only what you want to realize, because your declarations are the law and the enforcement of the law to the case. Man and law are one; man and opportunity are one. Expectancy is the answer to your prayer.

A Treatment

Man is governed by Mind, and this Mind is the law of perfection, completeness, activity, harmony, continued harmonious action, vigor and vitality to its ideas, to body and all that body includes. Mind is the power, the law, to this treatment. This treatment is the enforcement of law. Mind is the law of elimination and expulsion to the beliefs in the case.

Body and Perfection Immaculate Conception

Body is universal, infallible, immortal, available, ever-present, the embodiment of all right ideas. There is no private body. Man has (and is) this body now. Get an immaculate conception of body. Get an immaculate conception of everything; to do so is the Saviour. Body could be maintained forever if the output were equal to the intake, for then an equilibrium could be maintained. There is no reason why we may not maintain this body unimpaired indefinitely.

Law and Opportunity

Law is not something away off. It is present—**Our Law which art in heaven.** God's law is the law of boundless opportunity. There is no limitation, because of the availability, immortality, universality, infallibility and ever presence of opportunity. Declare this one hundred times a day. Mind is one. If a human could see (realize) all of Mind at once, he would be equal to Mind; but because Mind is ever unfolding to the Christian Scientist, he always exists at the standpoint of gain.

Animal Magnetism Handled and Destroyed

Eliminate the belief that animal magnetism can operate as law, rule or cause, whereby to impair or impede the harmonious action or functions of body, or anything that body includes, or to impair or impede any faculty of Mind. Animal magnetism is empty, hence it has no avenue; it is mindless, hence it has no avenue; it is mindless because it has no law. Deprive it of its sting by depriving it of its person.

Condemnation Cannot Argue

Animal magnetism cannot constitute itself a belief of condemnation, cannot be a law to me or my affairs. It has no law to transgress, hence no penalty to pay for disobedience to its erroneous belief called law.

We Should Be Agents of Redemption

We should all be dwelling so completely in Mind, holding the right idea, that the vilest sinner would be redeemed. A victim of rattlesnake poison does not need condemnation; he needs redemption. The same is true of the victim of murderous, dishonest, or lustful feeling, or impulse, whether yielded to outwardly, or not.

God and Man

God is the unlimited infinity of conscious Mind, Life, Truth and Love; and man is the immortal, indestructible and perfect activity of this infinite Mind.

Man the Perfect Reflection of God

Man is the conscious embodiment of Mind, and is therefore the perfect reflection or image of all that God is.

One Man, One Body

Man being the body of God, there is but one man, one body, for there is but one God. I am man, the compound idea of divine Mind, the infinite divine consciousness, the individual (indivisible) expression of infinite perfection.

Perfect Body and Treatment to Demonstrate It

Man is body, the infinite aggregation of spiritual ideas, and is therefore wholly spiritual, normal, complete and eternal, abiding ever under the law of Life, health, harmony and perfection in the Kingdom of Heaven.

My Immaculate Conception

I am the eternal embodiment of all that is good, true, real, enduring, beautiful and pure, and am therefore the immaculate conception of Divine Mind—its imperishable, immortal, spiritual idea.

Body Eternal

This perfect body never was born, because it has always existed; never was evoked, organized or composed; therefore it is under no law of disorganization, disintegration, decay or death; under no belief of age, maturity or degeneration.

Individual Completeness

This perfect body never has suffered, is under no condemnation on account of being falsely cognized as a human man or woman; for this body is neither male nor female, after the flesh, but both in Spirit, for it manifests the divine completeness of our Father-Mother God.

Perfect Blood, and Treatment to Demonstrate It

The essence of blood being Life, my blood is absolutely pure, free from every abnormal secretion, accumulated impurity or poison.

The Law of Mind and Its Results

The law of Mind is the law of Life, health, perfection, completeness, activity, vitality and vigor unto its ideas, unto body and all that is included in body.

No Displacement

There can be no displacement of any organ, because every idea is eternally held in the divine control, which is all-harmonious. The so-called physical organisms are the false material concepts of MIND'S spiritual ideas, qualities. It is, therefore, the Christian Scientist's business to exchange the objects of sense for the ideas, qualities of MIND. (See Science and Health, p. 269.)

Impurity and Discord Eliminated

The law of Mind is the law of elimination and expulsion unto all belief of impurity or discord. The law of Mind is a law of rest and repose to its ideas. The scientific sense of repose is all-harmonious action.

General Treatment for a Claim of Disease

The claim is not matter.

It is neither person, place nor thing.

It is not material substance nor a material body.

There is no body nor matter nor tissue that needs to be changed.

No time nor process nor delay is necessary to effect all the change that is required.

It is not something that has presence, occupancy, place or sojourn.

It is not something that has continuity in matter or ever was a material condition.

It is not something that was materially conceived, developed, organized or born.

It is not something that ever was subject to prenatal mesmerism or that was the channel for the descent of hereditary taint or impairment.

It is not something that is in consequence of any cause or thing or process or influence.

It is simply itself and is not in anything or of anything.

Everything that exists **is now perfect.**

Divine Mind is the law of perfection, harmony, to everything that is. It is the law of reconstruction, restoration, recuperation, recovery, elimination, to what is called the human body, but which is only an erroneous belief about body. Hence

Mind is the law of correction to the error, and hence the law of healing.

Mortal mind or malpractice is not a power and cannot govern you. It cannot cause you to malpractice.

A Handling of Malpractice

You know that the error called malpractice is nothing but wrong thought. *Mal* (Latin), meaning "wrong," therefore mental malpractice is wrong mental practice.

You know that wrong thought cannot project anything upon you. It never has done so.

You know that the thing that "counts" is what **you** know and feel, and that no form of human thought transference has power to do anything against your declarations and resistance.

It is better for you to declare: The claim that error can affect me through the belief of a channel, or through the thought (feeling) of anger, resentment, condemnation, etc., is annulled by this treatment.

Belief About Being Acclimated Handled

Deny the belief of law that you have to become acclimated.

Belief of Poisonous Secretions Handled

Declare that Mind is the law of elimination and expulsion to the belief of abnormal secretions or retention, also the belief of morbific secretions, etc.

Mental Depression Handled

Mental depression is mesmerism. Do not regard it as being your depression.

Basis of Treatment

All things are already perfect. Being is already perfect. The treatment is the activity of this right idea of the perfection of all things. This idea of perfection is the spiritual idea which heals.

Denial

1st. The denial must include the denial of any presence or substance that can be diseased.
2nd. It must deny all origin or cause for disease. It must deny the belief of an unknown or developed cause for disease.
3rd. Denial of so-called mortal law and its claim of enforcement for disease.

Law

The treatment must declare that it is the Word of God or Mind; that it reflects the divine power, the divine law, and therefore is the law unto the case. It has not been reversed and cannot be. Its effect or influence cannot be reversed. There is no law of reversal. There is no law or rule to prevent or interfere with Christian Science healing. There is no law of a return of old belief.

Malpractice

The claim of malpractice is:
1st. That there is a mortal mind.
2nd. That it has avenues or channels through which it can act.
3rd. That it has activity, power, influence.
4th. That it can act **through** or **as** law, rule, wish, desire, declaration, prediction, prophecy, curse, anathema, condemnation, prayer, or censure.
5th. That there is an object upon which it can act.
6th. That mortal mind and its activities have a past, a history.

Offset Malpractice

Deny specifically each of the above false claims.

Fundamental Points in Treatment

1st. **Mind**—substance, basis, noumenon, Principle.
2nd. **Manifestation**—ideas, man, body, etc.

3rd. **Law**—through which the government is enforced.
4th. **Power**—which is enforced according to law.
5th. **Action**—which is the result of power enforced by law.

Useful Declarations

Mind is the law of perfection, completeness, activity, vitality, vigor, harmony, normality, to its ideas, to body, and to all that is included in body.

Mind is the law of elimination and expulsion to the beliefs of abnormity, discord, morbific secretions, accumulated impurity, calcareous deposit.

This treatment is the enforcement of law.

Do Not Deny or Doubt Your Understanding

Through mesmerism we are tempted to deny our understanding, and every time we do this we deny our salvation and our Christ. If I were the devil, seeking to destroy the work of a Christian Science practitioner, I would argue something like this: "Oh, you are a live Christian Scientist, and Christian Science is all right, too; but then you do not have enough understanding to meet this," or "You have too much fear," or "You are not good enough." I would silently argue this until the Christian Scientist came to believe it, and thus hang him up to dry.

Limitation Is Mesmerism

This is what makes laws of limitation, and the great majority of Christian Scientists are mesmerized to believe it. What they must do is to recognize all limitation as mesmerism, and therefore declare: "I will stick my finger into you and you will dissolve." The devil is only afraid of the Christian Scientist who knows that it is only mesmerism which is hitting him square in the eyes. The "watching and working" Christian Scientist knows that the testimony of the five physical senses is mesmerism—mesmerism by material creation, so-called, concerning which Mrs. Eddy declares that it is "sometimes beautiful, always erroneous." (Science & Health, 277:31). When you recognize this, you will have something actively at work destroying the devil. There is no student on earth who is not swayed more or less by mesmerism.

Mind All-Inclusive

Mind includes all cause, law, power, consciousness, universe, man; Mind is the law of harmony and perfection to everything.

Take Your Troubles to God

Take your troubles to God. The operation of Christian Science acts just as though God were personal and took account of your troubles and needs. Error acts like a personal devil or a personal evil.

Human Will Hinders Our Receptivity of Good

What spoils our consciousness of receptivity is hatred and selfishness, the despotic and tyrannical action of the human mind. This human will permeates the whole fabric of human life and physical universe. We should constantly watch, guard against, and pray to be delivered from this monster of human will. No mortal is free from it. This tendency on our part darkens us always and dims our windows of receptivity. Learn to obey the divine precept—"Thy will be done," not "My will be done." Beware of and watch human will as you would watch a snake.

Love, the Great Accomplishment

The great thing to accomplish is the Science of Love. It means Life. It is the only corrective and is equal to every emergency and conquers every condition of discord. Our prayer should be for divine government, divine leading.

Love the Only Solvent, the Only Deliverer

Why, just think! what have we here? We have this problem of trying to live with each other, and not a saint among us. What will solve the problem? Not insinuation, nor recrimination, not accusation, not distrust or falsehood. Only Love will solve it. Destroy error through charity and mercy. We have to love our way out of hell and into heaven. Be merciful one to another, gentle, considerate and kind.

Error Not Overlooked, But Destroyed by Love

We cannot wink at error; we cannot overlook it or be deceived by it. We must destroy it with love. We must be patient with each other, and we must stop making ado about little things. Imperceptibly every one who is one-half or two-thirds honest is getting better. Strive for the complete elimination of anger. Love will heal and raise the dead.

Christian Science in the World Depends on Scientists

The cause of Christian Science is by no means assured. It is a very common thing for Christian Scientists to say: "Thank God for this blessed truth," and to think it has come to stay. I wish I could say that with assurance and believe it. **It cannot be cut down by any power from without, but beware of inward rot—dissensions, criticism and strife within the ranks.** Truth is here, but we must prove whether it has come to stay or not. A tree fallen is down. It makes no difference whether it is caused by being cut down or by inward rot.

Operative Christian Science Is No Better Than Scientists

The entire cause of Christian Science is in the consciousness of Christian Scientists, and is no better than they are. If Christian Scientists, so-called, are quarreling, it is the cause of the devil. If Christian Science is to be permanent, learn to live Love. Scrutinize every error and cast it out by forgiving.

Love Minds Its Own Business

Love minds its own business. If I had to write the ten commandments tomorrow, I would make the first one: "Mind your own business, for God's sake; this is the chief end of man." And the second is like unto it: "Do not backbite or criticise others."

Criticism and Censoriousness Condemned

If you want error, wind up your tongue and let your mouth talk for an hour. If you want Truth, sit still and let Intelligence manifest itself.

Love, Our Highest Good

Our highest good is silently voicing itself to consciousness as our God, or Love. Whence comes this Christ, the descent of the Holy Ghost? It is Spirit, which comes through our receptivity.

Handling Animal Magnetism

Christ, spiritual understanding of Good, alone can handle animal magnetism. The divine idea—God's idea—alone can handle it, know its nothingness. When a human being handles it he has a quarrel right off. Nine out of ten handle it as a person. All is Mind. God would know there is nothing to hate and nothing to be hated. Divine Love, by knowing itself, knows there is nothing to fight back. **Knowing** God, **living** Good, is all that will handle animal magnetism.

Clinging to Truth Saves from Error

Christian Science brings to light immortality. When error appears, it appears to disappear. Mentally cling to God, Good, to the true idea about the false claim, and this will save you from error.

Everything Is Now

Know this: Everything is now. The knowledge is not the is-ness, but knowing the is-ness saves you from every false claim about it, from the material sense of the is-ness of Life.

You Are an Executive

If error says, "I can't," Christ (your real self) says, "I can." All there is to us, scientifically speaking, is what we know that is true, and that is never under condemnation.

Immaculate Conception

The immaculate conception is that which conceives the right idea of perfection. It can be and is with us alway, if we watch and pray that our windows of receptivity be spotless, merciful and pure.

Nerve Troubles Would Be Aptly Named, "The Talking Serpent"

"Talking serpent" is about as near being a claim of nerves as anything. Under this head, belief claims that nerves mar sight, hearing, taste, sensation; and that all the functions of the body are induced or regulated by nerves. Then there is the generalissimo of the whole claim, called pneumogastric nerve, which is supposed to regulate heart, stomach, and nearly everything.

Treatment for Claims of Nerves—Solar Plexus

Then there is the solar plexus, nerve center; and finally here is the claim of nerve irritation, nerve degeneration and paralysis, as the claim of matter. These should be vigorously denied. It has been discovered that mental malpractice tries to reach Christian Scientists by arguing irritation of the nerves, of solar plexus and of the pneumogastric nerve. You should destroy the belief that this can be done.

Work for Efficiency and Protection

I urge the students to give more attention to the claim of mental malpractice, that Christian Science does not heal and cannot heal. Every student should constantly declare against this argument; and I urge them to constantly declare the truth about man, about body and all things. On the error side it should be declared: "There are no material nerves; whatever they mean in Spirit is perfect in God, and this idea destroys the false concept." I urge them to do more protective work, to prevent the action of error, instead of waiting for it to strike its blow.

The Devil, the Arch-Hypnotist

All evil is not disease, but suggestion. If the devil were entitled to a name, it should be hypnotist, because all error is hypnotic. Handle error, not as something, but as suggestion, belief, argument. Do not let the helpless babes dissuade you from mastering evil by foreseeing its intended action, and handling it before it can operate.

Time Is a Falsehood

The past is a lie; there is no truth in anything that is claiming to have happened. There is, and has been, and always will be, only the eternal now. Remember only the good, then you will be communing with God, and harmony will be the inevitable result.

In Dark Hours Persist in Declaring Truth and Good

Try to be conscious that God is with you every moment; and in the seemingly dark hours when error screams to be heard and would tempt you to your destruction, faint not, and know that man is governed alone by God, and Truth is the only voice to be heard. Poisonous influences from people's thoughts are nothing when you prove them nothing. Go right on and keep your thought on the real. Never for one moment look back at the past. It was a lie and never was, because God was not in it.

Let Not Thought Be Engaged with Error Unnecessarily

Do not go out in mortal mind company, for the sake of mere amusement, any more than you can possibly help. The arguments of animal magnetism will try to make you know of them, so that you will not be able to know your own sense of right, Principle instead of person.

Be Courageous, and Power and Success Are Yours

Take courage of every experience, and power will be yours. Go on, dear friends, and prove that you are the children of Him who cares for His own. Be faithful to Principle in all you say and do, and success will be yours.

Happiness a Duty—Depression a Sin

Be happy at all times and in all places; for remember it is right and a duty you owe to yourself and to your God to retain the right, no matter how loudly the senses scream. Depression belongs not to the child of God, neither is it real, nor can it affect one when his motives are right.

The Faithful Have More to Meet, But More with Which to Meet It

The more faithful we are, the louder will error scream, until, as Science and Health says, "its voice is forever hushed." I would rather you would make too much of error than not enough. You will have to keep awake if you rightly handle its claim of power; but you will be very apt to go sound asleep if you believe that there is no claim of power in error to be humanly recognized and dealt with. The world thinks that man is both good and evil, but it would be impossible for both of two opposites to be true.

No Separation

Mind is Omnipresence; and if we are each working in the right way we will have no sense of separation.

A Seeming Law of Reversal Needs to Be Met

There is no law of reversal or a return of a false belief. Now this belief of law stands between your case and your treatment every time, and interposes to prevent healing. Promise that by means of constant endeavor you will proceed to break that spurious law, and have your students do the same. The dependence is upon you and upon other teachers to educate the world how to meet and handle the laws of mental malpractice.

Antidote for Argument of Reversal

This treatment is the very Word, presence, power and action of God. It is the law of Life and harmony to this case. I cannot be mesmerized to doubt its power and efficiency. I cannot be mesmerized to hold in thought any doubt as to the power of Truth over all error. This treatment cannot return unto itself void. It does heal. There is no law that can impede, arrest, restrain or reverse it. Its effects cannot be reversed. It cannot be made to produce an effect opposite to that which is intended. There is no such law.

Mental Protection of Home

There is but one household: that is God's household. There is no avenue or channel by which error can possibly enter this household to create a sense of discord, fear, derision, anger, doubt, subtlety, lack, or straitened circumstances. Nothing can enter this household or consciousness to annoy or destroy; for all here is Life, and God, Good, fills it.

No Mental Attack

Error has no power to voice itself to you through any other personality, ignorantly or maliciously directed, for or against the all-power of Good. Personality is a lie. Divine Love is all Being, and every manifestation of Intelligence is a divine idea reflecting God, Love, Truth and Life to you everywhere. Let all flesh be still and know that God is all. I do not suffer for the sins of others, for sin is its own punisher, and I will not sin. Thus I am free from suffering.

Malicious Mesmerism Annulled

Malicious mesmerism annuls itself in opposing God and His idea, man; all is under the irrevocable law of Life, Truth and Love. Malicious animal magnetism and mental malpractice never did anything to man. They have neither place nor power. In the name of God and all of Good, declare that **it**, error, has no power, place, law nor anything wherewith to invade or molest the eternal harmony of man. God is All and All is Good. There is no danger nor fear of any evil claim put forth in its name. God's law enforced smashes all supposed laws of evil.

God Answers Prayer

God is not in you as person, but the knowledge or appreciation of God is within your consciousness. This does away with the old belief of a located God. Really, the only location we need to be concerned about finding is "God with us." When you appealed to a personal God, you could not appeal to more than a God who was willing to do a good thing in answer to prayer; and our God has already done that before we pray. Christian Science reveals "God with us"; and He will **in effect** enter into the mire and mud and desolation of daily life, and will do all that a personal God could do, and He does not have to be told to do it.

Activity of Right Ideas Saves

Jesus is to us an educational exhibit of the Christ overcoming temptation. He is the manifestation of a sense that takes cognizance of materiality, and being endowed with Spirit, anointed with wisdom, overcomes it. The essense lies in the Mind which is in Christ, in the activity, power and presence of Christ, destroying error. Activity always does something; it destroys error. A right idea is always Christ "coming to the flesh to destroy incarnate error." Every right idea is a saving idea; it saves from the wrong belief. For every wrong belief there is always a saving Christ. The process of activity of right ideas is your salvation. The science of salvation lies in the spiritual idea, which comes educating and transforming the mentality of man-kind.

Nature and Action of Evil Uncovered

The heavenward-journeying man must discern the falsity of evil. Truth unravels to the individual the mystery of iniquity. Entering upon Christian Science, you see more evil than ever before. Mesmer performed one service for the world in that he gave a name to that which is nothing, but which indicates what evil claims and how it acts. The term "animal magnetism" was in use before Christian Science was discovered, and is the best term that can be used to uncover evil as being evil human concept acting mesmerically.

Animal Magnetism Discussed

Christian Science scientifically designates evil as "animal magnetism." It is no new phase of evil, but the term indicates that we recognize evil in its proper light. This does not add to it, but begins the disarming process by exposing the nature of evil; and the term is a natural, rational one. This takes the sting out of the old submission to evil. **As evil** or **matter** you cannot get rid of the pretense termed evil. As animal magnetism you can. Evil resolved into and handled as animal magnetism can be demolished.

What You Are to Handle in Treatment

Suppose you have to treat an insane woman who believes she is covered with feathers. She says she has them. Would you treat her for the purpose of removing feathers? Are there any to deal with? Or would you know that you must abolish such a belief? Now then, suppose your patient says that his lungs are half gone. Do you work any more in the realm of decayed lungs than in the realm of feathers? Do you have such a bodily condition to deal with or have you just to abolish the mesmerism of belief in such a condition? Watch yourself. See that your treatments are not treatments for feathers. Unless you are wide awake, you are liable to make perfunctory declarations of Truth with an underlying sense of treating feathers. Resolve things into thoughts and emerge from the whole area of feathers.

Treatment Must Know That It Is God Manifest

To know the Truth, is to consciously realize the activity of right ideas in individual consciousness. Treatment is always activity of right ideas. Its activity is "God with us." God manifested. Because we think the treatment is ours, it does not know enough to know that it is good. Treatment must know that it is God's word manifested, and that it reflects sufficient good, activity and power to silence any lies. The active practice of right ideas destroys the wrong sense.

Destroy Dream-Beasts, or Awaken the Dreamer

We can abolish error only when it is resolved into belief, lies, a wrong sense of a right something which is ever present with us. A child protected in his parents' house might dream of wild beasts. Would the Christ-mind enter that dream and demolish those beasts, or would it awaken the child? **Could** the Christ-mind, the knowledge of Truth, enter that dream and find the beasts? No; but it could demolish the dream, the belief, and awaken the child to the truth about himself. So Truth, mentally enforced as law, does not deal with conditions and things, but it demolishes the mesmerism of wrong belief.

Enforcement and Protection of Treatment

The adversary, like Herod of old, lies in wait for every Christian Science treatment, before it is given. The laws of mental malpractice endeavor to suggest the belief that Christian Science does not heal, and that Scientists shall not think their treatments can heal. Scientists themselves use this big gun of the adversary by agreeing with it. You must work by means of constant endeavor to break this lie. To protect your treatment, know with every treatment that this treatment is the very Word, power, presence and action of God; that it is the very law of Life and harmony to the case; that you cannot be mesmerized to doubt its power and efficiency; it cannot return unto itself void; it does heal; there is no law that can impede, arrest, restrain or reverse it, or frustrate its operation or effect.

Right Thought Must Externalize Itself

The law of God is the only law that exists. Declare against any power of evil being ordained for you. Release your own career, routine and destiny from any and all entanglements of evil law. If pressed into the corner of adversity and you do not know which way to turn, go on. Utter God's word; declare it faithfully, knowing that it cannot return unto itself void. The coming of deliverance is an inevitable event, even if it seems delayed, for **right thought must externalize itself.**

The Lesson of the Crucifixion and Resurrection

Jesus was pressed into that corner on the cross. Was there not ample proof in the outcome of that experience that the saving Christ was with him? What is the saving Christ to destroy? "My will." It is found in the idea that in "Thy will" is the law of our extreme joy, satisfaction and perfection. Consciousness should turn eagerly to "Thy will" like a flower to the sunshine. It does not ask for the renunciation of "mine," but the discovery of "Thine."

Protection from Animal Magnetism. Prayer

Mrs. Eddy has given this illustration, though these are not exactly her words: Suppose a coiled serpent lay behind you and you did not know it was there. What would you do? God alone handles animal magnetism through Christ. What opens the door for the Christ? Prayer. Through this doorway enters that which handles the serpent we do not see.

What Causes Mental Clouds to Disappear?

A Christian Scientist's consciousness is like the sky in which are disappearing clouds, the windows of receptivity being opened. What opens them? The transitional, transforming state where consciousness reverently and piously yearns for God, Good.

Miscellaneous Falsehoods Denied

There is no mortal mind to argue that life, power, strength, vitality, energy and action are dependent on matter, and that substance, intelligence and Life are something apart from God. There is no power in the belief of laws of health, physiology, hygiene, human nature; and no power in the belief of penalty for the violation of any of these supposed laws.

Belief of Heredity Scientifically Dealt with

There is no power in the belief of inheritance, or physical or mental tendencies. Mortals have no history, no past, no present or future. All is the eternal now. Man has always been and always will be the perfect image and likeness of God. Mind is the law of action, strength, vitality, perfection, to body and to everything that pertains thereto.

Beliefs of Faulty Secretion and Elimination Handled

Mind is the law of elimination and expulsion to the belief of insufficient elimination and abnormal retention and secretion of impure substance.

Belief of Consequences Dealt With

Men are not under condemnation because of the belief of matter, or because of the belief of material body. Men and women are not under penalty for anything ever done or not done. There is no penalty, no suffering out of the flesh, no suffering for sin. There is no vengeance, no divine wrath; and there are no evil consequences for any form of erring belief.

How God Is Known. Individuality

God is the infinity of conscious Mind, Wisdom, Truth; and the only way to know God is by knowing that which expresses Good, by knowing and reflecting the right idea of God. What you know about Christian Science, Good, man, universe, constitutes your present spiritual identity.

Demonstration Defined. Treatment Described

The activity of the spiritual idea is declaring the Truth about God and man, and the uncovering and handling of error destroys the error; the "sign following" this scientific application is "demonstration." A Christian Scientist is one in whose consciousness spiritual sense is active. Nothing saves the Christian Scientist but the activity of scientific application in demonstration of God's laws. Christian Science treatment and practice is knowing, and to know that your treatment is the activity of God's Word does the work. How do I know that the treatment is good? Such knowing ought to know that the treatment is good.

An Important Declaration

Declare that your treatment is with power, reflects all power, is power manifested; this knowing annihilates evil. Declare: I do realize that all there is of man is to know God. I cannot be mesmerized to doubt or hinder the Word declared.

Divine Impulsion

We have the substance of Spirit, and the treatment must have the impulsion that enforces what we know. All is Good;

therefore there is no evil power to be afraid of. Knowing the omnipresence of Good will break fear.

Declare Truth Specifically and Actively

Declare Truth specifically and actively. There is no more **to** your treatment than there is **in** it. We must know enough to know that there is one Mind, and that it is good, and that there is no evil, no error, no carnality about it. We must know the same about Truth and Love.

Healing Faith Is Active Reliance Upon God

Every case of sickness is according to so-called mortal law. There is no such law. Everyone is governed by the law of God. In handling sickness, do not handle disease, but a so-called mortal-mind law. The Word of God is the one and only law. This treatment is a law to this case, to annihilate whatever you have to meet. It is the law of extermination. Faith does the work; not blind faith, but the knowing God that is active Mind —the one conscious Intelligence, your Mind.

Faulty Treatment Described and Corrected

A treatment is infirm when matter is treated. To the extent that you are mesmerized to treat disease as disease, you will lose confidence in your work. Mind governs the universe. Every living thing is governed by God's law. It is the law of Life to the body. You must get your body under the law of good, not evil. When you think you have something to do with the body, you are treating matter. If a man says: "Two plus two equals five," you do not look down his throat to see why he says so, or examine his vocal organs. If he has a fever you do not examine his tongue or pulse, nor ask him if his pulse is better after treatment. If you do, you are making it matter. That is a fatal mistake. Handle the fiction of belief and the mortal mind law, whatever that may be. To help break these laws is a sublime opportunity. It is the voice of immortality coming to our consciousness.

Discouragement, Fear, Self-Depreciation

The devil puts nine-tenths of the Christian Scientists on hooks by saying: "You are discouraged, afraid; you are not good enough to practice Christian Science," etc. Use what you have; you have enough; all there is. You are good enough; you are worthy; you are not discouraged.

Treatment for Pain

When mesmerized by pain, turn and say: "I know what you are. This is not pain or a belief of pain. It is a belief of mind in matter; a lie of belief without a believer, nothingness claiming to be something. I am not afraid. I am spiritual, and so immune."

Treat Until You Annihilate Fear

If in your work you have anything left that you are afraid of, begin over, annihilate the whole business. Evil is a wrong sense of right. We must not try to annihilate the body, but we must know what body is; the one perfect, spiritual body of infinite divine Mind is infinite divine consciousness—spiritual universe—the embodiment of Mind's ideas, perfect, complete, and all harmoniously active; this knowing is the Saviour. It is to know the body of right ideas.

Treatment for Belief of Eye Troubles

For eyes declare: Eyes are perfect; vision is perfect; sight is perfect, governed by God, wisdom, eternal Good. It is a wrong belief of substance in matter. Declare this two hundred times a day if necessary.

At-One-Ment. Purity. Self-Will. Right Desire

We must make our connection between God and man. Keep your own windows clear. Determination to have our own way shuts out God. Right desire is the opening through which God comes.

Charity in Judgment Commended

Humanly we are all in error; all have our smoking trails. Do not be critical and do not always be uncovering error. Be patient; error is in me and in you, humanly. Pray God deliver us both. Do not think about others' errors; you make it harder for them, harder to do their work. Thank God they are better men than they were.

Science of Love the Greatest Need

We need the Science of Love. It is Life. Better do without food than without Love. Love your husband; it is right. Envy, jealousy, anger, fear, form the atmosphere of death. Love is the atmosphere of Life. There is nothing to hate. Ask, "How would I like my brother to do this or that to me?" Find the way to the art of loving. Christian Scientists must not make much ado about little things. When you have overcome envy, jealousy, etc., then tackle coffee and fans. Do not think that the other fellow has to do it all. Go home and learn Love yourself. You miss the opportunity if you do not put your house in order. Be merciful, compassionate. The brutality of man is far worse than that of beasts. Learn charity.

No Self-Condemnation. Sin Versus Man

Do not condemn self. You are the understanding of Good. The right idea of God means right man. There is only one man, immortal man. Reality of man is rightness. Discriminate between claims of sin and the individual. Turn on sin and extirpate it. I am God's idea. An infinity of ideas expresses God. What we know about Truth constitutes our present spiritual identity. The spiritual idea is Saviour

Christian Science Does Not Treat Matter but Error

Knowing Truth is treatment. Only the likeness of God is man. Treatments are failures because we think we have a sick man or woman to treat. That is only a belief in mortal mind law. Christian Science does not demonstrate over matter, only over error. Resolve the whole thing into a material law, the realm of material belief. Do not treat fever any more than you would feathers in an insane woman. No pain, no claim of pain, only mesmerism, the action of mortal mind. Do not annihilate, but displace error with right ideas. The true idea is always the Saviour.

See and Cultivate Good. Human Love

Human will shuts out God's will. The desire to know is the open door. Accept the ten per cent of good in our brother, and wait for the ninety per cent of evil to disappear. To say that human love is all wrong is a lie. (This was said because a lady told him she was told she must not love her husband; and another that she could not heal the sick if she drank coffee.)

The Real Man. The Real Body

Perfect rightness in thought, word and deed is the real man. Evil is a wrong sense of a right thing. Human body is a counterfeit of the true body, the body of right ideas.

No Antagonism

We have nothing to fight. Do not think of the other one as a "brand plucked from the burning." Let us join hands and pray together, and not pull each other's hair. Obey the Golden Rule.

PART II
MISCELLANEOUS NOTES

MISCELLANEOUS NOTES

From Mr. Kimball's Teaching

Getting good out of class instruction is not a matter of memory, but of grasping the underlying Principle.

SCRIPTURAL CONDEMNATIONS: "The wages of sin is death." "Man that is born of woman is of few days and full of trouble." We are not held or bound by any such mortal-mind laws.

BIBLE: The Bible was conceived by humans, by men as we are, and they had and gave forth some woeful misconceptions of Deity.

PATIENCE: Do not speak of patience as an attribute of God; there is nothing for God to be patient about. All is well.

DUALITY: Do not speak of the idea, rose, and the objective rose. All there is, is the idea; that is the real.

REQUISITES FOR HEALING: All we have to do to be healed, or to come into our inheritance of good, right now, is to turn from evil beliefs, evil deeds, so-called wrong thinking, and grasp the ever-presence and immanence of good; that is, to have right ideas.

EMOTIONALISM: Class study is not acquiring some emotional traits, or any "Glory to God" expressions; but one should observe a quiet, serene, unruffled demeanor at all times.

HAPPINESS: Drunkenness—evil—gives all the pleasure and God all the pain—so it seems—to some. This is not reasonable. In order to secure execution, one must have a condemnation. Then seek to destroy the condemnation.

REFORMATION: Sheep stealing. Educate the man out of it, not punish him; then he will quit, and no punishment is needed.

SELF-CONDEMNATION: Cease self-condemnation. God, Good, does not condemn; does not hold or know error. It is Good you are seeking to know. What care you what error says! Giving this instruction, that each hearer may know how to take care of himself and lessen hell for others.

ETERNITY: Eternity is here now. **There is no "other life."**

SERIOUS CASE: Formerly taught, in every illness, to handle thought of death, but do not so teach now. Illustration follows: Called to treat man very low after others had failed. My treatments were not effective, but congratulated myself that patient was no worse.

Called in a hurry; only consciousness left--speech gone. Required patient to follow my audible treatment with lip motion as—"There is one Life; Life is eternal. That Life is my Life," until patient began to articulate and gasped: "I am so tired; let up." I said: "No; keep repeating." And so this went on until perfect action of the body was restored to the man.

DEATH—HANDLING OF: In thus stating, "Life is eternal," you see, no thought of death could enter. When man asked me to "let up," it was the cry of error, death, but I did not yield.

GOD—HOW HE IS KNOWN: God is defined as Principle, the basis of all manifestation. We know God only through ideas; hence to have "right ideas" is to have God, or Immanuel, with us. This is our Messiah, our Redeemer, our salvation. Jesus held the right ideas, hence he manifested his divinity, and we must follow the "Wayshower."

EXPECTATION: Be open, be willing, be receptive to Truth; be **expecting** good all the time.

SUPPLY: Do not be avaricious; but get—be getting.

POVERTY: Poverty is no part of a true relation to infinite Principle. Do not limit your supply to one avenue—as, a store, a certain business. But know that the channels of divine Mind are infinite. I have known demonstrations by this method to equal any given in the Bible.

SIN—HANDLING OF; TRUTH—POWER OF: Many Christian Scientists are always trying to get rid of something, some fault. Quit that. Get more "right ideas," and the error falls away.

When you grasp "Two times two is four," the old belief that "Two times two is five" drops away, and you don't strive to be rid of it.

MAN; IMMORTALITY: I am speaking truth to you. By as much as you are responsive to this truth, accepting, grasping it, by so much are you the idea of God, and so much do you express God. If you are not in this frame of mind, then you will have to plod on, until you become receptive to Truth.

PESSIMISM: A certain class of Scientists deplore the present state of existence; nothing is worth while—all had better jump into the lake. BE A BUILDER, not an iconoclast. By the renewing of the mind is the body renewed.

TIME; SPACE: There is no time; no space.

Illustration: Two fingers, objects of matter, held to view, apart. The distance is merely between the objectifications of mortal mind—between dreams—no distance at all. Time is noted by the beginning and ending of events. Mind is Presence, Truth, Life, Love, etc. It is self-existent, co-ordinate being—hence, no time. God is Omnipresence. This does not mean that God is in every place, here and there, filling all space; but God is Presence, and that is not present which is not good.

CANCER: There is no **place** for sin, disease, infirmities, need. This thought, presented logically by me, healed a cancer.

OMNIPRESENCE: God is Life. There is just one Life, infinite Life, and that Life is eternal; hence there is no death.

HEART: No fear of loss of heart action should cause death, because Life does not depend upon matter. **Know** that there is no power in evil.

KNOWING: We know that of which we are conscious, and no more.

UNCOVERING ERROR: Many quote with great satisfaction from Matthew: "Nothing is hidden that shall not be revealed." People sit around for error to uncover itself, when no delay is necessary. We manifest intelligence as the idea of Intelligence; hence, we can know at once in regard to what seems hidden.

INDIVIDUALITY: The human mind rebels at the assertion of there being one man only, and fears loss of individuality.

ONE MIND is enough for all. "Two times two is four," is known, accepted, and is sufficient for all. It is an ever-present manifestation of mathematical principle.

SUPPLY; BUSINESS: Law: Supply and demand govern the business world of mortal mind. Demand is the chief ruler. All this so-called law is no law at all. God is law, and it is God's business to be All—everything—supply.

DEMONSTRATION: A demonstration is not a case of miraculous intervention, but an expression of divine law.

TRANSPORTATION: Demonstration over time, space, friction, train wreck ahead, transportation. Each thought or law of mortal mind handled to keep my appointment—with fifteen minutes to spare, after being told that the train was six hours late.

REALIZATION DARKENED: We are here to present the postulates of Christian Science. No one has acquired the full knowledge. Demonstration follows the postulates and this requires realization.

We often accept the suggestion that we are not able to realize. Then and there, declare there is power in your treatment, and that you DO realize, and that there is no power to prevent your realization of **good.** In fact, we realize more than we seem to.

MATTER: Physicists of the day have resolved matter into about sixty elements, and then have gone further and stated that these elements are produced by an invisible, intangible, imponderable nothing, called ether. Some one has wisely stated in the Bible: "Dust to dust."

BODY: Life outside the body. Schumann-Heink, in explaining to a friend as to how she sings, says that she sings about six inches in front of her face; hence, not dependent upon throat.

HEART: By showing a patient that walking is not dependent upon physical heart-action, she got up and walked.

CHILD BORN—DEFINITION OF: A child born is simply animate matter.

UNITY OF EVIL: Consciousness is first perceived when the child begins to notice. All is now a flutter of excitement in the house, and so the education is a taking on of the same conceptions as all the rest of the world of mortal mind in regard to objects round about. In fact, this proves that, in the mortal-mind world, there is but one mortal mind, as we all do, live, believe, eat, wear about the same things.

TESTS: The test to apply to all manifestations is: "Is it good? Is it of GOD?"

PRINCIPLE: We are held in check in the making and execution of laws by "The Constitution," and so we are governed, and work out, solve, all problems through PRINCIPLE.

HEREDITY: So-called law of heredity is prenatal influence—mental influence—because matter cannot transmit anything. Heredity claims rheumatism, heart trouble, etc., and should be handled from the standpoint of pre-natal influence.

LAW: Law is spiritual—mental. All law is mental, but it needs enforcement. Illustration: Laws of land.

God would be a nonentity were He not expressed in ideas, and man is the highest expression of God. We must arise—awake—and state the immanence of Good. This is an exact Science and should be so stated. The right idea should be back of the words and our statement should conform to said idea; otherwise, we cannot expect perfect or desirable results.

PRACTITIONER: The Law has provided everything, but an actor is needed to enforce or put it in operation.

WRONG TREATMENT: Wrong statements in treatment: "No strength in the arm!" If this treatment took effect, the arm would remain or become useless.

Question was asked: "In case of faulty statements, would not the fact that there is no power in evil, save the patient?" Answer: No, not if there were no actor there to make the statement; but it might be that the student or practitioner had voiced enough of good to do the healing work.

MALPRACTICE: Mrs. Eddy once had a patient, who, according to materia medica, came with only a little of one lung left. She did not treat her for consumption, but against malpractice. She said that, had she treated against consumption, the patient would have been lost.

In such way, are many cases lost. In treating, realize the patient's unity with God; oneness of Life, of health. of plenty, of everything.

' It is a wonder to me that so many recover as do, in Science, because many treatments are given so ignorantly.''

MICROBES; GERMS; BACILLI; RATS; INSECTS; PESTS: Declare the usefulness of all God's created ideas, and further declare that none of these ideas desire to harm or destroy your house, goods, or flesh. This de-mesmerizes the insect or the animal. God does not kill. Love does not kill.

Illustration given: Worms on vines. Complaint made, and I declared the usefulness and harmlessness of all God's ideas. Worms departed; do not know where.

TREATING A BURGLAR: If a burglar died on the way to commit a crime, would that be desirable? No.

FINGER HEALED: I was trimming shrubbery; cut off one end of finger; tied same up with handkerchief, stating: "It is God's business to keep me supplied with fingers." The finger was restored to its natural condition in about three weeks, as you may see by examining.

GOD: God as Law, Mind, Principle, Love, Intelligence, etc., and as a Father or Mother with protecting arms ever ready.

Who would have a different God than Christian Science defines? Speak!

The most masterful, powerful, convincing, loving God, whose spontaneity and completion of all creation is beyond question, was presented.

CHEMICALIZATION: Eye trouble, treated by others. I was called; found practitioner had said: "You may get worse at first, but don't mind—good sign—chemicalization." Good treatment never causes pain. The activity of spiritual ideas dispels false beliefs. This mental upheaval is designated as "chemicalization." If the **human will** (operating as a law of violence unto itself) resists TRUTH'S ideas, pain is the "sign following," which precedes the elimination of poisonous secretions. Therefore, it is the practitioner's business to mentally abolish the so-called law of **human will**, thus preventing **any** suffering from chemicalization.

MALPRACTICE: If I knew some people were treating me, I would sit up nights and watch them. Many are unprepared for the work of treating, although all should be encouraged to try. Good workers are made from young students by honest application and by experience.

LAW; KINGDOM OF HEAVEN WITHIN; POWER: You are a law unto yourselves. Heaven is within. Kingdom of God is within. You have the power within—use it.

PATIENCE: Question was asked: "Mrs. Eddy speaks of 'a patient God.' If God is not patient, then why use the term?"

Answer: Mrs. Eddy made many concessions to the thought of the day. She is gradually eliminating such expressions from her book at the rate of a thousand words a year. Some day, she may deem it wise to express pure, metaphysical Science, as the world is now more ready to accept it than some years back. (This class was taught before Mrs. Eddy's decease.)

TEN COMMANDMENTS; HEREDITY: The ten commandments were not written by God. Think of God visiting the iniquities of the fathers on the children unto the third and fourth generation of them that hate Him! God doesn't know hate, iniquity, etc.

WAGES OF SIN: "Wages of sin is death." This is a mortal law, established in and by general mortal belief. Both sin and its consequences should be overcome by Science.

HUMANS: What we know about God is our real self; hence, a man may seem at the same time to be half good, half evil.

TREATING: In treating, treat affirmatively, followed by opposite negation. Saying, "Two times two is not five," does not add to one's knowledge. State the truth, and it pushes out error. Don't do as some practitioners, "Deny the error in order to make place for truth."

A woman with a sick child said she treated, seeing the spiritual child, the disease, God, and herself. Reply: "It is your business to know God. You saw no spiritual child; so move that off the board. Is disease real? No; then you could not see that, or should not have seen that. What is left? God, Good, and your consciousness of Good. God's idea is perfect. Now you can treat." [Four pieces of paper were used in giving this illustration.]

No one, unfortunately, has reached the point of rising entirely above matter.

KNOWING EVIL: Jesus Christ healed no one after his resurrection. He had ascended too far above sin, disease, etc. He could take no cognizance of it.

ARMOR OF GOD: For twenty-one years no one has spoken to me disparagingly of Christian Science. After my being healed from a miserable condition, I said: "Nothing can be said or done to move or shake my faith in or grasp of God."

TREATING: How could Spirit reconstruct the body—matter? It could not. That is a limitation of speech. I have used "elimination and reconstruction" in the printed matter, but I now say unto you: Spirit changes the belief of sickness, disease, poverty, and when this belief changes, it is like a rubber ball with the clamps removed—the body resumes its shape—that is, returns to a normal condition.

Student remarked: "When beliefs of age, limitation, etc., are dropped, then we will not grow old, etc.?" Answer: "Correct."

INVENTION: Man is not inventive. It is discovery all the time. We simply manifest these various qualities.

SABBATH DAY; SUNDAY: Each day is holy; not only one in seven. Concessions are made to custom.

ONE MORTAL MIND: Showed on previous day that we all had essentially the same idea about clothes, transportation, amusements, etc., hence, the same mortal mind, because we entertain thoughts about the same things; and that which we believe constitutes our mortal experience.

ONE MAN; BODY: Today we learn there is but one body, but one man, and we are that man. Illustration: Sameness of mortal bodies by reducing them to their component parts —water, salts, etc. All bodies alike—the same.

One body of Truth, and when we are conscious of good, we all have the same consciousness. To cognize or conceive of anything as a tree, a bird, beast, or landscape, is to make that part of our body of consciousness—and the consciousness of right ideas, as we have said, is our real self, spiritual body— our body.

TREATING: No sex, no mortal man, no woman, no matter. You never have to deal with either of these for your patient. You have a false belief to deal with. You affirm the presence of God's perfect man, and deny the erroneous beliefs of sickness, inharmony, want, or whatever the claim may be. Get the mortal woman or man out of the case and see God's perfect idea.

We have been told in class, under Mrs. Eddy, to meet cases in Love; but we never had love defined. I studied over this thought of love six months and found that while I held no personal hatred for any one, I hated my collar, my buttons in the back, fashions, the weather, etc. I immediately set to work to impersonalize love, and so to eliminate hate. When one does this, others cannot come into his presence without being blessed.

NEIGHBOR: Another incident in class, under Mrs. Eddy, was related by the instructor. The question was asked, "Do you love your neighbor's children as well as your own?" Those of us who had children looked a little "sheepish," and finally admitted that we did not. Then she said: "If you did learn to love your neighbor's children as well as your own, would you not love your own a little more?" Then we were shown how to love our neighbor as ourselves.

Our **neighbor** is the man of "right ideas," and by holding the same ideas, we must and do love our neighbor as ourselves; for the man of right ideas (the spiritual man) is our real self.

BODY: Do not despise the body, but improve it by taking on better beliefs, and so by degrees rise in the scale of being. Mrs. Eddy rebuked a student who had been denying the body in this way: "You say there is no body, no arm, etc., but Jesus said: 'Stretch forth thy hand.'"

IDEAS AND SYMBOLS, SEEN AND UNSEEN: A student out West quoted me as authority for his statement that, back of every invention, as well as natural object, there was a spiritual fact—spiritual automobiles, watches, livers, and what not. I had to deal with this carefully.

I wrote: "A man has a tree. He makes a telegraph pole, a coffin, a whiskey barrel. . . . Is there a real telegraph pole, a real coffin, a real whiskey barrel back of the material pole, coffin, whiskey barrel? No, but a material tree is back of these and back of this material tree is a spiritual tree, a spiritual idea, perfect, eternal and infinite, or boundless."

Evil is the lie about something real. Coffin meant death, and death is the opposite of Life, and it is plain to be seen that there is no spiritual coffin back of the material coffin, etc.

GREENBACK; WART; BLOT: Illustration of preceding thought: United States dollar, greenback, and a blot on the greenback. Dollar back of the greenback, but nothing back of the blot. A wart on the finger. There is a spiritual idea back of the finger, but none back of the wart. It is a diseased condition of the finger, an abnormal condition, with nothing back of it.

TALKING; MISREPRESENTING: Cautioned here not to get foreign ideas and attribute them to our teacher.

TREATING; SILENT TREATMENT; AUDIBLE TREATMENT: I asked: "Should one always treat silently, or should he analyze the claim or the cause of it to the patient?" Answer:

"That would depend upon the ability of the patient, as well as the power of presentation by the practitioner."

PRUDERY; PURITY; BODY: A practitioner once said she would send no patient to any practitioner who wore elbow sleeves. Faulty. She was condemning part of the body.

COFFEE; LOVE—HUMAN: After a lecture in Iowa, a woman rushed out in tears to me and said: "A woman in town says I can't heal people as long as I drink coffee."

Another woman in tears immediately followed this one and said: "A woman in town says I can't heal people and love my husband." (A woman in town—yes, there is always a woman in town.) She said she had tried not to love her husband, but he would not have it.

Well, I fixed her up so she could heal people and still love her husband.

Do not despise human love. Rather, by improving and enlarging on what we have, do we gain more.

ASCENSION; BETTER BELIEFS: Come to final demonstration, ascension, by improving physical body, better beliefs, and so on, *ad infinitum*. Even so did Jesus.

EYE LOST: Question by Londoner: "How would you treat a patient who had lost an eye? I declared for sight." Answer: "I would not do that. I would deny the belief that said I could lose an eye. This would mean restoration to normal conditions." Man, the consciousness of Mind's ideas, cannot lose an idea.

CONCESSIONS; SCHOLASTIC THEOLOGY: Was to give lecture in Iowa. It fell on Thursday, general prayer-meeting night. Committee came to me and said: "Could you not manage so as to get the orthodox people here?" I said: "Why did you set it for Thursday night?" . . . However, I helped them out by saying: "We can call our lecture fifteen or twenty minutes after the regular time, and this will permit other church-goers to come from their services directly here."

I knew better than to have done this and should not have done it. If they ought to have been there, they would have been on time. Well, they came in after their services. . . . I was awakened during the night by most excruciating pain in my chest. I recognized it as the error of orthodoxy striking at me. I at once made my declaration of Truth and it ceased.

MORTAL MIND; UNFAVORABLE DREAM: At one time I and another member of my family had an unfavorable dream in regard to Mrs. Eddy. When she was told of it, she said it was error or mortal mind trying to reach her through her nearest friends—Scientists. "All is infinite Mind and its manifestation."

CONSCIOUSNESS: All there is, is Mind and its ideas. What is mortal mind? There is no mortal mind. The activity of the ideas of divine Mind is all the consciousness we have. We have no such thing as something, a consciousness, or some kind of receptacle, to receive these truths of infinite Mind.

The activity of the Truth itself is our consciousness.

ONE MAN; CONSCIOUSNESS: Our consciousness should grow, enlarge, until we embrace all of infinity, and what more could we ask? "Two times two is four," is truth that does business for all of us. None desires this to be different.

When ideas are not active, we have no consciousness, as when asleep—save we dream. Seeming loss of consciousness: when we fail to cognize.

TREATING; HANDLING MORTAL MIND BELIEFS: The first thing to handle, in disposing of any trouble, is mortal mind,—that is, the **belief** that such and such can be. Matter is a manifestation of mortal mind. Control mortal mind and the manifestation yields. Mortal mind counterfeits Truth; hence, what mortal mind says is ever a lie about Truth.

MATTER: Matter is doomed to decay by its own law, made by mortal belief. Its effort at immortal life is in the process of births—a kind of continuity of lives or life.

Showing that everything material is evil: Analyze the rose—beautiful, fragrant; but, left over night in a room, may be fatal to a man. Poison lurks in it—death. None of this is found in Spirit or its ideas.

MORTALS; GENERATION: A mortal commences to die as soon as born—born to die. It is the law of matter. Biology tells us that the human man was originally bisexual. The Bible says that God made man in His image and likeness, but that man was not Adam. The next step says that woman was taken out of Adam. This man and woman were placed in a material garden.

The next step, they fell, and Cain was born. He stands for strife, blood, anger, cursings, etc. Adam and Eve fell, and so will all Adams and Eves fall unless instructed by Science.

Then we have Noah and the Ark; type of safety, righteousness. Next we have Abraham—faithfulness; Isaac and Jacob, and so on. Then Moses, who saw error and what it would lead to, and he formulated "Thou shalt not, etc." Then later came Jesus.

MAN; MINDS MANY; BODIES MANY: Man is the idea or manifestation of divine Mind. We have been told by error that we should be made as minds many. We have erred in believing that we have separate minds or separate bodies. We believe we can have a detached life. This ends in death.

BODY; LIFE: There is but one body, one Life, and Jesus meant this when he said, "I and my Father are one." We reasoned yesterday and concluded that we have but one mind, and today we shall learn that we have but one body. This one body reflects all of divine Mind, and as we attain—become conscious of that infinity—we shall be satisfied. "I shall be satisfied when I awake in His likeness."

MUSIC; HEARING: Beethoven, though deaf, heard, composed and wrote music. So much less of a man are we, because we have to hire some one to blow the air or beat the drum for us in order to hear music. We should have all this **within** us. We should not have to transport ourselves here or there to enjoy music. This is not necessary, for God is Self-sufficient, and His idea reflects Him in self-sufficiency.

IMPENETRABILITY: Question by student: "How did Jesus pass through walls and doors unopened?" Some one said that he beheld his body as nothing. ANSWER: Could he take nothing through nothing? NO. He handled the belief of materiality. It was as easy to lift or pass through it as it was to do anything else. Jesus consciously realized the perfectibility, substantiality, and omnipresence of MIND'S ideas which lie behind the aggregation of bodily organisms that go to make up the so-called physical or material body. This conscious knowing was the scientific overcoming of the beliefs of matter, time and space, and therby the enforcement of divine law. Jesus knew that where he was in consciousness (there is no place where consciousness is not) there the so-called physical symbol would appear at his bidding.

OBSTETRICS: In obstetrics, the child is not handled, in treatment. In case of wrong presentation, the belief is handled —no child, no woman, no materiality—all belief.

JESUS—DEMONSTRATIONS OF: Jesus demonstrated over every material claim, even re-presented his body after death, and finally ascended beyond the cognition of matter.

INDIVIDUALITY; REFLECTION: Man's individuality is the reflection of God, as the glow on the leaf is the reflection of the sun. The leaf has no glow of itself, but the glow proceeds from the sun, and so are we the ideas of divine Mind.

BIBLE INTERPRETATION: Question here, "Is this the place, where the seed is within itself?" Answer: I do not like to interpret the Bible. It has been interpreted so many ways; it has caused much war and bloodshed, and I don't want any killing in this class. I would rather hold to a purely **scientific** presentation of the Truth. The Bible should be interpreted as "Science and Health" unfolds it.

Mrs. Kimball said: "Some years ago, when we came into Christian Science, Mrs. Eddy told us not to read the Bible for a while."

The Bible is in some statements contradictory, and it literally **has to have a key** to be opened. Much in the Bible is simply mortal mind. I hold to the scientific presentation of Truth.

ORIGIN OF EVIL: "Two times two is five?" "No, two times two is four." "But where did you get 'two times two is five?'" Answer: "Two times two is four." "What conceives of two times two is five?" Answer: "Two times two is four." "When did 'two times two is five' begin to exist?" **"It never did begin."**

So here error turns away, when we stand firmly for the truth. Error can only question. It has no identity, no existence, no beginning. "Two times two is four," and so continues.

JESUS CHRIST: Jesus was not specially sent to us. It was his business to reach heaven as quickly as he could, and he did it. Jesus was the Way-shower, and Christ came to him as it will have to come to each one of us. "Christ" means **anointed,** — demonstrable understanding of divine law as practiced by Jesus.

DUALITY: Stop talking error. Don't talk of your real self, and your counterfeit. There is but one selfhood, and that is spiritual, pure, perfect, immortal.

DEAD MAN—WHAT CONSTITUTES: A man walking along the street may be more of a dead man than the one whose so-called physical body is already in the cemetery, for the reason that the one whose body is in the cemetery may have already awakened to the fact of Life immortal.

CREEDS: Science and Health, 471:22: Question: "Are doctrines and creeds any benefit to mankind?" Read answer from book—Science and Health. We have been held in the grasp of creeds, and even in the gloom of same—many of us. I was a Presbyterian. I had been taught heaven and feared hell.

EVERLASTING PUNISHMENT: Quoted passage wherein Jesus is purported to have spoken of everlasting punishment. He did not speak in this language. He dealt in metaphysics. He said "age-long punishment." The translators, having preconceived ideas, used "everlasting punishment" to fit their thoughts.

OTHER GODS; BODY; ONENESS: "Thou shalt have no other gods before me." But one Life, one Truth, one Mind, one body. Understand, God is not **in** anything. Mind is not **in** body or brain. It is not limited.

TREATMENT: Illustration of treatment: Lost valuable package on street car. Went on my way; dropped a note to Superintendent describing goods, and asked that I be called if package was turned in.

I handled the matter to know that whoever found it wanted to do the right thing; that avarice, greed, covetousness could not control him or her. It was returned.

Question was asked: "Had it not been returned, what would you have thought?" Answer: "That some one stole it." Question: "But what, then, about your treatment?" Answer: "It didn't succeed in affecting the wrong-doer."

FAILURES; URGING: Jesus no doubt gave more time to Judas than to all others. Error seemingly is not always reached. If it is on the ascent, we must always wait for the turn downward, before it can be displaced by the truth. Hence, do not urge Christian Science, or say "try it" to any one. Let them come, as they will, when all else has failed. That is the way I came. In some cases Jesus could not do his mighty works. I never said to but one person, "Try Christian Science."

LIFTED UP: "If I be lifted up, I will **draw, draw, draw,** etc." It is so much better to **draw** than to push people into the kingdom.

IMPERSONAL TREATMENT: Cablegram received—no signature: "Treat me." It matters not what the name of the person is. It is the belief of a claim I must handle. In order to be sure of reaching the trouble, in such a case, I make every statement of truth that I can recall at the time, and later, if some omissions occur to me, then I amend my treatment.

TREATMENT: The first statement always to be made is to counteract the rather popular belief and statement that Christian Science cannot heal, etc. Then proceed directly to the claim of belief, if you know it; and if not, make your declarations general enough so that they may even be specific.

TREATMENT: Question: "Must the first statement be repeated every time, if more than one treatment is necessary?" Answer: "If I felt the claim (malpractice thought) was met at first, I would not repeat; otherwise I would."

Usually, find out the claim of belief from the patient, if he knows, or he may give you the doctor's report. But to know this is not absolutely necessary.

My own case was slow in healing. Practitioner told me to take some cases, and in this way I would heal myself. She unloaded upon me some "old hawks," those who had been treated unsuccessfully by several practitioners. One I remember. I called upon the woman, and at my advent all attendants flew. She had had a very bad night and had harassed all.

She was in bedroom and I in parlor. I was suffering, but she was suffering more. I was scared. I did not know what to do. Error said that I could not do the work, I had not the understanding, etc. But I finally bethought me, I could say everything I knew in Science. I did. I began to get well, and I asked the patient how she was, and she replied, "Oh, so easy," and so the healing asserted itself.

Your mortal self doesn't do the healing, anyway. Nothing depends upon mortal self. The healing is done by the **active ideas** of Truth, and you surely can state the Truth you know. As a matter of fact, there is nothing to heal, no disease to be removed, or lack to overcome; but the *modus operandi* is as above described.

However, if any one asks if Christian Science heals, say, "Yes."

SPECIFIC CAUSES; CAUSATION: Some years ago, some practitioners had great long lists of certain sins as causes of certain diseases. The number of things which I have known the rheumatic to be treated for is astonishing.

Rheumatism: Practitioners comparing notes: "Well, what do you treat?" "I always treat pride." "No, I take self-righteousness;" and so on.

All this is folly. The root claim of all is in general mortal mind. Some practitioners have to make the patient a sinner before healing him. It is like the doctor who said that if he could only run the ailments of his patients into fits, he could cure fits.

ANIMAL MAGNETISM; ERROR; EVIL: Mrs. Eddy uses the term "evil." This does not cover all of materiality. She uses "error": that is different. She finally uses "animal magnetism"—another term for mortal mind—the mind of death. This term was used long before Mrs. Eddy was born. Animal magnetism has been classified, for the sake of analysis and easy handling, as **ignorant, fraudulent,** and **malicious.**

In my early teaching, I was afraid of this subject, but now I rather enjoy it. I have learned how to protect myself, as you must do.

"Ignorant animal magnetism" is that kind of thinking (so-called), which believes, for instance, in contagion of disease. We all have to contend against the effect of this and that universal belief of failure or success.

"Malicious animal magnetism" is exercised when one studies to direct evil thought or judgment with some specific intent.

When one does not know enough to know whether his treatment is good or not, or if the patient will have faith in it, it would be better not given.

SENSUALITY: Do not make the mistake of charging everything to sensuality. I look upon this more as one of the appetites of the flesh. Now, don't fall into this error.

REALIZATION; TREATMENT: Speaking of realizing, and feeling as if we are not in condition to give a treatment: We have come to a pretty bad state of affairs when we can think or talk of nothing but error. As said before, your mortal self does not do the healing. It is the **activity** of the Word. So, declare the truths you know. When we are able to rise above personality wholly, then for us will come the ascension.

FAILURES: We do not heal every case. Referred previously to Judas, and others. Jesus never took a case he could not heal, but we have no such perception—discernment. We should have, however.

AGE; TREATMENT: Referring again to practitioners comparing methods: One says: "I handled age." "How did you do it?" Answer: "I said there was no such thing as old age." This was of no use. The claim of mortal mind, materiality, atomic theory, decay, dissolution, chemical action, death, should be handled in your statement, and so break down the law of age.

BUSINESS DEMONSTRATION; TREATMENT: Illustration: I have a house to sell. If it is right for me to sell it, it is right for some one to buy; and it would be wrong for said party not to buy or for me not to sell. A desire to sell, to put the loss on some other person, is not honest. Supply and demand, scientifically understood, are one.

A banking firm had $500,000.00 worth of Mexican bonds. They were depreciating and the officials, knowing this, could not honestly urge them on their customers. One of the firm, a student of mine, came to me for consultation in the matter.

He was advised same as in the "house treatment" above. He applied same and in short time had a call for a large lot of these bonds from abroad. Quoted price; made a sale at a gain; and had the second call for the entire lot.

MINISTERS; CREEDS: Ministers: I do not like their introductions of lecturers. They are partisans—afraid to stand for progress. Christian Science is a religion of progression

All creeds are well enough, but they are only stepping stones, but some take a step and stay right there. A lawyer has a trained, judicial mind. He knows or searches both sides of the case, and is ready for either side. But the minister rarely knows any other presentation of thought or creed than his own.

CHRISTIAN SCIENCE PRACTICE; TREATMENT: Questions by class invited; answers and illustrations given. "I want you to learn how to work effectively NOW, and not have to wait fifty or sixty years. In the early days, very little was known as to how to get results.

"Indeed, much of the practice of the present day is mesmeric, hypnotic; and most of the early practice was faith-cure; whereas Christian Science healing is that of clear, pure, metaphysical understanding."

TREATMENT; IMPERSONAL TREATMENT: A person is never treated. After listening to all the error which a patient may present, **you** need the treatment most. Their story has been the suggestion of evil to you. Just so, does evil, animal magnetism, suggest itself to people at large, both by audible and inaudible suggestion, mostly the latter.

SUGGESTION: You should make nothing of the evil by striking at the claim of mesmeric suggestion. Destroy this and you silence the senses that report evil.

NAMES OF PATIENTS: You need no name of any person to treat, because it is not personality you handle. But the treatment, if in response even to an unsigned telegram, if given, will be received by the one attuned to your reply—or in such receptive mood of expectancy. There is a line of connection between the called and the caller.

IMPERSONAL TREATMENT; PERSONAL TREATMENT; FEMALE TROUBLE; TREATMENT: Never treat a man, woman or child. Treating a woman for diseases peculiar to women might rather fasten same upon her than relieve her. Change of name, as in case of a woman marrying, would not mean loss of connection in treating.

NAME OF DISEASE: Some practitioners feel need to know the name of the claim presented. This is a mark of limitation.

DIAGNOSIS: Sometimes, however, a diagnosis of the physical ailment may allay the fear of the patient, or may enable the practitioner to more effectively direct his work. When to ask or when not to ask for diagnosis by M. D. must be left to the perception of the practitioner. Jesus never needed such, nor did he always call the disease by name.

SCARLET FEVER—TREATING: Question: "If patient had scarlet fever and was treated for measles, would the work be effective?" Answer: "It would not matter, so that claims of fever, eruption, contagion, and elimination were covered."

CONTAGIOUS DISEASE: If in doubt as to contagious disease, call in physician and obey the law. No one need fear a physician or his opinion.

BRAVADO: In St. Louis, a man and his wife attended a lecture in the church. They asked to have a window shut, and they were told that no one could take cold listening to such a lecture. Illness resulted, and the husband, a prominent man of the city, loudly proclaimed the lunacy of Christian Scientists.

FOOLISHNESS: No Christian Scientist should say what another should do or not do. I know of practitioners who tell their patients to do anything they wish, brave anything, even before the patient has lost fear, and the practitioner is not strong enough to carry them. This is bravado.

HUMAN WILL-POWER: Much of the treatment currently given is mesmeric, or human will over the patient. WATCH AGAINST THIS.

ANXIETY: Thought transference is mesmeric effect of one mind upon another. If entertaining anxiety and desire for healing of certain persons for its effect upon the community, one is more likely to become mesmerized by the claim himself than to deliver the afflicted.

TREATMENT: MALPRACTICE: SELF-DEPRECIATION: It is well to open a treatment with some statements contradicting mental malpractice or self-depreciation,—such statements as: "I cannot do this work," "I am not equal to it," or fear of the criticisms of the public, or a particular class of persons who disparage the healer's ability, or the efficacy of Christian Science.

HEART; HEART DISEASE—TREATMENT OF: SPIRITUALIZATION: A heart is a human concept or manifestation of mortal mind counterfeiting something real. I do not say counterfeiting a heart (a spiritual heart), but counterfeiting the right idea, or quality of divine Mind.

Life does not depend upon heart or its action, or any body of matter. But the claim of mortal mind is that life depends upon this action. So, my treatment is directed to this mortal mind belief or claim. Lift that, and the clamp is taken off the heart, and the heart resumes its normal action. This is improved belief, and when we finally grasp the "unseeing" of matter, our patient will vanish into heaven and we will follow.

CONDEMNATION; SIN; MATERIAL REMEDIES: Question asked by one of the students: "Should one be 'damned,' or condemned, if he remembered in the night that he had a headache powder that formerly helped him, and he took it?" Answer: "No, nor when a practitioner fails to meet a case, should he say that it is because of some uncovered sin of the patient. How does the practitioner know it is a sin? What right has he to condemn?"

KIMBALL'S HEALING: My healing was very slow. Indeed, I was not healed until I learned the way myself. But after being under treatment for some time, I suffered so much in my head and back, that I determined to steal out in my coachman's quarters and resume the use of a rubber ice-cap for head and back, and did so, thereby catching cold. I lay down on his bed.

After this, or just before, I went back to my physician. I asked him what he thought of Christian Science healing me. He said he thought it could. So, after being re-examined, heartily discouraged, and made much worse, I went back to Christian Science to stay.

MEDICINE: One who goes back to medicine, it should be explained, while he may be helped, is only further mesmerized by evil at the time, and is liable to a recurrence of the complaint.

MATTER: Matter is an expression of evil; medicine is material; evil helps evil; it is doomed by its own law of death.

HELPING ON A CASE: If a practitioner asked me for help on a case, most likely I would take the case away from him, but not tell him. I would treat the patient directly. Again, I might handle the malpractice and fear for the practitioner.

IMPERSONAL TREATMENT: If treatment were personal, a name would always be needed. A person would have to keep the practitioner notified every time she married or changed her name. All treatment should be impersonal. On way to business—hear a lot of error—deny it and go on; impersonal treatment.

TREATMENT: LAW: Christian Science rests on this foundation:

All being and everything real exists now, and is forever complete and perfect now.

All is Mind, mental, spiritual.

All by way of substance, presence, and occupancy exists now.

All by way of law, power and action exists now.

And this allness is ever-present and available.

Christian Science practice is not for the purpose of doing anything to anything that exists.

This allness of existence includes everything in the entire range of infinity.

Christian Science practice is not for the purpose of creating or constructing or re-constructing, or repairing, or altering anything that exists.

The practitioner need not think he has to "bring out" something.

Everything is governed by law.

Fundamental law enforces harmonious action, and is always the law of Life and health.

There is no other law. That which seems to be law or rule of discord is but a belief of error.

Christian Science practice is the enforcement of divine Law, and conversely, stops and abolishes the enforcement of spurious belief or law.

The practice of Christian Science recognizes the claims of mortal mind, but does not admit any validity to them.

To ignore a claim does not mean progress. Some people are afraid to tackle the error, and hide their heads in the sand like an ostrich. Others give a flat denial. The activity of metaphysical logic scientifically proves the nothingness of error from the standpoint that evil has neither presence, cause nor law because it is not a manifestation of Omnipresence, Omnipotence, Omniscience.

The requisite recognition on your part is that mortal mind, in belief, is the sole cause of every error, and that it alone projects that error, and that the sum-total of mortal mind is animal magnetism.

ILLUSTRATION: Doctor visits a case; makes a law, as you say, for the case. You speak of this as the doctor's law, and so you give it personality. In this way, one takes umbrage at creeds, philosophies, doctors, etc. You should see the whole thing as a belief, a suggestion of mortal mind. Hence, the necessity of making some such declaration as the following:

"This is neither person, place, or thing; but is a mere argument, a statement or belief of mortal mind, and it is a false statement about that which is true, and it has neither presence, cause, nor law. God is All—Omnipresence, Omnipotence, Omniscience."

All there is about Christian Science practice is the mental *modus operandi*, whereby the falsity is silenced. No matter what the claim is, your immediate recourse is to know that Mind is the rule of perfection and harmony to everything, and is the law of expulsion and elimination to every erring belief about a substance, a presence. Mind is a law of power and action.

ERROR ANALYZED: In the statement of the claim of disease, it is essential to cover three points, as follows:

First: That there is a place or substance that can be occupied by disease.

Second: That there is a cause of disease.

Third: That there is a law to enforce it, and to procure a *modus operandi*.

These three beliefs must be annulled in every case.

REMARKS: Cause of disease perceived, then specific treatment should follow.

MALARIA: Handle weather conditions, decay, disintegration of animal, mineral, or vegetable matter, so as to form poison. **Please note:** If you put in operation No. 1, above, there is nothing left for disease or mortal mind to operate upon.

HEREDITY: If a case presented itself in which heredity played some part, then I should begin to reason out that the law of heredity was and is a falsity, a dictum of cosmic mortal mind by which the patient has subconsciously become so mesmerized that it is a rule for him; hence he has become a victim.

The father, or germ, of mortal man is, according to physiology, $1/125,000$ of an inch in length, and the female ovum is $1/25$ of an inch. Now, how could this one particle of moisture carry in it such far-reaching tendencies and dispositions as hereditary claims? All members of a family healthy and virile until forty years of age. Then, hereditary claim commences to operate fatally. The mortal mind that, through its own presence, brought forth life (counterfeit) now ultimates in death.

SUBCONSCIOUS MIND: There are three strata in mortal mind; namely—matter, unconscious mind, and active mind. Unconscious mind is sometimes called the subconscious mind.

SEX DISEASE: "Sexual disease does not bring contamination." There is great need that this should be declared often, because, to sense, the blood of almost the entire human family is more or less contaminated, through belief of heredity, with syphilitic taint.

TREATMENT; GOD AND MAN: A treatment that is all affirmation about God may not meet the case. We know God only through His idea—man; and we need not despise man or be gloomy in mentioning him.

"Man is effect. There is one complete body, which includes all that can possibly be included in body. Body is the complete representative of Mind. The real man is shown forth as real body, and the real man is whole and complete as the wholeness and completeness of body."

TREATMENT: MANIFESTING BODY: I would let this be a very frequent declaration, with the purpose of producing immunity: "Owing to the fact that body is mental or spiritual, it contains no inherent disease, and disease cannot be imposed upon it mesmerically."

The idea of the body being spiritual removes the idea of matter upon which mesmerism would act. We need to manifest spiritual body.

WEATHER; RAIN: I have lectured twelve or fifteen hundred times; have had it rain, particularly on two trips through Illinois, a number of times. Once it seemed that all the water —the entire supply—would drop down. I needed to go about seventy miles to another appointment, so I thought I had better go to work, and I did.

About 4:00 p. m. the sun shone out and all was well. I was met by a committee of some importance in the town, who rather saucily said: "We have looked for you all day." Said I: "I was trying to insure a pleasant evening."

One or two of the ladies took the cue and said: "I worked on the weather—why didn't you leave that to us?" Answer: "Because I did not think you or any one else here knew how to handle it." After a little cross-fire, I said: "Well, now tell me how you treated." One replied: "I declared there were no clouds in heaven." Had this been effective, we never would have had any more rain. Another said: "I just said, if anybody did get wet, it would not hurt them."

I did not tell them how to treat—did not think they would understand me if I did—but you will.

MAN: TREATING: I don't know anything about clouds in heaven. To cure boils, one need not say that God has no boils. What we want to declare most is what we know about man. . . . Man never fell. Man is complete, perfect body, the idea or manifestation of divine Mind. Declaring the scientific truth or fact about man and body, you are nearer your patient than when declaring about God.

TREATMENT: The ten lepers yielded their beliefs, but not the cause. Jesus said: "Go, and sin no more." You may not heal in one treatment, for several reasons, but keep at it. Always handle contagion, infection, electrical effects or cause, temperament, or so-called chemical causes.

INSOMNIA: Treatment for insomnia: Man is forever conscious. He, being the idea of God, this consciousness must be good. There is no interruption in this consciousness. Man is the consciousness or manifestation of Mind, Spirit, and God never sleeps. Therefore, really, man never sleeps: so stop being afraid of consciousness—and the patient will sleep.

TREATMENT; MOTHER-IN-LAW: Here is a case of X Y Z. In the course of my treating him or her, I discover his hate for his mother-in-law. I handle this, and he is healed.

I have another case of X Y Z. I find, after some time, hate of mother-in-law. I handle this and the patient is healed.

Another practitioner, talking over cases, says: "Now what do you handle in case of trouble called X Y Z?"

Suppose I reply: "Handle hatred of mother-in-law. I did it and it healed." "Yes, but my patient has no mother-in-law."

A lesson was enforced here, showing a common error, namely, a supposition that a given physical disease always has the same mental cause.

TREATMENT: Mesmerism, hypnotism, psychology, telepathy, thought transference, mental theories, theosophy, false philosophy, false science. Treat against such as having intelligence, substance or power. The "Osler" thought carries death to the ultimate. False theology, destructive and murderous. It teaches that God ordained the death of everybody, agony for all time and eternity, etc. Handle false theology particularly.

IMPERSONALIZE ERROR: Many Scientists are so small as to take umbrage at a person on account of his creed, opinion, or philosophy, when it is their business to impersonalize error, to see the effect as nothing and the belief as the evil. Declare against such belief as a law or rule to govern men; for man is perfect, whole, harmonious, reflecting only that which is good, and does so now and always.

HEREDITY; RACE-IMPROVEMENT: The way to insure a better, superior race, is to treat daily, from the time of conception, against heredity. This should insure immaculate birth. The sub-conscious mind is the channel for the heredity thought, and its existence or capacity to be a channel should be denied.

MALPRACTICE; TREATMENT: Malpractice—worst form—intentional exercise of the thought of murder.

First comes recognition that all mental malpractice is based on the supposition that there is mortal mind.

Second, that it manifests itself through what is called avenue or channel or instrument.

Third, that it can impart to thought, which it must manifest through its channel, both action and power.

Fourth, that it can enforce its belief or declaration, its rule, wish, or desire, by means of its law.

Fifth, that it has an object upon which it can act or impress itself.

It is never Mind, or power, or law.

It has no mortals, nor mortal minds, no persons, no personalities, no men, women, or children, through which it can act, or upon whom it can devolve any power to act.

It is not law, and has no law-maker.

No law can be erected by the belief called a malpractitioner.

A treatment against malpractice must never hold the thought of a malpractitioner or a person in the treatment.

The whole purpose of a treatment against malpractice is to disclose it as being not a person, but as an erring belief only, and as being of no more consequence than an erring belief.

The treatment, therefore, denies the primary claim of mortal mind, and the following claims of avenue, law, power, action and objective.

Deny also the power of malpractice, claiming to act as hatred, envy, jealousy, malice, revenge, anger, and fear.

Example given, and difference shown between raw hatred and declared hatred. May be likened to difference in potency between water and steam.

Hold no person in your thought during treatment, especially not the thought of a malpractitioner.

ILLUSTRATION of erroneous treatment: I have pain in back. I recognize it as from malpractice and at once give treatment which is personal. Hence, the other party has pain, and sees me as the sender. He resumes work, and the one who is most personal, can hate most, wins. Usually, the Christian

Scientist would lose, because he could not hate as much as the other party.

Love the so-called malpractitioner; see the claim as nothing and as not being the activity of the so-called malpractitioner, but of satan, error, which is neither real nor powerful; then the claim of malpractice would be destroyed for both the so-called malpractitioner and yourself.

ASTROLOGY: Solar system is governed by law of materiality. Astrology—any law of cosmic mortal mind—may govern you until annulled. Handle belief of horoscope and heredity.

Truth is propelled by push. So it has been said the falling of the apple is by push. So, truth comes to us; it is "pushed" on us.

Declare for yourself annulment of all astrological law. This is a belief attached to the conjunction or opposition of planets, when child is born. . . . I am saying more to this class on astrology than I ever did before. I would emphasize, it is important to **recognize** astrology in treatment, for the purpose of annulling its false claims.

PALMISTRY; SPIRITUALISM: Palmistry is a belief that if a person has certain lines in his hand, his character is indicated and fixed thereby.

Handle beliefs of phrenology, fatalism, destiny, doom, superstition, witchcraft, thought-transference.

Spiritualism is a belief that another, present or departed, can impress himself upon you. Napoleon Bonaparte is an example of the belief of fatalism.

COURTSHIP PERIOD, DISEASES PECULIAR TO: Many young girls "run down" during courtship, before marriage —bad liver—indigestion, etc. The desire of another to possess her all the time, also the desire to give herself to another is the false desire or belief to be handled.

TRUTH, HOW LEARNED: Just here was asked: "By what faculty of the human mind do we apply truth? Is it through reason? You have just used that term." Answer: Yes, and it is the Truth coming—"pushing"—to us. There are persons of different grades of mentality, some logical, others more or less so, and others quite vacillating. That mind that is the most logical, and has developed to the highest standard, is the one that is the best transparency for Truth, and so truth comes to such an one, as the sun shines through a rift in the clouds.

MENTAL MALPRACTICE—COMBATING: Mrs. Eddy said that, for the first twelve years in Christian Science, not a case was lost; but after this, mental malpractice had to be combated.

MAN IS ACTIVITY: No spiritual selfhood floating around. Man is active, right thought. Immortal man is activity, the aggregation of right ideas. I am my own true self, right here and now: "I Am" is man,—is the activity of right ideas.

TRANSITIONAL STATE: We are in a transitional state, and in proportion as we are transformed do we express right ideas.

ORIGIN OF EVIL: Philosophies have been wrecked in trying to account for the origin of evil. I would jump into the lake if I found the origin of evil, because then it would be true. There is no origin, source, or foundation for evil. "Two times two is five" is a lie about "two times two is four." This silences error.

TREATMENT: Omit the word "you" in treatment, but if you can't, then use it. . . . Better than no treatment. Your case is a claim or belief of error, not a man or woman. Argument is used simply to attune your own thought. All is Good, and Good is All; one spiritual body, perfect man. The rule of harmony is perpetual, eternal. The sin or disease to be handled is a false claim and it is not true.

In treatment, always contemplate claim, not the believer. The belief and believer are one. Whether or not to talk to patients depends upon the nature and condition of the patient and the ability of the practitioner.

TEACHING: Right kind of talk of great advantage. "Teach by healing and heal by teaching." Instruction by a practitioner would be better than class instruction, if the practitioner is well instructed and knows how to teach, to impart Truth's ideas.

INDIVIDUALITY; TREATMENT: Do not hamper the individual. Let a person follow his own light, his own initiative, even if he has sometimes to retrace his steps. MOST IMPORTANT RULE: "Declare the truth; deny the belief."

TREATMENT; GERMS; MICROBES; PARASITES; MEAT-EATING: Claim to be handled is any form of life organization acting by reason of hunger; invasion by colonies of germs. It is not death of organisms that should be sought in treatment, but demesmerism of invading organisms. "Get them to stop eating and go to Sunday School." One insect preys upon another. Dragon fly upon spiders; spiders upon flies, etc.; and man upon them all. Note how buffalo, deer, and all wild game have disappeared. Men are the great murderers. They believe in being sustained by the death of other living creatures and things.

Question asked: "How do you justify meat eating?" Answer: "I don't. I eat less and less meat all the time. The body is 85 per cent water, and we do not need so much solid foods as we commonly use."

Paralysis, consumption, burglary, mistletoe (a parasite plant), used in illustrating above thoughts.

TREATMENT: For treatment of disease, Dr. Hammond advocates elimination of poisonous secretions through proper exercise, perspiration, etc. Lack of elimination by skin, liver, lungs, and evacuation through proper channels, is cause of most disease. This would cause retention of morbific (death producing) secretions.

"Recognize the claim of belief and do not admit its verity."

TREATMENT; EXERCISE; MAN: I know a woman, a Christian Scientist, who had this and that ailment. I inquired into her habits. She took little or no exercise, when formerly she used to walk miles. She now covered but a few necessary blocks.

No need to read "Science and Health" and the Bible, and sit with your hand to your brow, because you are a Scientist, until you become pale and wan. . . . I used to belong to that class.

I called the woman's attention to the fact that man is the activity of right ideas. Natural, normal exercise is proper and pure air and food are proper.

TREATMENT; LAW: Mind is the law of completeness, perfection, harmony, life, strength, vigor, vitality, action unto its ideas.

Mind is the law of elimination and expulsion to the belief

of deficient elimination, abnormal secretion, or retention of the belief of morbific secretion, poison or impurity.

All Christian Science treatment is eliminative of error, and one must see to it that the *modus operandi* is one directed to the elimination of any kind of a false belief about any kind of a thing, and annul the so-called law of that belief.

MANIPULATION; MALPRACTICE: Remarks: Kennedy, an early pupil of Mrs. Eddy, taken by Mrs. Eddy at urgent request of his mother, proved dishonest and a hypocrite in Science. Was cast out. Having learned to manipulate mortal mind, vowed he would follow Mrs. Eddy until death with persecution. He joined a band of hypocrites, and some one of them projected this thought, that afterward became a law of reversal (so-called) in mortal mind: "All healed patients in Christian Science shall relapse to their former belief, or their mucous membrane shall become diseased."

RELAPSES: After this, relapses occurred with Christian Science treatment, and for a while everything went wrong with Mrs. Eddy, even to the fitting of a dress, the making of her shoes, and her business. Later she discovered this evil. Some one of the perpetrators told it.

Dictation: Important: "Handle the belief of a return of an old belief." Called to a patient. Discovered this trouble. Treated for same—recovery.

REVERSAL; TREATMENT: Handle belief of reversal —important.

"This treatment is not reversed, and it cannot be made to produce an effect contrary to that which is intended. The belief of the law of reversal is annulled by this treatment, and cannot be made to apply to or to influence anything."

At one time the mesmerists formulated this law: "Every treatment given in Christian Science will be reversed." For instance, if you treated for "life," death would ensue. Christian Science practitioners lost patients until this law of malpractice was uncovered; hence, we treat against any law of reversal, as previously explained.

HYPNOTISM: Spoke of "adepts" in Asia. Physician sent there to meet one of them. He told the adept that he had acquired something in hypnotism, and could protect himself. . . . Most terrific storm arose suddenly; physician pale with fear; then the sun broke forth. . . . Next the Doctor was climbing an endless ladder into space. When he had had all of this that he could stand, again conditions were normal. The adept said to him: "So you think you can protect yourself." This uncovers the limit of a claim of false activity in mortal mind which may operate unless scientifically met, and should not be ignored. Declare: There is no evil or mortal mind; for God never made any. Therefore, it cannot exercise any hypnotic power. It cannot mesmerically impose the belief of this, that, or the other evil upon me or any one else.

TREATMENT: The nub of all is the **conclusion.** I do not use long argument. I arrive at the conclusion early. Mrs. Eddy says: "Let the Spirit bear witness."

ASTROLOGY; HOROSCOPE: This subject having come under my notice more directly lately, I speak of it to the class, not with the view of their taking up a study of the subject, but that they may be aware that mortal-mind has made astrological laws that in some cases have to be annulled. It is not necessary to have any horoscope cast. Indeed, I would not. If it is desirable, you can refer to some work on the subject, and get tables of horoscopes there.

One is inclined, in reading his own horoscope, to condemn the bad, and be delighted with the good, and accept that part. But we should deny the natural good, forecast in the horoscope, as well as the bad.

RESUME: Today is a resumé of our week's labors:
1—We considered God as substance, presence, cause, and law.
2—Function, activity, power, outlined.
3—The opposite of good is a lie. This seeming is evil. Deny it. The human mind is transitional.
Everything that is, is good. Expel wrong belief. The application is mental activity of right thought expelling false belief.

Man always existent, always harmonious, always perfect.

TREATMENT: To a Christian Scientist, error appears only to disappear. It has no place, is no person, no thing. I am not afraid. I can master any error that presents itself.

FEAR; BELIEF: Belief of fear is itself a belief.

INSANITY: Insanity is generally accompanied by the belief of a diseased body. It is a belief that mind can be in body, and should be handled from that standpoint.

MALPRACTICE; POISON IVY; PNEUMOGASTRIC NERVE: Malpractitioners (wrong thinkers) made a law that poison ivy should cause irritation, distress, etc.

Pneumogastric nerve: Irritation, and by sympathy, a claim may touch head, back, chest, heart, or stomach; causes fear and great distress.

The truth about pneumo-gastric nerve is some divine manifestation, idea, activity, which cannot be interfered with, and there is no nerve which can be, or any belief of any such nerve.

POISON; TREATMENT: Poison has no active principle, no chemical modus operandi or effect; there are no consequences of poison.

CHILDREN—TREATMENT OF: Young child: Nearest avenue is mother. Her thought either mesmerizes or demesmerizes the child, as the case may be. The child and mother often treated together; but if mother is unscientific, protect child against mother's thought.

MALPRACTICE; BOILS: At one time mental malpractice declared that Christian Science readers should have an accumulation of morbific substance in their bodies because of their lack of proper outdoor exercise and normal activities. At that time I was "Reader," and when I treated against it, a boil came on my person and discharged. I am not given to boils.

BODY: Each conscious being is individual expression of body, the body of right ideas.

TREATMENT—CO-OPERATIVE: "More than one treat a case?" Answer: "I should say, not more than one handle a case at one time. If practitioner is good, no more needed; if bad, two bad ones would not help matters."

TEACHING AND ADDRESSES

When several have treated on a case, the way has usually been for one to outline the line of treatment to be adhered to by all, thus avoiding error and insuring application of the law correctly. I have seen as wonderful miracles performed as are recorded in the Bible.

REMUNERATION: Any price is too dear for some work, and other work is not properly compensated. Distance, location, etc., govern charges.

Hold a poor thought, and you reap it. I always expect patients to pay. I should look askance at myself if I attracted poverty thought. I must be paid, if it takes the student or person twenty years.

PROFESSIONAL ETIQUETTE; SECRECY; CONFIDENCES: Talking of patients: The confessional is respected; lawyers respect their clients' disclosures; doctors their patients'; and a Christian Science practitioner who talks about his patients should be debarred.

CLASS INSTRUCTION; WISDOM IN TALKING; TEACHERS—OTHER: Class instruction: Some will rejoice with you; others feel aggrieved, etc. So quietly go your way, and be kind and respectful to other teachers. This will protect you most. The older Scientists have least to say.

KIMBALL'S TEACHING ABSOLUTE SCIENCE; CLASS TEACHING; DELAY UNNECESSARY; INSTANTANEOUS UNDERSTANDING: You, no doubt, will hear much opposition to the way I have taught you, but let it pass. I make bold to say that I have given you absolute Science, and

I want you to avoid errors made by those inexperienced, and get this Truth and its application **now,** and not be fifty or sixty years getting it.

LAWSUIT: A certain lawsuit was referred to. Management and detail of handling same afforded valuable working information to the hearers. Obstacles surmounted equal to any miraculous work recorded in the Bible.

QUESTIONS: When questions were invited from class, we were told to ask and they would be answered, if it required seven or seventy times seven different phrasings in order that we might grasp the replies; or if unable to answer, this would be frankly admitted.

UNSCIENTIFIC CHRISTIAN SCIENTISTS; APPLICATION, ERRONEOUS: One class of Christian Scientists, along with other forms of crystallized thought, such as Theology, Medicine, Theosophy, Astrology, Spiritualism, etc., are making false laws for themselves by their erroneous thinking and faulty statements. Some Scientists have beliefs peculiar to themselves. Beware of falling into such errors.

MALPRACTICE DEFINED; WRONG THINKING: All malpractice resolves itself into this: "Some one is thinking wrongly about something that is true."

INACTIVITY; REPOSE; RESULT OF MATERIA MEDICA'S DECLARATIONS: The M. D.'s are already declaring that restful repose or inertia of the Scientists is yet going to be their undoing, as such a state arrests elimination, secretion, and the result is depletion.

ACTIVITY; EXERCISE: Even the counterfeit man, to be a good counterfeit of the right idea, should be active.

BODY, DESPISING; ASCENSION; BELIEFS, BETTER: Do not despise your material body, nor throw stones at it. We attain the "ascension" only through better beliefs, and as our beliefs improve, our bodies respond and manifest or externalize these improved beliefs. A healthy sense of a material body is a better belief than a sense of sick body, because material body is only one falsehood, while sick body involves two falsehoods. The primary claim is the so-called physical body, while diseased conditions are secondary claims.

TREATMENT; DECLARATION; LIFE ETERNAL; BODY, PERFECT: Declare a hundred times daily: "I have eternal life and perfect body"; and if you have time enough, declare it a hundred times more.

GOD—HOW KNOWN; MANIFESTATION; EMBODIMENT; AFFIRM GOD AND MAN; AFFIRM PERFECT MAN: God is known only through man—this manifestation or embodiment of "right ideas"; hence, it is essential that we should not only affirm God, but should declare daily for the perfect man, and the same will be externalized on the human plane by improved physical conditions.

COFFEE; TEA; MALPRACTICE: Some people abstain from the drinking of tea and coffee because they don't care to work against the malpractice or wrong thinking of some people about the use of these two beverages.

SUPPLY; EXPECTANCY; RECEPTIVITY: One who keeps himself in a state of expectancy keeps his avenue of "opportunity" open, and in this way does not limit his supply. BE RECEPTIVE TO GOOD. If I were more receptive, I would not be hampered by this "stuff." (Referring to some notes he had written in case of inability to be present at the Association and give the address personally.) Some one remarked: "Give me the 'stuff.'" (Laughter.)

BIBLE, CONCESSIONS; SCIENCE AND HEALTH, CONCESSIONS: Remarks repeated about composition and interpretation of the Bible; also about the concessions made to mortal thought in the phraseology of Science and Health.

EDUCATION; ETERNAL LIFE, ATTAINING; RIGHT IDEAS; SIN, WAGES OF: "Wages of sin is death." "As ye sow, so shall ye reap," etc. "We must give an account of every foolish word," etc.

To attain eternal life is a matter of education, pure and simple. The "wages of sin" is **learning** "right ideas." It makes that a necessity, for mortals to be rid of sin.

PENALTY: God knows not sin, sickness, or death, or evil of any kind; hence, he has attached no penalty. Mortal mind counterfeits Life, and then tries to insure its own extinction through penalty.

PUNISHMENT; SUFFERING; CONCESSIONS IN SCIENCE AND HEALTH: "We must all come through Science or suffering," etc. (S. & H.) We do not better ourselves through suffering, do not gain anything other than the educational culture to do right. This, along with some other expressions in Science and Health, are simply concessions to human thought at its present stage of development. To have expressed Science plainer in times past might have resulted in its decapitation.

BIBLE, INTERPRETATION: It were better not to read the Bible at all, unless one uses spiritual discernment and can give the proper interpretation.

APPRECIATION: Those who are not capable of properly appreciating what I say here and in my classes have no business here until further study has prepared them to receive.

REVELATION: Revelation is the revealed truth about God, man, universe—immortality brought to light. Revelator and revelation are one. The spiritual thought always precedes the scientific action.

REFLECTION: "Revelator" and "Revelation" are human terms, of present usage. In due time "reflection" will be spoken of, instead. Man is God's reflection upon Himself.

REVELATION, THE: When a thing is to be revealed, there is always one mind more ready than any other to receive it, one higher in thought than anyone else—just as in a mountain range there will be one peak higher than the others, which catches the rays of the sun first.

MIND AND BODY: Mortal body is in and of mortal mind. Spiritual body is in Mind, and not Mind in spiritual body.

IDEAS: Mind finds full and complete expression in ideas. Words do not last forever, but spiritual ideas do.

MIND AND MATTER: Mind does not need matter. It is impossible for matter to express Mind, God, because it is capable of discord, evil, and is finite.

DYING MAN, RECOVERY OF: A man supposed to be dying was made to keep repeating: "There is one infinite Life, that Life is eternal Life, and that Life is my Life." He recovered.

ONE MIND IS MINE: There is one Mind, and that Mind is the Mind of man—the understanding of Principle; just as there is one 6, and that 6 belongs to the understanding of the principle of mathematics.

FALSE PRACTICE: Insanity and aberration might be produced by declaring, "You have no mind."

SPIRITUAL BODY, PARTS AND FUNCTIONS OF: There is strength in arm, in muscles; you have a stomach, lungs and arm. These are ideas of Mind and not forms of matter, infinite and not finite. There is strength, health, power, in them and these belong to man, an inheritance from Mind. Man is immortal. "Now are we the sons of God."

FALSE PRACTICE: A student tried to heal an unused arm by saying, "There is no strength in it." That was wrong. Someone made the statement, "There is no power in **physical** arm to be lost." That is correct.

BODY, SPIRITUAL: There is one body in Mind, perfect, spiritual, and that is the perfect body—the body, or sum-total, of right ideas. Body is this "compound" idea of divine Mind.

SPIRITUAL BODY UNPICTURABLE: You cannot depict spiritual stomach, arm, etc.; for these are infinite, illimitable, and therefore unpicturable ideas.

LIFE DEFINED: God is Life, because Life is Mind. Reflected Life is consciousness of God, knowing God, and not knowing that which is not included in Him.

GOD, FALSE SENSE OF: The world says God is both good and bad. However much they may try to avoid it, in effect they say that He knows evil.

EYES, TREATMENT FOR: In case of belief in sore eyes, the physical eyes are not treated, but declare that all the eye there is, is in Mind, intact, perfect, spiritual, cannot be touched by or impaired by *materia medica* law, so-called. There is but one sight, and that belongs to all. Sight is spiritual discernment.

HEART, TREATMENT FOR: Declare one heart, perfect and belonging to all, a perfect, harmonious idea, manifestation and activity of divine Mind.

TREATMENT, NATURE OF: It is not necessary to **say** that man has no pain, etc., but to **know** that man, the consciousness of divine Mind, has no pain, that man is the image of infinite Good, which includes only good. **To know,** is treatment.

PATIENTS, INSTRUCT THEM: Give patient something to grasp. Expect everyone to become a Christian Scientist. Mrs. Eddy says, in "Science and Health": "Explain audibly to your patients, as soon as they can bear it, the complete control which Mind holds over the body. Show them how mortal mind seems to induce disease by certain fears and false conclusions, and how divine Mind can cure by opposite thoughts. Give your patients an underlying understanding to support them and to shield them from the baneful effects of their own conclusions. Show them that the conquest over sickness, as well as over sin, depends on mentally destroying all belief in material pleasure and pain."

"HEALER," DO NOT USE TERM: Say "practitioner," not "healer."

HEART TROUBLE. FEAR, LEGITIMATE TO USE MEDICAL OPINIONS TO ALLAY: You can safely say to one who has heart trouble, that, according to the best medical opinion, nine out of ten cases of supposed heart trouble are only stomach trouble; and it is legitimate to allay fear in this way.

PNEUMOGASTRIC NERVE: A certain nerve (pneumogastric nerve) seems to get deranged and will in belief cause pain in lungs, back of the neck and different parts of the body. But, in fact, the pneumo-gastric nerve is a manifestation of Mind, and its substance, functions and activity cannot be impaired.

SLEEPLESSNESS, TREATMENT FOR: Man wanting sleep, treat thus: "God is all. All is Mind, which neither slumbers nor sleeps. Man must know that, since he reflects Mind, which is ever-active, he does not sleep, does not want to sleep. Sleep is a penalty for mortality."

INSOMNIA: Thus fear of insomnia, fear of continuing to be conscious, is allayed. The patient is satisfied and sleeps.

UNSELFISHNESS, RESULT OF: Mrs. Eddy asked her students if they loved their neighbor's children as their own. She said that if they desired other children to have what they wanted, their own children would be more apt to have what they wanted.

"CHRISTIAN SCIENTISTS," GENUINE AND SPURIOUS: Two extremes. The loveliest sight is a Christian Scientist who loves. The most pitiful sight is one who has malice and calls himself a Christian Scientist.

ANNIHILATION DOES NOT OCCUR: Nothing is annihilated. The sense of things is transformed. The elements of mortal belief are gradually displaced by spiritual ideas, and so things are not destroyed, but seen aright—found to be spiritual, not material.

The consciousness of Mind's ideas is God's man. To know God is to know man. A bird only knows that it is a bird;

the oyster that it is an oyster, and would not be anything else.

SINNER, BEST PROCEDURE FOR: The best thing that a murderer can do, even while his hand is red with blood, is to get to God as soon as he can. Not condemnation but salvation is his extreme need.

PURE UNAFFECTED BY IMPURITY: A man suffering from impure air objects because he is impure. If he were perfectly pure, impure air could not affect him.

ANIMALITY CLASSIFIED: Animality is classified as sensuality and sexuality.

SIN FUNDAMENTALLY COSMIC, NOT PERSONAL. SUBCONSCIOUSNESS: Mortal mind in solution is sin before the human concept of sin appears. It is termed subconscious mortal mind. From this source come mental transmissions, telepathy, mesmerism, sexuality, heredity, death.

DISEASE, SEAT OF: All belief of disease is in the subconscious mortal mind.

TREATMENT, POINT IN: Do not treat scrofula, but the subconscious mortal mind. Mortal mind is always the culprit.

MORTAL MIND A LIAR: Mortal mind does not need or want matter. All it wants is lies, lies about God and His creation. One of mortal mind's concepts of an expression of the one Life is horse, and, scientifically speaking, what there actually is to horse is the qualities of divine Mind which are expressed by this concept, such as obedience, loyalty, strength, love, etc.

DOMINION, HOW GAINED: Dominion over all things is had by understanding, knowing. To have dominion over a horse is to know that there is no fractious horse; for horse is a divine idea, manifestation and activity, governed by the one Mind.

CONCEPTION, MORTAL AND IMMACULATE: Man born of woman cannot be wholly spiritual. Jesus represented an improved belief of conception. Christian Science is the only wholly immaculate conception. It is wholly apart from matter.

EVE, THE MISTAKE OF: Eve yielded to the belief of good in matter. From that came Cain and Abel, who ruptured the brotherhood of man, and so it continued until error brought on itself the flood—the flood of evil consequences.

NOAH AND THE ARK: Then arose Noah, whose thought of good drew beyond others, and was uplifted to safety, or the Ark. Whatever the destruction, Noah would have been saved.

MOSES AND THE LAW: Then came Moses, who caught glimpses enough of the Messiah to see that evil is opposed to good, and brought out the "Thou shalt not."

PROPHETS: Then foreseeing by the prophets of the coming of truth, and so on down until—

MARY, AND HER CONCEPTION: Mary, whose thought arose to such a height that she perceived the fatherhood of God, and that perception so overshadowed her that she brought forth Jesus. Christian Science is the perception of the divine Fatherhood and Motherhood, and is purely spiritual.

SPIRITUALISM: Spiritualism, in that which constitutes its "ism," is always mental poison, and will react and manifest as disease. In treating a person who is a spiritualist, he needs to be healed not from a disease, but from spiritualism. Handle the assertion that Christian Science cannot heal; know that Christian Science does heal.

ANIMAL MAGNETISM HANDLED: Animal magnetism reaches you through any door you leave open. Watch and pray. Handle the serpent behind you. "God with us"—

that handles malicious animal magnetism. The consciousness that is with God, Power, does it.

DISCOURAGEMENT: Discouragement is never yourself, always a lie, and must be met as mesmerism.

ANIMAL MAGNETISM, HOW IT REACHES US: Animal magnetism only reaches us through an element of error within. The arguments and suggestions of animal magnetism do not go to God or to man, but to itself, always to itself. The right man has always the perfect thought and feeling, and it cannot touch him.

MORTAL MIND, A HANDLING OF: Mortal mind cannot argue that you cannot heal, or do right, or overcome pain, disease, disloyalty, or any error. "Now are we the sons of God."

HYPNOTISM: All mortal thought is hypnotism, either as mortal cause or mortal effect. Hypnotism claims to do anything that mortals can do. An Eastern adept produced the appearance of a terrific storm. (A storm is the involuntary action of fundamental error.) The limit of hypnotism is to voluntarily reproduce in experience the involuntary actions of error. Christian Science uncovers hypnotism, so that Christian Scientists know more about its false claim than a hypnotist does.

ANIMAL MAGNETISM MUST BE HANDLED: Jesus was the only one who succeeded in demonstrating both the letter and the Spirit, when he declared: "There is no death." Until we can do likewise, we MUST handle animal magnetism, by scientifically knowing its nothingness, and refusing to yield to its solicitations.

DO NOT EXPECT TO GAIN SOMETHING BY DYING. Talking about passing on, etc., is mortality coaxing Christian Scientists to die. Everything that reconciles Christian Scientists to death is the rankest kind of animal magnetism. Because of having destroyed some fear of death, the Christian Scientist is often a more easy channel for it, if he believes he may get something better after dying.

INSTANT IN THE TRUTH: There is no God of tomorrow, but a God of now. This breaks fear.

BUSINESS: A man and a woman were depressed about their future business. Broke it by treating the seeming presence of fear, the basis of treatment being OMNIPRESENCE; the only time there is, is **now**.

DEPRESSION, TREATMENT FOR: God is not depressed; hence, man is not; God is harmonious Mind, Truth; hence, man is peaceful, conscious knowing of Truth. No such thing as "dying in the Lord," but LIVING. Every step heavenward here helps one now.

VARIETIES OF ERROR: Mortal mind takes certain specific forms. False theology, false philosophy, false science, spiritualism, mediumship, clairvoyance, hypnotism, mesmerism, esoteric magic, white magic, black art, oriental witchchaft, diabolism, demonology, thought transference, phychic force, etc.

TREATMENT, POINT IN: You must know there is no patient to heal, no sick man. A Christian Science treatment is not the influence of mind over matter, nor mind over mind, but the power of Truth casting out error, the government of mankind by the one Mind.

MEMORY: Pre-existence is not a matter of memory. In Mind, and therefore with the real man, spiritual consciousness, nothing has to be remembered, because all that is, is always coincidently present to consciousness. Consciousness, being the embodiment of all ideas emanating from Substance, is everlastingly the possessor of all creation at the standpoint of idea.

PERSISTENCE IN TREATMENT: More than ever does Mrs. Eddy see that there are no mortals. She says, "Treat three days for one who has seemingly passed out."

TREATMENT, IMPERSONAL: A telegram received, a man dying, no name, knew nothing about him. Did not treat the man, but a claim that said, "It's a man's mind, the belief of error, going against him." The declaration of Truth, thrusting out error, reached and destroyed the falsehood, leaving the man free. Hearing of a sick man in the next block, to declare that there is no sick man, is a treatment. Every declaration of truth helps individually and collectively.

TREATMENT, POINT IN: Even if the case is simply a case of disease and no sin, yet include the moral in the treatment—thus: There is no sin, no temptation to sin, no fall; no penalty; hence, no form of suffering.

SUFFERING, EVEN FOR SIN, NOT TO BE MENTALLY ENFORCED: To declare that a person has got to suffer, even for sin, is mental malpractice. God does not provide either sin or suffering, and to mentally declare for or enforce what God does not, is malpractice,—wrong mental practice.

MALPRACTICE ILLUSTRATED: To say that an injury of any kind will pursue and overtake, is mental malpractice. To give reasons why a person is not healed is mental malpractice; for God is the only Cause.

CLAIMS NOT MET: You need not be disturbed because a certain case is not met. One of the rankest errors is to blame either practitioner or patient. Sometimes, in a present human situation, a case healed is worse than one not healed. Other problems may need to be worked out, by a given person, before the problem of healing.

PERSISTENCE: Endeavor to know that the first treatment has done the work. But, one or fifty, keep it up. Never give up so long as one wants help.

LONESOMENESS: Alone with God is not to be lonesome.

TREATMENT, POINT IN: Admit a claim only as a false belief; then see its nothingness.

MENTAL WORK, GENERAL: It is not meant that every specific form of sin should be handled daily, but one should be ready to handle any one of them.

MALPRACTICE, TREATMENT FOR: Handle mental malpractice thus: "There is one infinity of Good, one Mind, one Life, and that is man's Life." The consciousness of at-one-ment with God handles mental malpractice.

EXPECTATION OF GOOD: Hopeful expectation, based on the understanding that God is with us, is continuous treatment.

SEXUAL POISON: In almost every case, treat against sexual poison, because there is a belief that the blood of all humanity is more or less tainted with this poison, through heredity. There are three appetites through which mankind is sustained—for food, for sleep, for procreation. So there are three conditions to be met in any case of belief of material existence.

POISON, TREATMENT FOR: For any poison, handle the spurious law of chemistry which claims to act as active principle of that poison.

PLEURISY: The one action is God, which cannot be lost or impaired.

NERVES: Especially take up nerves. "All the nerves there are, are divine ideas, manifestations and activities of Mind, and are eternally perfect, and their functions cannot be impaired."

PAIN: Pain and mesmerism are one, one in mortal mind.

ANIMAL MAGNETISM, FORMS OF: The forms of animal magnetism. Ignorant. Malicious. The wickedest is deliberate mental malpractice—premeditated mental assassination.

SCIENTISTS AND CHILD-BEARING: It is mental malpractice to criticize Christian Scientists in regard to bearing children.

GOD WITH US: The only God there is cannot forsake us at any time. We must have our anchorage in that thought, must acquaint ourselves with Life, Truth and Love. God never fails in His promises, and the only reason we think He does, is through a faulty concept, which is being destroyed. The only reality is, "God with us."

BASIS OF HEALING: To be spiritually minded is to know the Truth and demonstrate it. The basis of all healing is the declaration of the fact that all is perfect now. God's work is finished and good. We can accomplish nothing apart from that, or with any other means.

ORGANS AND FUNCTIONS, TREATMENT FOR: Every organ or function of the body is an idea, manifestation, and activity of God; so what there is to stomach, for instance, is the truth about it. It is all right at all times, imperishable, perfect. God's ideas are never subject to disease. Because the only law of being is perfect, no law can interfere with or disturb the harmonious action of any function or any organ of man.

DEATH, CAUSE OF: The belief of life in matter, is the cause of death.

DEATH, PREVENTION OF: Now we must know that Life is God alone. We have no mind in our body. The only Mind is God. Humanity without Science is hurrying into the flames of destruction, like the moths about a candle.

SALVATION THROUGH MENTAL ACTIVITY: To us comes salvation, through mental activity, the activity of the Mind of Christ. God's grace is sufficient for every need, and we must know that good thoughts are power, and evil beliefs powerless **when met with Truth.** It is our privilege to have all good now.

YOURSELF, HOLD CORRECT SENSE OF: Stop thinking that evil is yourself. It is not, and no matter what suggestions come, saying your work is in vain, or you cannot treat, or you are discouraged, or you have too much to meet, etc., know that this is malicious argument and not yourself, and no part of you, and you have nothing to do with it, except to destroy it. It cannot disturb your mind or body. "Get thee, hence, satan." Dismiss it all, with the certainty that it can do nothing that it is trying to do, and you have no ears to hear it, no mind or body on which error can depict itself; that malicious mesmerism has no substance which it can control or use, for God is the only substance.

SEGREGATIONS OF ERROR HANDLED: Declare, over and over, that there is no mental argument in the guise of so-called material laws, laws of mental transference, laws of materia medica, no false theology, no hypnotism, no malpractice, no apostate thought, no priestcraft; none of these have power to harm a Christian Scientist or to interfere with or thwart Christian Science treatment. None of these seeming errors can make God less than infinite, nor man as anything other than God's likeness and governed by God alone. We must wage this war for all humanity and in that way gain our own salvation.

STEPPING STONES TO HIGHER THINGS: Every claim of evil that comes to us can be, must be, made a stepping stone. The more that is coming to us, the faster we are climbing up and out of it all. We can meet it all fearlessly, because Intelligence is meeting and destroying all these claims for us, if we actively rely on Him. Intelligence is healing all our diseases, etc. Mortal mind cannot make any law to reverse God's law.

HANDLING ADVERSE THOUGHT: Do not care who thinks about you, or what they think. Our safety lies in recognizing such claims as false, then rejoicing in knowing their nothingness and destroying them. The operation of Truth is here at all times and in all ways. Be systematic in handling all these claims. Know that no evil power in belief can effect Christian Science patients, nothing can impede your own progress nor the progress of Christian Scientists.

HANDLING ARGUMENT OF RELAPSE: The claim of the return of an old belief is a humbug. Stop believing its lies and deny it. Truth's work is perfect and complete; you are healed and you know it. We have no physical body that can be distressed, so do not be afraid that error can do anything to your body, for it cannot. God controls our body; we are spiritual and not material.

UNCOVERING ERROR: Uncover error as unlike Truth, having no substance, no mind, no action, no laws, no cause, no effect. God is ALL. Take everything away from error, and know that all belongs to Truth.

CONFIDENCE REQUISITE: Have confidence in your declaration of Truth. Rest in the assurance of Truth's certain triumph. Through active reliance, put all responsibility upon God. He is capable of taking care of the whole business. God is infinite, so good and loving, that all we have to do is to declare the Truth, deny the error, and abide in Him. Man is **the understanding of God** and is perfect, and has no capacity to receive or manifest error, sin, sickness, or death, in any form

PART III
DESTROYING EVIL

THE GREAT GIFT OF GOD
Methods of Taking Possession of It

Christian Science is revealed to us, and we are studying it for the purpose of accomplishing for ourselves and all mankind righteous dominion over materiality, a more satisfactory existence, more complete salvation from sin, sickness, poverty, and death, greater happiness and strength, wisdom and courage. It is the true realization of the true brotherhood of man and man's relation to God. We learn that doing good sustains life. Our natural, rightful and inevitable heritage is satisfaction, when we awake in His likeness.

Christian Science opens up to us greater possibilities, takes off mortal limitations, breaks mortal laws and shows to us that men's true relation to God provides for every need and includes all that is good; and we can accomplish this through better living, whereby we learn the Science of Life, Truth and Love.

Christian Science is provable and is being wonderfully demonstrated by Christian Scientists, but we ought to do much better in every sphere of our work. Christian Science is absolutely attested Truth.

Suggestions of slowness of growth and questions of "Why?" come to all of us, but looking back we can see some gain from last month or last year in calmness, in sureness and better satisfaction. We must be grateful all the way that Intelligence has been with us helping us.

In order that we may get our anchorage, we must know that every treatment we give is profitable and is helping us along. Our source is inexhaustible. In God we have an abundance that never changes. All good is eternal and ever-present. Everything that man needs is already accomplished. Life always was and is joyous. Our salvation is assured and accomplished.

We find God ever present, Good ever present, Life ever present control, government. We know the Science of Being,— **the oneness of God and man, Mind and consciousness, Soul and body.** Nothing can ever dim our perception of it or disqualify us from demonstrating it, **for man is the understanding of divine Science and I am that man.** The foundation of Science is one supreme God, tangible, real, good, intelligence, power, action, substance, the only Creator and law-giver. When we turn for power from matter to Spirit, we move mountains, surmount all obstacles, achieve success, and overcome fear.

The only Mind and might is the forever Mind, self-existent and adequate, ever active and perfect, governing its own ideas in the only perfect way. Mind is always conscious and is Life, and Life is not in matter.

There is no animal, mineral or vegetable poison, no active principle to poison. Nothing can poison the being or body or flesh (spiritual **understanding)** of man. No form of mesmerism or evil argument can operate through a belief of poison. Know that mental malpractice cannot make use of the belief that electricity can poison nerve centers.

Willingness to die is suicide. **Willingness for another to die is murder.**

"RISE IN THE STRENGTH OF SPIRIT"

The great aim should be to sufficiently grasp the idea that all is Mind, and that matter is nothing and is not to be feared. This is the spiritual consciousness that saves by destroying error. Persons trying to heal themselves often say, "I cannot realize that I am well when there seems to be a continual sense of sickness." Anticipating that you may say this, let me give you a few points.

The universe of God is the only universe, a universe of Good; and whatever organ or function is, is spiritual, and is therefore perfect, and is a part of the eternity of Good. Man is the manifestation of Truth, and all of his conditions, operations and being are eternally perfect. You are spiritual, perfect, and all that seems otherwise is error. Declare that you are spiritual, and this great truth will begin to manifest itself in the destruction of the fear arising from the belief that you are material.

What you fear is, that you have a material disease that may lead to physical death, none of which is true. All this trash is of the kingdom of illusion; and when you begin to realize it, instead of your material body being demolished (in belief), you will find that you still have, in belief, a material body, minus the supposed action and power of error. God is supreme; His law and power are supreme; and if you will stop believing lies parading as laws, God will keep perfect what seems to be a mortal or material body, until such time as men realize that they have a spiritual body, whose functions are far different from what they have supposed the functions of the body to be.

The faith cures are occasioned, not by understanding, but by absolute faith that God will heal. Such absolute faith shuts out all power from mortal opinions and laws, and the patient supposes that God has interposed with a special dispensation of Providence, when God will do the same thing for every one who will trust His supremacy and not be afraid of matter.

Work on the claim of obstruction, and at the time of giving a treatment, spend more time in destroying the lies of mortal mind claiming to be laws. In relation to the treatment, be sure to know that mortal mind is the lie, and has no self-existence and can not arrest or exert any power or influence, or mental malpractice, or malicious animal magnetism, nor in any way obstruct or interfere with your work, nor delay nor put off the consummation of it.

FAITH, INTUITION, SCIENCE

God Working with Us

Mrs. Eddy once said to me: "And always remember that God worketh with you." I replied, "Oh! Mrs. Eddy, if I could only know that, but it seems that God knows nothing about it." **"Your understanding of Christian Science is God working with you,"** Mrs. Eddy replied. I think we may see that no person ever had a personal God that was ever so near to humans, even in belief, as is the God of the Christian Scientist; for God is his very Mind, inasmuch as Mind, Good, is governing his thought.

I find that I have been trying to save myself; but, inasmuch as there is but one Saviour (the Son of God or Truth), I am now trying to let the government be upon his shoulder, and let Intelligence, as manifested through Christ, handle the errors of false belief.

The people who cannot accept Christian Science through intuition, and manifest faith first, must sooner or later come to know its science. What is more logical, more rational or more exact than the Science of Life. Mrs. Eddy once settled this question for me by saying: "You cannot have faith in that which you do not understand." A vast amount of healing that has been done in Christian Science has been faith cure, and today many of the students are mixing the mesmerism of faith in their treatments to a large extent.

Of course, the element of faith that is based upon and warranted by understanding is very desirable, and I should say is the energy of a treatment and is a great destroyer of fear.

little understanding operates to change belief at first, and faith becomes an alterative, but finally **scientific understanding alone will save us.** And what is that? Is it not true consciousness, absolute, positive, exact? I think that a woman's intuition is a great assistance at first, but, after all, Christian Science is science, and neither faith nor intuition.

TALK ON SUPPLY

I feel that, while you are not after money in the ordinary sense of the word, there is every reason to know that you are entitled to adequate provision. Everything that is involved in that which people call supply, maintenance, etc., is a thing of thought. What we need to do, is to reach out toward unlimited thought, in this respect. Humanly, it would be natural for you to think that, while you are in the practice of Christian Science, your supply should come through your practice; but just see what a limited thought is that! Inasmuch as supply belongs to infinity, and is really a manifestation of infinity, how woefully scant is the thought that ignores infinity and limits supply to one narrow channel.

On the other hand, think thus: Supply is omnipresent and unlimited, and is always where you are and what you want. It is liable to show itself to you through millions of channels. Therefore, open up all of the channels and let it come in. Keep yourself in a state of non-surprise. Gain a mental attitude in which nothing in the way of supply will surprise you, not even if you found pieces of silver in the mouth of a fish. You are not the victim of any circumstance; you are the child of God. You have an infinite income commensurate with the grandeur of your thought expressing the infinity of being. No sense of man or woman, or any belief of occasion, event, or inexplicable fatality, or any other belief, can hold out against your treatment, which is the very presence and power of the only God there is.

Infinity is wholly accomplished. Life is established, and all law and power are established. Reality, or the divine Mind, includes nothing but perfection. All the possibilities of being are yours now; there will never be any more. You need not wait for deliverance; today it is yours. You may as well express dominion now as to wait. Declare everything good **for** yourself. Expect everything good **now.**

AN OPEN LETTER

December, 1889

"Cast thy burden on the Lord." These words are not simply in the way of advice or suggestion, but are in the line of scientific demonstration and are definite and mandatory.

God-reliance

Now when we have a burden do we endeavor to cast it on the Lord, and learn that he demonstrates the truth and casts out error, or do we hunt up some friend or acquaintance who is working out his own problem of being in the midst of supposed difficulties, and cast it on him, thereby adding to his sense of evil which he is laboring to diminish?

Help, When Entitled to

If we find that we cannot scientifically cast our burden on the Lord, after an honest endeavor, we are entitled to help and we can and will get it; but to voluntarily and unnecessarily involve some one else in a burden that we can ourselves destroy, is cowardice; it is a sin that will suffer while it continues.

Voicing Error

It is no less a sin for us, under similar circumstances, to unload this burden on the little group of Scientists, or the association of which we are members and with whom we meet occasionally, with the supposed object of mutual benefit and spiritual uplifting.

Beneficial Association

These meetings of Scientists, even where only two or three meet together, can be made very beneficial, if only the truth is declared and spoken. But in how many, many such meetings is this possible benefit utterly prevented by the introduction of all sorts of erroneous topics, mostly of a personal and irrelevant nature, which are discussed on the lowest plane of error, are nursed and made much of by those whose avowed object in meeting was to realize and demonstrate the unreality of error, and lessen the sense thereof. Students who indulge, although unwittingly, in this propensity should be warned that it carries its penalty.

LETTER TO A PATIENT

Directions for Working

We as Christian Scientists are constantly missing God because we do not realize that He is with us. All humanity has sought Him and never found Him until Christian Science demonstrated His presence.

Christ, spiritual understanding of Truth, says: "Come unto me," and leads us to Life, Truth and Love as the only realities. We have to see God through that which manifests good. Then, gaining the right idea of anything, we find God with us. Truth is victorious with us, the only God, Good, cannot, shall not forsake us at any time.

We must have our anchorage in that thought, acquaint ourselves with God and be at peace. God never fails in this promise, and the only reason we think He does is through a faulty concept, which is being destroyed. The only reality is God with us. The greatest demonstration was Jesus' crucifixion and resurrection. We must cling to the Truth no matter what error may say about failures. We know God is proving the allness and might of infinite Love, Life and Truth. The only satisfaction is knowing God, and we are learning Him. The only growth is knowing God—God with us.

It is God with us that supplies all wisdom and power and strength and need, silences grief and exterminates poverty. This is being spiritually-minded—to know the truth and demonstrate it. The basis of all healing is the realization of the fact that all is perfect now, God's work is finished and good. We can accomplish nothing apart from that or by any other means.

Every organ or function of the body is an idea of God, and all there is to stomach is the truth about it. It is all right at all times, imperishable, perfect. God's ideas are never subject to disease, because the law of being is perfect; no law can interfere with or disturb the harmonious action or function of any organ of man.

The belief that life is in matter is the cause of death. Now we know Life is God alone; we have no mind in our body, physicality. The only mind is God. Humanity without Science is hurrying into flames of destruction, like moths about a candle.

To us comes salvation through mental activity, the mind of Christ. God's grace is sufficient for every need, and we must know that good thoughts are power. Evil thoughts are powerless when met with Truth. It is our privilege to have all good now. Heaven is with us. Malicious mesmerism in its various forms seems to work faster and more industriously than we do. Handle the law of reversal with every treatment by knowing that there are not minds many, no evil minds, no law to support nor channel for malicious mesmerism, and the work of God cannot be reversed and we know Christ, **spiritual understanding,** comes to break every yoke or law of evil, and does it.

These beliefs of law touch us more or less, unless we bar the door of thought and know they are powerless, nothing. We have first to recognize them as false claims, then give them no place, cut them off, and know that Truth is destroying all these claims for us. Intelligence is banishing diseases from us. Mental malpractice cannot make a law to reverse God's law. Do not care who may be holding a belief, who thinks about you nor what they are believing. Our safety lies in recognizing such a claim as false belief, then in knowing its nothingness and destroying it. The operation of Truth is going on for us when we operate it.

Church Quarrels

Be systematic in handling all these claims. Know that no evil power or belief can affect the Christian Scientists. Handle belief of factions in church by knowing and scientifically declaring the definition of church in Glossary of "Science and Health," and that man is under divine government alone. Rise to the grandeur of manhood in Christian Science.

Directions For Treating

The claim of a return of old beliefs is a humbug. Know and prove this. Truth's work is perfect and complete. You are healed and you know it. We have no body that can be diseased; so do not be afraid that error can do anything to your body, for it cannot. God controls our body, the body of right ideas. We are spiritual and not material. Overcome error as unlike Truth, having no substance, no mind, no motion, no law, no cause, no effect. God is all there is to us. Take everything away from error and know that all belongs to Truth. Have confidence in your declarations of Truth. Rest in the assurance of Truth's certain triumph. Malpractice has no object, no subject, cannot operate through any law of occultism, and you cannot be mesmerized by evil in any way. It is nothing, for God is the only Mind.

Man is the understanding of God and is perfect and has no capacity to receive or manifest error, sin, disease or death in any form now or forever. Stop believing evil of yourself. It is not you, and no matter what suggestions come to you, saying your work is vain or you cannot treat, or that you are discouraged, or you have too much to meet, know that these are malicious arguments and not yourself, and you have nothing to do with them, and they cannot disturb your mind or body. Get thee hence, satan. Dismiss them with the certainty that they can do nothing they are trying to do, and you have no ears to hear them or a mind or body on which error can depict itself, for malicious mesmerism has no substance which it can control or use.

God is the only substance. Declare over and over that there is no mental argument in the guise of material law; laws of mental transference or materia medica, false theology, hypnotism, malpractice, apostate thought, priestcraft, vibration, astrology, physiology, osteopathy, etc.; none of these seeming errors of belief can make God less than infinite nor man as anything but God's likeness and governed by God alone.

How to Meet Fear

We must wage this battle for all humanity, and in that way gain our own salvation. Every claim of evil that comes to us can be, must be, made a stepping-stone. The more that comes to us, the faster we are climbing up and out of it all, fearlessly, because Intelligence is meeting it all for us. It is a help to remember that fear is always about something that has no existence; that it is a lie and a liar at all times; that it has no principle, mind, intelligence, law or power, no language, motive, effect or result, and that it never has had and never can have a place in mind or in consciousness.

TREATMENT OF A TREATMENT

Animal Magnetism Annulled

Now let us examine this animal magnetism and see if there is anything in it to be afraid of. It has no source, no mind, no principle, no life, no presence, no power. It never made a channel of any one. It never made a malpractitioner. It never made a mortal. It never made anything. It is a myth. It has no existence. Now what is there to be afraid of? But it must be denied; the claim of its existence, power, law and works must be **proven** false.

The word spoken goes forth with power and cannot return void, but prospers. Born to consciousness, it is eternal, indestructible. It casts out, rejects and destroys the lie and the liar.

My consciousness cannot be disabled or read or manipulated, and I know it. Intelligence, power, action, law, substance, reality, are spiritual. Any false claim governing in belief is rendered null and void by the law of God, and I know it.

Substance is Spirit; it cannot absorb, secrete, accommodate or manifest poison. Order and harmony prevail. Love and Truth govern the entire universe, system, business, disposition, surroundings, and relations and manifest the true substance, and I know it. There is no belief of polarity, earth currents, vital, electric, or other fluids that can operate as law of disease or disorder unto men; no material nerve centers, no magnetism or magnets, no material force. There is no injustice, ingratitude, no misrepresentation, no erroneous influence from Christian Scientists.

There is no anxiety or fear of the future, no fatalism. Malicious animal magnetism has no mental capacity or **laws to operate, and I know it.** There is no belief of thought apostate from Science, no demonology or black magic, no animal nature, no impure thought, no bacterial germs or microbes or poison, no betrayal or telepathy of thought, no clairvoyance, that can operate as a law of disease or disorder, or fatalism to men, and I know it. Therefore, **I am not afraid.**

Do Not Handle Malpractice as Personal

Never address the person who errs by treating him mentally or by treating yourself for protection against him. Never recognize a person in your arguments. You must not. Never doctor the error much, but make yourself so conscious of the opposite truth that the error disappears. Know that nothing can come to you or go from you but what God sends; therefore no mortal can influence you, for only one Mind exists, and that is immortal Love. Overcome the evil with Good, Love, and do not feel that any other person exists.

This will deliver you. If you dwell in thought on any person, it will hinder you in overcoming personality in your healing and casting out sin. There is no personality, and this is more important to know than that there is no disease. Drop it, and remember that you can never rid yourself from a personality while holding in mind this personality. The way is to put it wholly out of mind and keep before your thought the right **model.**

ANIMAL MAGNETISM DESCRIBED
How to Deal with It

Now that we are beginning to see that God and His universe are already perfect and complete, that man is now the spiritual embodiment or expression of all God's perfect ideas, it is time for you to handle evil as animal magnetism, universal false belief.

One Man

The **one** scientific man is divine consciousness; and as God, Good, is All, man is conscious of good and good only. There is but **one** man, the man who knows good and does good, **and you are that man.** "The Scientific man and his Maker are here, and you would be none other than this man, if you would subordinate the fleshly perceptions to the spiritual sense and source of being"—"Unity of Good."

Prove this now to a suffering, sinful world, and, one by one, all will agree with you that Good is, indeed, the only presence and power. This is walking by faith (spiritual understanding), and not by sight. Look (spiritually) at things unseen (to mortal sense) and not at the things seen (by mortal sense). Know men no more after the flesh, but know man in his spiritual individuality. But how came all that the senses seem to see? Through belief, and that is why we seem to have material, mortal men, a material universe, sin, disease, death, etc.

A belief! The first belief was a seeming power apart from God—evil; the second, fear of this supposed evil. Then came the offspring of this fraud,—sin, disease, etc., envy, anger, hatred, malice, revenge, jealousy, etc. All these beliefs Mrs. Eddy names animal magnetism, as that name indicates their nature and action,—animal, because all is based on matter; mesmeric in action, because they mesmerize you into believing they are real. You will see that this term "animal magnetism" is the most comprehensive and applicable that can be used for that which it represents,—namely, evil and its action.

No one ever really destroyed an evil until it was known that evil is a belief. Animal magnetism includes all evil, but you need not fear it any more than you would fear the belief that two times two is five, supposing all the world believes it **is** so. But it must be denied. Power, Mind, Principle, Life, are law. Animal magnetism is really mental malpractice, wrong mental practice, and has no power or authority to make laws for men or anything. Mental malpractice itself is only a belief, because there is but one Mind. Mental malpractice is a myth, and the sooner we overcome believing in its presence the happier we will be.

By denying its claims to presence, power and law and knowing the truth and the truth only, its mists of fear will fade away. Love alone is present and governs all in harmony. When you say this, you know that you mean all the false beliefs in which we seem to live today. These beliefs Mrs. Eddy likens to a mist or cloud. The declaration of Truth acts as a ray of sunshine, dispersing the darkness of error. When you have denied the error in this way, knowing its nothingness and declaring God's presence and power, knowing the reality of that Presence, your responsibility is over. Love does the work.

If you lose something, handle animal magnetism; if your dog is ill, handle animal magnetism; if you hurt your finger or toe or knock yourself in any way, handle animal magnetism. If you feel a pain, handle animal magnetism.

One mistake that young Scientists make is to say that the claims of error are their claims. They say, "Oh, I have so much fear!" but the fact is that they do not have it. We are God's children; then there is no fear in you, in me, or in another. It is animal magnetism; never you. The same is true of discouragement, sickness, envy, jealousy, everything unlike God. They are always it, animal magnetism, never you.

A treatment must consist in knowing that the statement declared is the truth. Without knowing this, no mental argument is a treatment. Of course, it is better to declare the truth than to admit a lie; but, in order to have good results, there must not be left in the mind of the practitioner any sense of the claim which he denies.

You have no material, personal patient; there is only a belief to destroy. It is not the patient's belief, or your belief, nor any one's belief. Nobody has it; it does not exist. It has no origin, no reality, no power, life or law, and it is nothing and can do nothing. It has no channel or manifestation. Then rise above all material sense testimony and realize the true creation and man, as Jesus did when he saw the perfect man where mortals see the mortal.

Never treat matter or disease; always destroy the belief of it. If the practitioner believes the patient has a sick body or a sick place in his body, he will not help him. It is always a false sense of mind in matter. Have confidence in your treatment and its results. Know that your declaration is true and will do its work. Your treatment is the Word of God. "He sent His Word and healed them." The Word of God is power. God is power. God is omnipotent and His omnipotence means the omnipotence of Good. How much power has a treatment? All the power there is. How much life have you? All the life there is. How much intelligence have you? All the intelligence there is.

Spiritual growth of the individual Christian Scientist is regeneration. There is but one universe, and that spiritual, eternal. The veil of belief seems to hide it. All we have to do is to overcome, as fast as possible, the mistakes of a false education.

MALICIOUS ANIMAL MAGNETISM

The very worst form of malicious animal magnetism is that which offers itself to us in the guise of truth through the avenue of recent circumstances. In belief, it presents itself to you in the guise of an accusing angel.

I dare say that whenever you declare that you are the child of God, perfect and sinless, it immediately suggests that you are a child of satan, rather, wholly unworthy to claim any relationship with God, and incapable of realizing any of the truth that is for the children of God. It haunts you with a personality all distorted with mortal suggestions, makes itself hideous and hateful, urges you to adopt this as being yourself, and to consider this kind of an "I" as an outcast from God, bereft of hope and merit.

If it suggests all this and much more to you, then, dear friend, you have followed my experience and that of many others who have stood face to face with the sum-total of indescribable evil—the aggregation of envy, jealousy, resentment, hatred, malice and revenge called "malicious animal magnetism." Surely we need the whole armor of God to meet this "son of perdition." The claim of it is bad enough when it appears in its own appropriate ugliness; but when it seeks to dethrone God and reason, to stifle the benevolent and tranquilizing voice of divine Mind, then, yea then, does the heart seem sick indeed.

I have been through it all, and have discovered that it is nothingness, and so you will discover, for you have the armor of God. What you want to do is to recognize all this trash as the statement, argument, or suggestion of evil, and not the voice of God, who is infinite Love. Do you think God would make himself known to you in such a damnable way, that your loving Saviour would harass and torture you thus, and afford no gleam of hope, no avenue of escape, no reward for your honest intentions and endeavors, no chance for a fruition of all your holy aims, desires and aspirations?

You and I do not understand the divine Mind and His idea, when we accept and make real this apparition of fictitious, suppositional mind. This so-called mind calls itself matter; it outlines itself, in belief, as a material personality, with laws, shapes, forms, conditions, circumstances, events—all the phenomena that are embraced in the term "material life;" and yet, not one atom of its testimony is true; not one thing, thought or assumption is true; not one of its so-called events. There is not one solitary **fact** in all this whole fabric of evil.

Now, can this caricature of Mind, that has not a particle of truth in it, say anything that is true about you? Not a thing; and yet this is what has been deceiving you. The truth is, that, during the eternal past and now, you have ever been the perfect, sinless child of God; you never sinned and cannot.

Animal magnetism offers you a dream of material self, arrays it in a certain amount of belief of imperfection, and after bidding you adopt it, it urges you to accept it and follow out its supposed laws, etc.; it is not you, and you need give yourself no concern over its supposed past. It is the self of animal magnetism, it is animal magnetism and not you, that says, "I am a sinner," "I am unworthy," etc.

Christian Science declares: When you are perplexed as to whether you are hearing the voice of Truth or of error, you may use this guide to a conclusion: If there is any doubt whatever, you may know it is animal magnetism. Truth is peaceful and certain; it leads us with a loving hand. The voice of Truth never pains or causes any despair or doubt to him whose affections are fixed on God.

The knowledge of this rule has enabled me to detect and uncover the enemy. It rescued me from much misery, and has protected me against many similar suggestions. Just as soon as I realized that all this stuff was a bald imposition, and that God—Truth—has nothing to do with it, I rejected it. I refused to think about it, and very shortly the whole claim subsided. I had met this claim of evil, and the simple uncovering of it which the Truth made possible, utterly destroyed it. I was harassed a long time before I knew this rule, and it seemed to me that I would carry a consciousness of sin throughout all eternity. After my demonstration I concluded to take Paul's advice: "Forget the things that are behind." I knew that I was trying to lead a sinless life, but I was actually keeping alive the sense of sin and evil, by poring over the beliefs of sin and making them real. Now I am losing the sense of evil, to do which is according to Science.

Penance is not Christian Science. Intelligence demands that we destroy the sense of sin, and not perpetuate it by mourning over and distracting ourselves over that which never happened. I now refuse to dwell on the past, and am having much success in "putting off the old man." There is no food or virtue in this habit. The demand is that we address our thought to the eternal now, and not to the dead past.

Now, the voice of Christ, our Saviour, says to you through his demonstrations and through the demonstrations of Christian Science, and through his Word, that you were created by a good God, an infinite, good God (no evil in infinite good), and that this infinite Good is omnipotent; and, therefore, there is no power but the power of Good. This is the saving truth of Christian Science; and if there is no evil and no power but Good, there is nothing to be afraid of. I am not afraid.

What, then, is this phenomena called fear? Nothing but a suppositional mind. There is no fear. At most it is the image of the false, mortal mind, a phantom of error, nothingness. "God hath not given you the spirit of fear, but of power, and of love and of a sound mind." Never admit that you are afraid; it is only a lie. Neither are you a sinner, and you waste time and effort in contemplating yourself as such. The truth will find its way gently to our understanding. It will lead us to relinquish the desire and affection for all that is unlike Good. But when we seem to be conscious of a compound of fear, perplexity, discord, or any kind of evil, remember that Truth knows no such methods.

What Shall We Think About a Scientist Who Has "Died"?

Now as to the Scientist who "passes on," in belief. So sure as God is God, that personality that you are contemplating never lived and never died. Belief claims that there was life, substance and intelligence in that supposed physical outline. But was it there? Not a particle. Belief afterwards claimed that life had ceased; but was that true? Not at all. The sum-total of the whole thing is a changed belief. There has been no change with the grand facts, ideas of God. The kingdom of heaven is just the same, and your mourning is all for naught. Notwithstanding the impulse to sympathy and sentiment, try not to hear that error as a reality. There is no death, absolutely none.

It is righteous for you to resist the temptation of evil to be discouraged because the claims of belief are not overcome in each specific instance. The risen Christ would be but briefly honored by us, if we allowed evil to dissuade us from continuing to do good, because our new-born understanding was seemingly not equal to overcoming all the arguments of error. Because you are conscientious, malicious error will endeavor to reach you through this sensitive avenue. Remember that, and if you are invited to believe anything evil of yourself, know it is a lie come to torment you, and not the voice of God. Never yield to this suggestion, but think of what Christ, spiritual understanding, knows you to be.

MENTAL WICKEDNESS DEALT WITH

Man's Mind is God, or scientific Mind; and It is infinite and eternal, knowing no lapse from nor return to harmony. God has chosen us and not we Him; and we can rely on Wisdom's judgment that we are worthy to attain perfection, and we are good enough to heal and overcome all false beliefs. We have God's responsibility back of us, and can do the work of resisting all false beliefs; and we can dwell in being, body, the Christ body, which is eternal.

There is no belief in any law of horoscope, fatalism, astrology or clairvoyance to govern life or the affairs of God's man, his body, thoughts, or in any way whatsoever to govern the man whom God has made. Neither do these beliefs exist with power to influence or govern humans, in their health or any of their affairs. I am the man whom God has formed. I dwell in the spiritual realm of the real.

The law of divine Mind removes all belief of stoppage or stagnation of functions or organs of the human body; and Mind dissolves, removes, expels and eliminates all impurities, poisons, gases, accumulations of stuff, and equalizes the action of secretion and excretion. The law of divine Mind is the only law of my being and the only law to all that is called human body. Any false belief of stagnation cannot produce discouragement or mental apathy, for my spiritual senses are exercised by the divine Mind (my Mind) and cannot be stagnant.

Light cannot be perverted to kill through mirrors, producing electric waves. There is no such system known as hypnotism to promote or promulgate any law against Christian Science. Mrs. Eddy says on page 259 of "Science and Health," "Vibration is not intelligence; hence it is not a creator. Believing error gives it all the life it seems to have, so far as you are concerned.

Digestion is an activity in Mind, not in matter. Blood is a divine idea of God and cannot be poisoned. Eye is a divine idea; ear is a divine idea, forever in the bosom of the Father. Foot is a divine idea. Every divine idea is divinely active.

Christian Science reveals the whole of Being; it is the activity of the spiritual idea which heals the sick and the sinner. Man is the individual (indivisible) operation of one Mind. Man is not sick. There is only a belief which calls itself a sick man.

Malignant mental malpractice cannot act through a belief of ecclesiasticism, hypnotically associated with electric currents or electric vibration, to cause anything—death, hell, accident, perpetual insanity, a morbid desire for death or suicide. It cannot produce any so-called law or power or energy, force or desire. Mind alone governs Its creation, and Mind is all the power, energy, force or control there is.

There is no evil psychic anathema, no ecclesiastical curse, that can wreck my life or disturb my harmony, my home, my church, or create any discord among Christian Scientists.

There is no material substance to be sick. There is no cause for sickness. There is no law to enforce sickness. Break the belief that men can be sick. Specifically declare the Truth of being. This declaration of Truth denies the error.

The faith which is understanding is confidence, assurance, voluntary truth; and this is the divine impulsion in Christian Science treatment. There is no substance or place to be occupied by disease. There is no cause of disease. There is no law of enforcement to procure a *modus operandi*. It has neither presence, power, nor cause. All false claims are annulled by the perfect law of harmony.

Man is the active aggregation of right ideas. Man is forever spiritual. Man is under no law of obscuration; there is no such law fettering the one who is asking for Christian Science treatment. There is no cessation of right ideas, no lull or period of inaction. Belief is constantly being overcome; Truth is ever operative.

A Christian Science treatment is constructive, reconstructive and eliminative. Mankind stands at the door of unlimited opportunity. Declare for universality, availability, spontaneity, abundance, this very instant, unlimited opportunity. A receptive, expectant attitude receives and demonstrates results. The supply of good is infinite, unlimited, inexhaustible. spontaneous.

There is one body, the body of all being, the body of God. This body is perfect in identity, comeliness, beauty, for it expresses God. Malicious animal magnetism cannot operate to suggest or produce doubt or fear or irritation in a Christian Scientist. I have a right to demand of Mind the uncovering of this error. Mind is ever imparting perfect modes of expression to the mentality of mankind, so that it outlines beauty, form, color, grace, symmetry, refinement, delicacy, beatified being.

SOME "WILES OF THE DEVIL"
How to Circumvent Them

Knowing the Truth is treatment. We must break the law of relapse and return of old beliefs. Be exact, expansive, progressive and go ahead. Don't be fifty or sixty years breaking the claim of false laws. Be correct in every word. Incorrect work has been known to result disastrously. True thinking does the work, and all thought externalizes itself. All that mortal mind can do is to believe, and all its believing is a lie.

Deny the claim that mortal mind is a law-maker. There is no mortal mind, no occultism, no superstition or suggestive therapeutics. Handle the asserted claim that Christian Scientists and their patients shall have a return of old beliefs, or shall have irritation of the mucous membrane. Handle the claim that you cannot heal. Handle the claim of reversal, that your treatment shall be reversed, that it shall have an effect opposite to that intended. No hypnotic treatment can be destructive to Christian Science treatment. Handle moral questions, as well as physical and mental.

The next best thing to realization is declaration. The realm of disease is the realm of mesmerism. A claim is always a lie of belief without a believer. The only change that is necessary is the change of belief and the ultimate extinction of the belief.

No intercessory or supplicatory prayer or curse of the claim of ecclesiasticism can hurt me or mine, nor invade my divine rights of health, holiness, happiness, harmony, freedom, usefulness, prosperity. Neither can it molest my environments, such as business, social, domestic or family relations. Neither can it manifest itself as accident, sin, disease, death or discouragement in any form. Neither can it depress me nor use my consciousness, for it has no power, no law, no authority, no existence, no action, no life; for there is no power apart from God—the great I AM.

Sometimes a personality will parade before us and lead us to a blind attack; and then we find that anger, wrath, malice, evil speaking and revenge have entered like foes in the rear and have stolen from us our good, and have deprived us of the daily bread of Love on which we might feed, could we have seen where was the real danger; and that, for the Scientist, is not where the clamor or threatened attack seems to be made, or where the obtrusive personality is seen, but, rather, is detected as aggressive mental suggestions relative to person, place or thing, which come for adoption from without, but which seem to arise within the heart. The adoption of such evil suggestions as one's own thought and feeling defile a man or woman and tend to promote hell rather than heaven.

Definition of "person"—**a mask.**

Scientists cannot suffer through claims of law of poison ivy, arsenic, arterial, venereal or morbific matter. A claim of suffering with heart trouble, sharp pains in the head, back-ache, debility, prostration, is often from law of mortal mind acting on sympathetic or pneumogastric nerves—two nerves of the stomach—deceiving into belief of physical trouble.

Communion with God is treatment. To make one's self at one with the Father through communion with God is prayer. Then handle error carefully in all its forms. Scientists are apt to believe that they must be so good when about to handle error, but we must be smart enough to know evil as evil, and never call evil good, nor be so mesmerized as to be fooled by it.

Do not believe pain and handle animal magnetism, but uncover animal magnetism and handle it. Hatred is hatred; no matter whether it manifests pain in the head or foot, it is just hatred. We need to make haste to overcome hatred and all claims that go with it. It is the millinery of evil. Our lives are trimmed with it. Pray every morning for the unspeakable blessing of being delivered from hatred.

There is no thinker inside of me; we reflect Mind. Either mortal mind or divine Mind rules always. Mortal mind means death; divine Mind is Life. Mortal error has no capacity to lie, defame, misrepresent or slander. Do not treat defamation as somebody, but as a lie. No defamation can hinder the action of Truth.

Some Scientists want to lead, to be readers, etc. That is because they do not know what they are doing. Jesus is the example. He was crucified. If they understood that a Christian Scientist taking an office is mounting the cross instead of wearing a crown, so many would not be after the job.

A lady reader once asked what to handle when it seemed as though she could not stand to read. She was asked how she handled it, and she replied, "It is a lie." That is why she did not make the demonstration; for it is malicious animal magnetism that she should have handled. A lie would imply anything. Then wondering why the demonstration is not made, is animal magnetism.

Work specifically. Where is protection? Where is peace? Where is power? Within. We might say the same of the claim of suppositional evil. Our work is to settle the combat within.

Question was asked if there was anything in particular to handle when, in giving a treatment, one becomes so nervous that he has to stop and handle that. Yes; handle malicious mental malpractice vigorously. Its work is to get you to stop your treatment and argue with it as claim of nervousness or anything else, except malpractice. The only Christian Scientist that evil of any kind fears is one who spots it.

All things are mine. I reflect the allness of infinity. I reflect the abundance and supply of all good. There is no law, belief or circumstance or fate that can separate us from the allness of God. There is no law of malpractice that can interfere with my welfare, my possessions, my family or my business, for God alone governs.

"QUENCHING FIERY DARTS OF THE WICKED"

Animal Magnetism Handled

Animal magnetism is a lie of belief without a believer.

I know what you claim, but I am not afraid of you or any suggestions that you offer. You are neither person, place, nor thing. You have no power, presence or personality. You cannot reach me, nor influence me through envy, hate, fear or error of any name of nature.

The deceiving power of the universal thought or law is rendered null and void by the law of divine Intelligence, which is absolutely the only law and power. Animal magnetism cannot present itself to me in the guise of contagion, lack of time, lack of patience, lack of funds or any other lack, materially or spiritually or physically, for God is the source of all supply, and this supply is never limited.

I am not bound by any deceiving personality. I am not restricted in thought, capability or work. Error, animal magnetism, has no power to misrepresent me nor hinder my advancement in any way.

Envy, dislike, pride, hypocrisy, lust, self-will, self-justification, self-pity or self-love have no power or place in me. The claims of sickness, nervousness, or weak back, contraction or poor circulation, are unreal and have no power or place in me.

Life, Truth, and Love are laws of annihilation to anything unlike God. I am spiritual; for I am the image and likeness of God, Spirit, and reflect all that is pure, upright, and true.

The acceptance of material body as personality apart from

Mind is but the engine of mental malpractice and does only mental malpractice's work. Let the divine Mind illuminate and abolish mental malpractice until there is not a dark corner; then we shall **know that neither food**, climate nor any seeming condition can affect the body in any way; for there is but one cause, God, Good. God is the only doer, the only actor, and the only Saviour, the only governor of man. There is no confusion in Truth.

Malicious animal magnetism cannot separate me from my best and greatest good nor limit my supply in any way. It cannot touch me with any claim of poverty in myself or in any one else. Spirit is my unlimited source of supply. I am not dependent on any personality for my needs. Malicious animal magnetism cannot hide my work from me nor make me feel failure or lack. God gives to each and every one of His children abundantly all they need, and the supply is not, cannot be hidden at any time by mental malpractice, law or claim, for all the claims of mental malpractice are false and have no real existence; they are destroyed by Truth. I am born free, not in bondage to anything nor any one, for divine Principle leads me.

There is no power in anger, ill temper, scorn or contempt. There is no power in prejudice or superstition. There is no power in selfishness, envy, jealousy, pride, hate, malice or revenge. I am a law against all that is false and foolish and I declare the influence of all such passions null and void in me. I declare all such passions powerless to harm any one. I deny the reality of matter, because God is the only power, the only Substance. God is Spirit. I deny that the appearance that we call matter has any life, substance or intelligence, because God is the only Life and Intelligence, and God is Spirit. Only the good is true. Only the good has power. God is my health. God is my strength. God is my wisdom. God is my life. God never made me sick and sinful. God is the only creator and He did not make sickness, sin and death; it was never made and is not here. The belief of sickness is an untruth, brought on by animal magnetism,—universal false belief.

I am not subject to the laws of mortal belief in sickness, sin, and death, and the belief lasts only while I believe in the power of matter. Fear of sickness has not affected me. The many and manifold lies of mental malpractice have not affected me; for I deny that heredity in the above beliefs has caused disease to be imaged in me, for the reason that God, Good, immortal Spirit, divine Mind, is the only Power. I deny that I am sick or suffering, or that I am denied any manifestations of Good. I affirm that I am well, strong, happy and successful, Mind's idea, a prince of the King of the Universe and an heir of God, perfect and strong in every way; brave and happy. God is All, my health, my mind, courage, intelligence, understanding, my everything. All there is in me or of me is perfect and harmonious, and I was aways so. God is my Life, God is Love, and I fear no one. "Perfect love casteth out fear." All we need to do, to remain in perfect health and harmony, is to learn to pray aright and never forget our rightful heritage as the Prince of the King of the Universe.

I am "hid with Christ in God" where no mortal sense can find me and where no mortal belief can reach me. Mind sustains man in God. I am renewed daily in the image and likeness of God and cannot lose one faculty which expresses my divinity. I am free from false beliefs that have claimed to hold me in bondage. I am free. There is but one Substance, one Power, one Intelligence, one Life, one Love, which is the one God of the universe, who is Spirit, the all Good which fills all space and is omnipresent. I am the child of God, made in His image and likeness. I live, move and have my being in Mind. I am spiritual and cannot be sick, sinful and suffering, and no evil can come to me.

I deny the Reality of sickness, of sin, of suffering, and of error, of loneliness. I deny the power of evil in every guise. I deny the false beliefs entertained in sickness and nervousness, in misfortune, poverty or discouragement, or fear or doubt or foolishness. There is no law to hold me in bondage to lust and sensuality of any kind or degree; deceitfulness, treachery or hypocrisy are powerless to affect me. Error is powerless and mindless; therefore it must be speechless, and cannot make me an avenue or channel through which any discord can be expressed, for there is no reality in evil and it cannot voice itself to me or about me, or use me to voice itself. I will not be the instrument to be used by the devil to express error of any kind.

God is all abundance. There is no good or quality in hypnotism, mesmerism, self or foreign, ignorant or malicious, theological or medicinal, that can have any power over me morally, mentally, physically or financially.

There is only one Mind in or near me, and there is no personality in the kingdom of God; hence error has no power to enforce or inject into my thought any mental poison or set in motion any law or action that can interfere with **Truth and Truth's demonstration anywhere within the radius of my thought.**

PART IV
PUBLIC LECTURES

PROOF OF THE EXISTENCE AND NATURE OF GOD

Extract From a Lecture

The real naturalness of man is supersensible, above the senses. We are to learn that we may know all things.

Your Starting Point for Knowledge Is That You Are Conscious

I delivered a lecture in Kansas City last week, and was introduced by a lawyer. This gentleman was afterwards asked what he thought of the lecture, and he said that the lecture was all right; that it was perfectly logical, and that if one admitted the premises he must accept the conclusion. A premise of Christian Science is this: Everybody in this room is conscious; that is the starting point. Christian Science starts with the proposition that you are all conscious. Every man is conscious of something. What is he conscious of? Of the things that exist, of the things that are. Everything that you and I are conscious of is already made; it has already been made. This church, these walls, these floors have been made; they have been produced; not one was self-produced. Then something produced them. Some noumenon or cause produced everything that exists. Then everything that exists has a basis, foundation, cause, origin, or source, and exists because its Principle exists.

That You Are Conscious Proves Intelligent Cause

What is it that has induced all this? What is it that has produced it? It has been a question, and might be a difficult one, if it were not for one thing. Everybody in this room will admit that he is an intelligent man or woman. Inasmuch as we have to admit that our intelligence exists at the standpoint of effect, something is the cause of our intelligence, because it is a scientific proposition that no fountain can rise above its source. The very fact that you and I are intelligent, or by courtesy call ourselves intelligent—that mere fact carries with it the indisputable conclusion that we are the offspring of some intelligent inducer or animus; so it is clear that the cause of the universe is an intelligent cause.

A Divided Primal Cause Is Impossible

Is that intelligent, conscious cause good or bad, or both? The **infinity** of God topples, the moment we admit that He is both good and bad, because He must be either infinitely good or infinitely bad. A divided infinity is impossible in logic and in fact. Some people believe that God is good, but sometimes uses evil for the purpose of accomplishing good in the end. So the mother is consoled, according to this philosophy, for the death of her child. Some people say that God knows all about evil and sanctions it, but is not responsible for it. All this is apologetic; it really begs the question. There is a proposition in theology that God is omnipotent, that He is all will and volition, and that the possibilities of His activity are unlimited, and yet that He creates or makes use of or sanctions evil.

God Neither Is Evil, Uses Evil, Nor Knows Evil

Christian Science teaches that God does not create evil, does not make use of or sanction it, does not know it. Some people will say: "Don't you think God knows as much as I do?" How about the man with delirium tremens? He thinks he knows that he has snakes. Does anybody in a normal, right state of mind know that the man has snakes? It is simply a perverted sense of things, simply an illusion. And so it is with sin and pain and disease. They are all just snakes, all based on error, all based on an aberrated condition of the human mentality, and have no more substantiality in Science or Truth than those same good-for-nothing snakes. If God is good, and because He is good, and because He has never induced disease nor any other form of evil, because He has never ordained anything for your discomfiture whatever—for these reasons you need never again be afraid of God.

God Potentizes His Ideas

God as power means the power of good. God is Good, and that means that every right idea carries with it the very power of the universe. A right idea will move a mountain, because it is entitled to do the deed, and there is no adequate competition and no rival by way of power that can stay or obstruct or interfere with it. God has no other law for us than Life.

We Are Not Minus the Supply for Our Needs, but Simply Minus Understanding of Its Presence

The only law that is entitled to rule you and me one minute is the divine law of Life, and this law is wherever and whenever a sick man seems to be. The trouble with us is not that we are minus law, minus privilege, but are minus the understanding that law is at hand, and that we may lay hold of it this very instant. Our God is the law of Life and harmony and health and perfection and strength to all men, and there is not a person in this room who has any sense of bodily impairment that ought not to lose it this very minute.

Recovery Is the Only Law for the Sick

The only law there is for you is the law of recovery. There is no law of nature, no law of disease, no law of God, devil, or hell, against you; nothing but an aberrated mental condition on the part of humanity which calls "law" that which is only belief.

THE ENFORCEMENT OF LAW
Extract from a Lecture Delivered Feb. 7, 1907

The wisest men in the world would be most ready to admit that they know comparatively or practically very little or nothing. They would tell you that the vast realm of knowledge lies as yet unexplored, and that our progress as a race will be coincident with our discovery, with our perception of Truth; and they would urge you to be on the alert to learn, to investigate and discover, and to become reconciled to the abandonment of old theories.

The Chief Enemy Is Fear

The great pest of humanity, the torment of this race, that which makes for wretchedness and woe and poverty and sickness and death, that which is the chief procurator of nearly all the agony of humanity, is fear. Fear comes pretty nearly being all there is to devil, hell and damnation, and everything erroneous and discordant put together. Fear is absolutely outrageous, unnatural, un-Godlike, unscientific, absolutely contrary to Truth, and is an absolute fraud upon you and every person that lives.

Our God-Given Dominion

Christian Science alone reveals the possibility of man's dominion over fear. On almost the first page of the Bible is the declaration: "And God gave man dominion over all the earth." Is that true or not? If it isn't, then it is a mockery; and if it is true, then it follows that we are making a wretched mistake and have fallen vastly short of the possibilities of our lives. If it is true, what must it mean? It ought to mean that that which is entitled to be called God, origin, source, foundation and cause, the Principle by reason of which all things exist, that which is primarily creative, that which is primary power and action and purpose and rule and will and law and government—it must mean that this ordained and procured, even before men ever were born, that man should have a natural, indestructible right or function or privilege that is described as dominion over all the earth; it should mean dominion over your health, your body, your life; it ought to mean dominion over your environment, your circumstances, your conditions, your surroundings. It should mean that, if it is of any consequence at all. We have a right to be the masters of our circumstances; we have a right to stand up and live and be men and women, and **do and perform and achieve, to rise above poverty and distress.**

Dominion Through Mind

This dominion comes not through matter. Mind is the only adequate impulsion, force or animus of the universe; the only power of the universe. The Mind that is God, that is omnipotent, is volition and power and will and purpose. Salvation is something to achieve, not something to hope for.

Tension Induced by Fear Overcome

The men and women of this earth possess bodies, today, that are invariably in a state of rigid tension all the time. The world, today, is in a state of bodily tension all the time. If we knew enough to know that we have righteous dominion over all the earth, and that we can exercise it, that would be the end of such tension. The Mind which was in Christ Jesus means indestructible equipment.

Your Ordination

All the great discoveries in the future will be in the realm of Mind. You, just as you sit here on these seats, were ordained into the manifestation of a vastly superior intelligence and vastly superior intellectual grasp and comprehension, a more vast use of power, a grander equipment and a comprehensive and adequate dominion, whereby you are to achieve for yourselves a perfected and satisfying state and continuance of existence.

The Supersensible Capacity

By reason of Mind, I have developed a supersensible capacity whereby I can comprehend the substance of an idea; and this supersensible culture or study, or progress, means a true, spiritual sense of life. This supersensible culture has changed me from a position where I could not get one single idea out of "Science and Health" to where it is just as simple as sunlight; in fact, the only simple thing I know anything about.

Primal Cause

You did not create yourself, nor did this universe create itself, but the universe is the phenomenon of some cause; and that cause existed before a material universe of any kind appeared, and it existed and exists as Intelligence, as Mind, as Omniscience, as Law, as Power, as conscious, supreme individual capacity. Now, before the universe appeared, could you have traced that Mind, could you have measured that power with a yardstick, could you have taken the law of God and put it in a quart measure and told how many quarts there were of it?

Human Philosophy False

The human race has evolved a philosophy which means, not Life, but mortality; not Mind, but insanity; not health, but sickness; not dominion, but fear. Mortal man believes he was manufactured for the purpose of being killed. Would you be afraid of anything if you knew you had dominion over it? No, not one thing. You would know that you are master; that you need not endure, need not go down; and that you could annihilate, extinguish the foe, and you would be utterly devoid of fear.

Dominion Is Your Right, Your Ability, Your Possession

You must learn, first, that it **is** your right to exercise dominion; next, that you **can** exercise that right, and do exercise it, the right to cast out fear. Christian Science has put me upon ground where I never could manifest such fear as I used to; and if I ever got in hell again I would get out, because I know how to get out of hell. I know that my Redeemer liveth; and I know, and Christian Scientists are gradually learning, that, no matter what may befall us, we possess a knowledge and a power that will ultimately deliver us from any kind of hell that may present itself for our entertainment. You are entitled to have and include and to manifest that which will be an adequate equipment unto your health and your prosperity and your life.

A Competent Saviour

Christ has abolished the law of sin and death. This means that he has abolished the law of sin, disease and death, because death is but the ultimate of disease. To abolish means to annul, to exterminate, to extinguish, to undo. Christ literally smashed the law of sin and sickness and death. Do you believe for a moment that it was the purpose of Jesus to abolish divine law? If the law of sin, sickness and death is the divine law, is there anything that could abolish it? If God ordained the law of death, do you think that Christ could have abolished it? These errors have no right to act as law or seem to be law. Jesus the Christ was sent to seek and to save that which was lost. Is that which is sent to save that which is lost competent to do it? Have we a competent, irresistible Saviour, or not? When Christ Jesus abolished so-called law, he abolished no law of God, no law that had a right to operate, no law that God provided or instituted, no law that was included in the divine purpose, intention or plan; but he abolished something that was unnatural, spurious, unGodlike, and that is the teaching of Christian Science at this very point; namely, that disease does not afflict humanity because of natural law or divine ordination, but because of a spurious, erroneous and utterly outrageous impulsion. It teaches that all the so-called laws of disease are but the laws of this carnal mind, the substratum of ignorance and belief and fear, and that every bit of it can be annulled, and that, through Christ, **you** can do it.

What Is Law?

Something caused your existence, caused the existence of the universe. Everything that is, is because of God; and that which created the universe is its law. What is the science of law? The law of God for you and concerning you is the law of Life to you all the time, the law of health, the law of strength, the law of enduring and continuing faculties, the law of your prosperity, your achievement, the law of your dominion; and there is no other law whatever in the universe. This is the only law there is. All fundamental law, all that means either God or nature, that means Truth or Science, that means intelligence or wisdom, all this law makes for your health and your life now and forever, and there is no divine or natural law against you.

Sickness Not Because of Divine Law

If you are sick it is not because of law, but because of belief, ignorance, superstition and fear. God has not provided for your illness; there is no basic law that provides for it or procures it. There is a fable that, many years ago, a plague visited the city of Bagdad, and as a result ten thousand people died. Some one met the plague outside of Bagdad and reproached it for killing so many people. The plague answered: "You wrong me. I killed only one and fear killed all the rest." Did the other 9,999 die according to divine law or according to fear operating as law?

The Counterfeit of Law

Everything in the material universe happens according to a semblance of law. No measles, no law; no law, no measles;

but this is not law. The so-called laws that seem to govern mortals are absolutely gratuitous, illegitimate and abnormal, and are in no wise laws nor anything that you need to observe.

Christ Enforces Law Against Spurious Law

Christ Jesus annulled a mere pretense or abnormity that seemed to be law, that seemed to govern. He demonstrated, he proved, he set forth certain fundamental truths. He stands for the enforcement of law; he stands for the enforcement of the divine, eternal law of health and life; and he stands for the annulment of any so-called law that is operating to your discomfiture.

Operative Christian Science

Operative Christian Science is precisely the same thing; it is the enforcement of law. Christian Science means the annulment of these so-called laws of disease. Whenever a Christian Scientist heals a case, he does so by smashing a so-called law. Every demonstration of healing proves that disease is illegitimate and abnormal, that the so-called laws governing it are abnormities, having no intelligence and no right to exist and no power of continuance. If humanity had never departed from the normal, there never would have been any disease.

No Heredity But Good

There is no law that can bind you or bind upon you any hereditary disease. You may give up the belief now and forever that you are under the doom of any such law. God never provided for any such law. Declare in the name of Christ that you are under no ban, that you are healed, because you no longer need, after this hour, to be afraid of it, nor believe in it, nor expect it to master you. Be not afraid. You do not have to be afraid of anything. The law of being to you means dominion; and when you begin to exercise it, you will find that you have a larger equipment.

Present Salvation Possible

Christ Jesus stands for the possibility of salvation unto every man **now,** stands for the way and rule of that salvation, for the proof of it. The foundation of being is God and a divinely provided life for man and an eternal law for his life, health and prosperity. Christ has abolished and always will abolish the so-called law of sin, disease and death. You could not get away from the fundamental law of recovery to you if you tried. You only need to know that God's work is done, and that every provision necessary for your recovery has been made long ago, and that you are to stop believing something else. Humanity is sick according to a spurious and outrageous activity. **The proof of the divine nature and will is Christ.**

ACTIVITY IN THE TRUTH
A Lecture

The Object of Christian Scientists

As Christian Scientists, our object is to emerge as rapidly as possible from an evil, inharmonious sense of existence, into the understanding of life harmonious, good and eternal. Each and all must achieve dominion and sinlessness; so the best thing for us to do is to get to work and keep at it vigorously and courageously, knowing that God, Intelligence, is working with us.

God Our Helper

We each and all have the same God, Good, Intelligence, to help us. The only Truth there is is our Truth, our Good, our Life, our wisdom, our friend, our God, who is no respecter of persons. It matters not who voices the Truth, or who the mouthpiece is; it is for each and every one. We each have our experiences, and they are more or less valuable, as we make them occasions for demonstration. We have lessons to learn, and they may have to be learned by hard knocks, but we have the Truth to help us to learn them.

Let Us Be Awake and Working

Humanity is fooled all the time by error, and as Christian Scientists we are fooled too, if, instead of getting ahead and keeping ahead of error, we trail behind, and then grumble because Christian Science does not do more for us. We are deceived and defrauded most of the time unless we are awake and working.

Be Not Deceived by Mesmerism

The belief that we have a mind of our own which is telling us all sorts of lies, is all wrong. Mortal mind is wrong and we are but reflecting beliefs which are more or less mesmeric as we allow ourselves to be swayed thereby.

"Choose Ye"

We are not original thinkers, but, all the time, we are reflecting good thoughts of God, divine Mind, or erroneous beliefs of mortal mind, and we are choosing whom we serve. Thoughts are not in our body, nor do they emanate therefrom; nor do they come in consequence of some bodily condition.

Alertness

We must ask ourselves, whence come the beliefs that seem to be in our consciousness. Error cannot defraud or cheat us long when Truth is instructing us, and we are declaring and realizing the reality of God. The illusion of the carnal mind, the unreality and nature of evil, has been uncovered to us and revealed to us, and we should rejoice all the time, and be not discouraged by the lies of mortal mind.

Government, Good and Bad

The government of the one Mind means life and health; the other means sin, sickness, and death; one means strength and joy; the other means sorrow and weakness.

Wake Up!

Christian Scientists are fooled when they do not see error as error, nothingness. To make something of error is the biggest mistake possible. Do not be indolent, procrastinate, or be inert. A Scientist who is not working is lagging behind; he misses much of joy, and often turns and blames Science for not doing more for his comfort. The work of Science is to wake us up, not to solace us into inactivity and selfishness and ease.

The Source of Dominion

There are fifteen thousand million people believing sin, sickness, and death all the time, and all these beliefs are mesmeric, and constitute the claim of mortal mind atmosphere, and this miasma grinds all who accept it into misery, with the grave as a goal. Now comes Science as a ray of light penetrating the darkness, and as we see the light we lift our heads above the clouds, and begin to have dominion. The surging suggestions are easily met by the mental enforcement of Truth and Love, and we are not helpless victims any longer. We must all, sooner or later, work out our own salvation.

The Right Idea Destroys False Belief

We have this glorious revelation, that the right idea about everything destroys the false belief about it, as truly in Christian Science as in mathematics. The right idea of Truth is our Saviour. Don't reject it, but let it direct your thoughts and acts every moment, and it will console you, and bring you into union with God consciously, and you will know the Truth and the Truth will make you free.

The Right Idea Is Our Saviour

The right idea of Life is the Saviour from disease. When the Saviour has done his work, salvation is accomplished and we are consciously in the kingdom of God, and His kingdom is within us. The kingdom of God is within us, and the only antidote for error is the right idea of the same subject.

We Must Be Masters

In the process of salvation we must watch our thoughts and be on the alert, and detect these suggestions and reject and destroy them, and break down doubt and discouragement and apathy and false laws. We must look this predicament of humanity squarely in the face and master it and know that it cannot master us. Instead of being bound for the grave, we must know that we are on the eternal road to Life, that has no sense of death.

Evasion of Life's Problem Is Impossible

No evasion of the problem is possible. We must know that we can never die. We have to know this some time, and now is a good time to begin. We do not need to mourn that this seems to be so, but rather rejoice because we now know the way out. It is wrong sense that makes us feel sad and burdened, and we should rejoice that evil is unreal, and we do not work in vain, and it has no ability to stand up against Truth. When governed by Truth we are always strong and forcefully equipped, always hopeful.

Activity and Glorious Progress

When anything goes wrong, get to work in the realm of thought and fearlessly meet and destroy the claim. Appropriate the blessings which Truth has given you. Persistently declare the Truth about everything error is lying about, and know that the declaration of the Truth breaks the claim, as the truth is always positive and effective. Declare yourself in heaven in every treatment, and out of error. Know that Mind is always true and that lies have no mind to emanate from. Do not dally with the subject. Our deliverance depends upon how we cling to God and His ideas, and how fast we stop believing lies. Declare the Truth as instantly as you would step out of perdition into heaven, and you will know that the way out of every claim you meet and master is like another step out of hell into eternal life; but when we let ourselves get annoyed by a claim, we are cheating ourselves out of progress. Each demonstration gives strength and courage to meet the next one, and progress is glorious.

Attacks Not Needed Are Not Experienced

If we are spiritually minded enough not to need these knocks, to make us grow, we won't have them; so be wise and scientific enough to prevent these claims, and to forestall them in the better way. Cross swords with error and win your way into heaven. We must be loyal to our Saviour's spiritual understanding. We must depend fully upon our God, who is omnipotent Good.

Do Not Blame Others

Stop believing any circumstance or person is to blame for your failures or short-comings or slow growth. Our God is our best friend and deliverer, and will deliver. Hate flies when confronted with Love; Love is the best transparency. When our thoughts are clouded by resentment, hatred or error, the Truth cannot shine there; so keep your windows clean.

Wash Your Mentality Before You Wash Your Hands

If there is any resentment or hate in your heart, stay at home, pull down the blinds; don't wash your hands, until you have cast it out. Know that evil suggestions coming to your consciousness can gain no momentum there, nor can they gain force or power when met by Christ, who casts out devils. Hate brings death; Love is Life sustained.

Banish Waywardness to Make Room for Healing

A treatment cannot effectually enter a person's mentality when error is willfully persisted in. Some claims are not the result of sinful feelings, but are projected by general belief, and are quickly healed when our windows are clear, and Love rules our feelings. It is vain to expect good and blessings when we are harboring evil feelings. We do not get the benefits we are seeking because we do not overcome self-will and wayward conditions of belief. We must have these destroyed, as we are not amenable to Truth when we are wayward. Love is never jealous, envious or hateful. Love is transparent and receptive; Love presents the avenue for demonstration to be realized. What are we obeying? Are we rejecting error as we should, and gaining dominion and power and perpetuity of perfection? If not, we are not saving ourselves as fast as we should from the attacks of error.

Fruits of Scientific Living

Happiness is rightness and goodness and prosperity. Christian Science lived means grandness, strength, health, peace, and all good. Mrs. Eddy was told recently that a boy in Texas had been healed of a most terrible disease and redeemed from death. She said, "Well, that demonstration, if there had been no more, repays me for my years of hard labor."

Hard Problems Force Progress

When we are pushed into tight places and have to face the most serious problems, we are gaining big steps in our progress heavenward. Mrs. Eddy said, when raising one who had seemingly died, that she had never seen so clearly the truth of Life eternal, and the perfection of its manifestation.

Banish Apathy

There is too much apathy on the subject of breaking the claim of mortal belief that it has laws. Be systematic about that, every day. When you recognize the false laws, you must know that the Truth, mentally enforced, can and does break them. Let us glory in and abide by the declaration and realization of this:—That all is infinite Mind, and that its manifestations are all good, all spiritual, all in perfect action, all in perfect harmony.

God's Government Is My Government

There is one law-giver, one government, one Principle, and this is my government and my Principle.

"Awake to Righteousness and Sin Not"

All action is Mind, all reflection is good, and I reflect health, life, everlasting dominion; and the kingdom of heaven is within; all being is perfect; there is no evil or error or sickness or sin in the mind or body of man. I cannot be mesmerized to sin, to be sick, or to be sorrowful or weak. I cannot be afraid of anything at any time. Love is infinite and ever present; there is no hate, no resentment, no curse, no lust, no selfishness in man's Mind. God is All-in-all. I cannot be made the dupe of error in any way, for I am the idea, the manifestation of God, free, spiritual, harmonious.

Seeming Obstacles Scientifically Denied

There is no law working adversely to the law of God. There are no evil minds; there is no mental malpractice. There are no mortal influences that can turn me from the path of Good, Truth, or interfere with my progress or demonstration or usefulness.

Stagnation Scientifically Impossible.

I cannot be stagnated mesmerically; I am in action with Truth; I am alert to the demands of Truth, and know the Truth, and am protected by it. There is no false theology, no false philosophy. Turn on and destroy the claim of fear, that you can ever be made to believe that you cannot demonstrate Christian Science.

Method of Dealing with Pain

Fear is mesmerism and mesmerism is nothing, and must be disbelieved in, rejected and destroyed. Your body can never give you occasion to be afraid, and mesmeric waves cannot touch you when you guard your thought with Truth. When experiencing a belief of pain, don't waste time just handling pain, but declare against erroneous claims of malicious animal magnetism, and the claim will cease.

Malicious Mental Malpractice Annulled

If anybody hates you, you will find it out; if you are realizing the nothingness of the claim, you will learn that no hatred can harm you but the hatred you harbor for another. No one can make us suffer by their seeming hatred of Christian Science.

Immaturity Should Be Scientifically Denied

We perpetuate the claims of error by saying that we have not grown sufficiently to overcome these claims. Error seeks to bind us by making us believe that we have not understanding enough to demonstrate. Evil slays itself, and if we are reflecting evil beliefs we suffer for it, in consequence.

Hatred and Resentment Chief Obstacles

When we master hatred and resentment, we can move mountains. Pray to be delivered from hating, and from all evil, and help lift this load from mankind as well as from yourself.

Falsehoods Scientifically Handled

Handle defamation and false criticism and misrepresentation, prosecution, persecution and slander. Operative Christian Science must stop this wholesale slander that is being voiced through the pulpit and press, and we can operate it. This is especially required of us now. Know that these agencies cannot publish opinion against the Cause and its Leader or Christian Science, nor do anything that they aim to do. They are only a lot of lies that no one can or wants to believe, and Christian Scientists cannot be discouraged and stirred up and made fearful or doubtful by them. None have as yet quit business that we know of. We know that all this is a lie and powerless, because God is supreme. His kingdom is come, He is the only power and reality.

False Security

Bid the advisers cease when they try to make you believe that you do not want to talk about malicious animal magnetism. Get some working Scientist to hit you on the back and wake you up. Not wanting to handle malicious animal magnetism is equivalent to wanting to stay in hell. Don't be afraid, knowing that you can prove its claims false. Here is the law of God that gives you power and authority. Declare that you know it is nothing, therefore it is proving itself a liar. Declare for unity in the churches. Error cannot rule the members. There is no strife for power or place, no contention among the leaders. God's wisdom and government control all. Pray to be delivered from seeking a high place. Be childlike and obedient, unselfish and meek. You must know that you can never be blinded to Truth, but are always amenable to God's laws.

Defamation and Slander Annulled

There is no mental or moral contamination. God is the dominating Mind. Christian Science is the great physician, and Truth will diagnose the case for you, and you need not consult the doctor-books nor an M. D. We are bound to win in this continual effort in the right direction. The more error talks, the more it insists on its claims, the more it is a liar, and it knows it is a liar, and cannot deceive the Truth, and I am governed by Truth. Declare that the claims of defamation and slander cannot hinder you or your works, or injure your health or affairs. It cannot assume power in any way; for **God is all-power.**

SCIENCE OF MIND AND THOUGHT
Lecture Delivered in Denver, Colo.

Progress in Discovery
People are forever congratulating themselves on the measure of their enlightenment, their discoveries, their increased knowledge, and the vast development of the possibilities of existence. By reason of the natural process of discernment, of revelation, different individuals have made known to the world things that were before unknown or have been misconceived, or that have been considered unknowable or impossible.

Revolutionary Effect of Discovery
Many of these revelations have overturned established conditions of human belief, and have revolutionized the world. They have exposed the utter falsity of, and have reversed, previous conceptions, methods and action.

Hunger for Knowledge
In the exact ratio of this increased knowledge or perception is the conviction that finite mind has a very imperfect and limited conception of the Truth or Science of Being and that the vast range of knowledge which is beyond its perception is Infinite. Hence there is a great yearning for further revelation, a constant searching after the Truth, by a people whose hopes and prayers are that there may be more light, and that the real facts of existence may be revealed.

Rejection and Triumph of Truth
It is noticeable that this same people, who thus pray for the revelation of the Truth, usually reject and resist it when it is

first made known, and often revile and persecute the exponent or revelator; but, notwithstanding this, the Truth of Being is gradually impressing itself on the mentality of mankind in spite of all opposition, and will continue to "turn and overturn until He whose right it is shall reign."

Science of Life Needed

One writer, realizing the imperfection of human knowledge, has said, "We have no exact or absolute knowledge except the science of numbers." This is hardly true, but it is true that only exact and demonstrable scientific knowledge can be relied on for the government and welfare of humanity. In the same sense that we have a comprehension of and the satisfactory benefits of the science of numbers, we would also comprehend the science of everything that is included in the Infinitude of Being. Humanity must surely learn that, as there is the science of numbers, there must also be the science of Life and the science of health, and that this science wrought out in actual demonstration, will remove from humanity the discords of sin and disease.

Recognition of Need Makes Ready to Receive Truth

We shall, therefore, the better prepare our thoughts for a helpful consideration of our subject this evening, if we remember that the world is confessedly awry, is confessedly in a state of conflict and confusion; that it admits that it is the victim of ignorance of the laws of Being, and is incompetent to accomplish for itself a state of harmonious and satisfactory existence. If we do this we shall be more ready to look for and to discern a possible remedy and more willing to hope and admit that such a remedy may be at hand. That condition of mentality which most clearly detects the errors of human belief is the most receptive of the true ideas and the actuality of the science of life. It most easily grasps the Truth which leads to all Truth and is the mighty deliverer.

Advent of Christian Science

Over thirty years ago, the most extraordinary woman that ever lived, after a life and experience that fitted her in the highest degree for so grand a ministry, and by reason of her spiritual nature, her high mental attainments and deep insight into metaphysical science and the things of God, stood out far in advance of the common frontage of human mentality and announced the discovery or revelation of the Science of Life, which she afterwards named Christian Science. Not only this, but she announced that she had demonstrated beyond question the Principle which she had discerned, and gave such an exposition of the science as enabled any conscientious student to attest its verity by healing the sick and by obliterating thousands of ills that are just as abnormal and contrary to the science of Being as "two and two are five" is contrary to the science of numbers.

Christian Science Sublimest of Discoveries

When humanity's plight shall have been fully realized, and it shall have been learned that the true Christ-knowledge of Life and all that it includes is really the Saviour of the world, then it will be seen that this revelation of Christian Science through Mary Baker Eddy is one of the most sublime spectacles of all history.

The textbook of Christian Science by Mrs. Eddy, "Science and Health with Key to the Scriptures," is absolutely unique.

No Varieties of Doctrine

Notwithstanding this, there are people who never gave any heed to the subject until long after Mrs. Eddy's works were published, who profess that they also discovered Christian Science and that they are sponsers for a different school thereof.

Mrs. Eddy's Discovery of Christian Science Is Established

I am not here to engage in a controversy concerning this defective and presumptuous claim, which is really falling of its own unsustained weight, but will say that the fact that Mrs. Eddy was the discoverer and founder of Christian Science is now formulated history; is declared by encyclopedias, by dictionaries and biographical works; by the Parliament of Religions and its records, and is confirmed by the palpable fact that every statement written by any one may be found substantially in the previously published writings of Mrs. Eddy. I do not recall one salient statement on the subject that was not better stated by her years before.

Fruits of the Discovery

There are in the ranks of the Christian Science denomination, and in immediate affiliation with it, hundreds of thousands of people who, in consequence of this revelation and the unparalleled service of its discoverer, have been rescued from graves, lifted from beds of pain and disease, redeemed from the depths of intemperance, degradation and sin to a state of health, happiness and morality. History does not portray a solitary creature, since Jesus, in whose train may be seen such vast thousands as have been the beneficiaries of this discovery and the superhuman, God-directed labor of Mrs. Eddy, whereby its beneficence has found its way into the affections and weal of mankind.

Now in the face of all this, there are people who, in assumed behalf of the race, are protesting that we are making too much of Mrs. Eddy. This comes with strange inconsistency from those who make much of Calvin, Wesley and the Pope of Rome; of Swedenborg, Voltaire and others. It comes with poor grace from the laity which makes much of its clergymen; which accepts the minister as spiritual guide and interpreter and regards his opinion and wisdom as law. We might dismiss the claim with the retort that it comes to us with unclean hands, but I will make use of this reference to it to emphasize the fact that "Science and Health" teaches just the contrary. It exalts thought to the recognition of the allness of God. It leads the way to absolute loyalty and obedience to Him alone. It teaches the disciple to turn from personality and personal models to God, who alone can guide men aright.

Mrs. Eddy's Practice Consistent

Mrs. Eddy's practice is in strict accord with this teaching. Her constant efforts with her followers and students have been to turn them from reliance on her and from all attempt at the exaltation of her personality to the understanding of impersonal Christian Science, which is the true guide and wayshower. Her teaching in this respect has been effective, for her students do have a rational and scientific understanding of her work and relationship to the cause. It sometimes happens that sick people or neophytes in Christian Science, who have been healed, give vent to their gratitude in extravagant forms of acknowledgment and admiration, but this is neither inculcated nor encouraged by this science, by Mrs. Eddy, or her students generally.

Christian Science Infinite

Christian Science, or the Science of Being, is infinite. There is no beginning or ending to it. It covers all the phases of mind, law, government, substance, power and action. Do not expect that I can tell you all about this Science in one evening and do not be disappointed if you do not leave here with a complete understanding of it and fully equipped to move mountains. To grasp Infinity in an hour or two is obviously impossible. I have known people to complain because I did not tell them all about Christian Science and the work of healing, whereas if they had grasped one-tenth of what I did say, they would have gone away rejoicing.

Science of Mind and Thought

I am glad to say that Christian Science is a vast subject and covers a limitless area. It follows, therefore, that, at such a time as this, we can only consider certain phases of this Christian knowledge, and my object is to speak to you tonight concerning the Science of Mind and of the action and influence of thought on the affairs of men.

Sin Is Thought Before It Is Action

The statement is made in "Science and Health" that "sin is thought before it is acted" and this statement can successfully resist every conceivable argument to the contrary. If, indeed, you will give the subject very little scrutiny you will discern its verity for yourself and know that sinful belief is the impulse and animus of every sin.

Thought Primary in all Activity

All the strife and war among nations is primarily false belief. All the business affairs of the world are thought expressed. Continents are discovered, explored and colonized, nations are founded, cities are built, the earth is made to bring forth its produce, goods are designed and manufactured and all of the vast ponderous transactions of the world are procured and continued by the action of thought.

Results of Good and of Bad Thought

Thought establishes social relationships, and, on the other hand, it murders and commits suicide. It brings forth the manifestations of music, art and invention, and again, it demolishes and destroys. Without thought all human activity would cease; the earth would become depopulated, the wheels of industry would abruptly stop, crumble and decay and the work of men's hands be obliterated. Gaze where you will upon the scene of humanity and you may know that its visible presence on the earth and all its possessions, all that it does or has ever accomplished, all of the minutiæ and immensity of its doings,—indeed, all things of whatsoever phase or nature that are included in the entire compass of its career,—are but the phenomena of thought; and you may also know that mortal man and his affairs, which exist because of thought, would be a nonentity without it.

Wrong Thought the Procurer of Disease

I do not suppose that there is one person here who does not comprehend that this is true,—not one who does not, to some extent, grasp the apparent dominion of thought over all that concerns the destiny of mortal men, and because you can and do comprehend this, I expect you to patiently and intelligently listen while I tell you that part of the revelation of Christian Science, which our textbook explains with great amplification, is, that thought and its phenomena, acting either immediately or remotely, is the procurer of all disease.

Mental Origin of Disease Not Incredible

I do not expect or ask you to believe this on the strength of what I am saying. You cannot possibly know it until you study this Science and get an understanding of its Principle and the rules for its demonstration, and then prove it for yourself, so that no vestige of doubt remains; but in the presence of this apparent control of thought over humanity, this statement to which I have referred cannot seem to you to be very astounding.

Mind Heals Disease

Having prepared you for an admission that possibly the human mind, by means of its many ramifications, does institute and maintain diseased conditions, I will also add the correlative declaration from "Science and Health" that "Mind rightly directed heals disease."

Aggregate of Mortal Thought Acts as Law

Now let us retrace our steps a little and explore still further the Science of Mind, which not only reveals the fact that the thought of mortals externalizes itself on the life, health, happiness and destiny of each individual, but that our thoughts influence others as well, and further, that the aggregate of the universal thought acts upon humanity, on its present plane of existence, as law and government.

Good and Evil Thought Externalizes Itself

Going still further, you can learn, if you will, that all good or evil thought externalizes itself according to its nature. In other words, the Truth of being manifests itself as life, health, harmony and happiness, whereas error, or an erroneous sense of being manifests itself in sin, discord, death and the myriads of disasters which disfigure humanity and continue its strife, calamity and despair. You may learn that man governed by God does manifest life and happiness; he is indeed the very likeness of God and has dominion over all creation, instead of being subject to creation.

Salvation by Changed Thought

Now if the normal, God-ordained state of man is one of harmony, and we behold, instead, that mortals are environed by and manifesting every conceivable evil, and if we know that evil is but the paraphernalia of erroneous belief, then how shall we describe the only possible way of deliverance; the only process of redemption, whereby humanity may escape from its appalling agony and travail and manifest that which is infinite Good? Do you not have at hand a logical and easily comprehended answer? Does it not palpably appear to you that, in order to save the race, thought must be changed; that all of the individual and universal error, which by its action prostrates and kills mortal men, must be supplanted by the true or scientific sense? If erring thought is the cause of human evil, is there anything else to do but to change it and thereby establish different results?

No Salvation without Knowledge of Principle

At this point, let it be assumed that the suggestion occurs to you somewhat as follows: Well, suppose that I take it for granted that this is true, that the woe and mortality of mankind is in consequence of ignorance, superstition and misconception, false belief, theories and control; suppose that I admit that it is a false sense of life which begets sin and its desolation; how am I then any better off, unless I can have some faultless standard whereby to judge between the false and the true? How am I to know that the beliefs which are influencing me and others cannot bring me to mortality and its doom? Am I not still with Pilate, who typified the complexity of human dismay and need and longing by the inquiry, "What is truth?" Yes, you are! and so is every man who has no understanding of the demonstrable Truth which reforms, redeems, revivifies and sustains and which is revealed in Christian Science. This Science is chart, compass and beacon light to the mariner on the sea of trouble and without it he cannot accomplish his own salvation. It must be a great satisfaction to you, however, that you are unlike Pilate, in that you have the blessed lot to live in an age and under a condition of thought wherein it is possible to be lifted somewhat out of the besotted materialism which environed him.

Truth of Being Now Knowable

It is your privilege to live in the era of Christian Science, when divine metaphysics asserts the facts of Being in the consciousness of men who can, at least, understand the language of Spirit. The men of nineteen centuries ago could not comprehend Truth, and Jesus was too wise to utter it in their dull ears; but the men of today can hear, understand and demonstrate the Mind which was in Christ Jesus and which saves.

Radical Changes Necessary

It will be readily understood that, if the millenium, or the kingdom of heaven **within,** is to be established in individual consciousness, all, by way of false belief, must be abolished. When Nicodemus asked Jesus, "How can a man be born when he is old?" the answer was, "Except a man be born of water and of the Spirit, he cannot enter into the kingdom of God," indicating thereby the necessity for the discernment of an entirely altered sense of life. Jesus and all who understood Him admonished mankind to be transformed by the renewing of the mind; to put off the old man with his deeds; to put off mortality and put on immortality, to have that mind which was also in Christ Jesus—the mind which heals the sick, annuls the temptation and which discloses that "the kingdom of heaven is within you" and "whosoever keepeth my sayings shall never taste of death."

Mortals Have Been Resigned to Misery

The measure of human misery indicates the extent to which mankind is straying from the Life which is Good and indicates the necessity for and the degree of transformation which must ensue. At this stage of discernment, we are at first liable to demur because there is so much to do in order to restore ourselves and the world to health, peace, and concord. Mortals have struggled so long and unsuccessfully against evil that they have come to regard it as inevitable and irresistible and have sought to be reconciled to the many enemies of life and happiness by the strange, futile hope that the last enemy, death, would bestow a peace upon them which the lesser enemies had despoiled. In gloomy abiding, men have sinned, suffered and gone to an unresisted grave under the delusive expectation that in some way God would be more merciful in death than He had been to life. When urged by conscience to a more exalted state of being it has only seemed like an invitation to give up the pleasures of this life and enter upon a career of reluctant sacrifice and of resignation to sickness and death with the uncertain prospect of a post mortem heaven.

Christian Science Discloses Deliverance

Now Christian Science shows conclusively that mankind has nothing to give up but misery and that which causes it, including both sin and disease. It reveals the self-punishment and self-destructive nature of evil. It shows how to detect and master it; it discloses and makes available the natural dominion of man; it equips men with the understanding and power which enables them to know that they are surely working out their salvation from evil, without dying, instead of merely hoping for salvation after death. Moreover, it effaces the mystery which always surrounded this entire subject and men gain a comprehension of the rationale of their deliverance. Lastly, it begins forthwith to manifest itself in benefits, and confers the assurance that it is leavening the entire lump.

The Fundamental Nature of Sin

It has been said that the only way to get even with a life insurance company is to die. It certainly seems, also, as though the only way to test the common theories of salvation is to die. But Christian Science bids men live, and the true understanding of life which it bestows endows them with an endless continuity of benefits. Inasmuch as Christian Science explains that sin and disease, as well as other human disorders, are occasioned by abnormal thought and erroneous belief, and that the only remedy is Christian Science Mind healing and the possession of the Mind of Christ, I will allude briefly to the fundamental nature of sin and the reason why sin and error cause a sense of suffering. The advancing thought of this age, rapidly progressing under the light of Science, "is grasping the fact that the Truth **is** and that it is Good," and that God alone is natural and lawful. When this shall have become self-evident to the people, it will be seen that all evil and all that results in evil is abnormal, unrighteous and unnecessary.

All Unlike God Is Harmful

Christian Science still further reveals the fact that all that is unlike God is evil, regardless of what the seeming may be to human sense; hence we are led to the statement that all evil, whether it is called sin, ignorance, error, misconception, or by any other name, and in spite of all opinion to the contrary, is harmful, inevitably harmful. Some forms of evil are manifested in what we call sin, the transgression of the moral code of conventions, others in sorrow, sickness, misfortune, destitution and in various other ills, but they are all the offspring of the one evil, the "carnal mind," which is enmity against God, against Life, Truth, Love and the power and action of Good.

Christian Science Uncovers Sin and Its Consequences

It is generally acknowledged that men are sinful, and there is some apprehension of possible punishment therefor, but the continuity of sin is encouraged by reason of the established belief in a system of sorrow, repentance and cancellation. If men really believed the statement that "whatever a man soweth, that shall he also reap," they would, through fear of suffering alone, refrain from sin. If the drunkard had only known, when he lifted the first intoxicating glass to his lips, that he was really imbibing delirium tremens with all its horrors, he would most likely have hesitated long and successfully. If the sinner who "finds satisfaction in sin," as described in "Science and Health," only knew that every sin reacts upon itself and causes inevitable suffering, he would be appalled by the prospective anguish which evil entails upon itself and turn from it. The mission of Christian Science is to make known to mortals this very nature of evil and to reconcile him to his own deliverance from it.

Why Does the Sinner Suffer?

The question may be asked, "Why is it inevitable that sin begets suffering? Why do not men sin, if they choose to do so, and then stop without ill effects?" This question is answered more fully and better in "Science and Health" than I can do it, but in order to bring this subject home to each one of us, I will partially explain, for example, the effects of envy, jealousy, anger, malice and revenge on the person who manifests them. Humanity is at present living on a plane of law and control whereupon envy, hatred and malice are antagonistic to physical well being—as poison would be. The Bible says that "He that hateth his brother is a murderer and cannot inherit eternal life," and Christian Science shows that these evil beliefs are not only murderous, but that the most deadly effect is on the perpetrator himself, for they kindle and feed the fires of hell for him. He cannot inherit eternal Life because his own course is suicidal and by reason of the bodily effects produced by sin he is destroying his own sense and manifestation of Life. Such a sinner is operating on a plane which evolves penalties upon him in the way of disturbed circulation of the blood, obstructed bodily functions and the impairment of organic action. These things interfere with and repress the healthy secretions of the body and clog the system with morbific substance. All this and much more are among the consequences of sin and this suffering is not imposed by a wrathful God who is bestowing vengeance on the sinner, but is simply a part of the evolution of evil which decrees its own penalties even to the extinction of human life.

Sin Must Be Healed to Remove Disease

It follows, therefore, that a man who is sick because of his sin needs not medicine, but transformation, mentally and morally, and the legitimate and efficacious annulment of the imposed penalty. When the Christian Scientist has to heal a case of sickness caused by sin, it is necessary to remove from the patient the sin, or cause of his condition, and also to annul the penalty. Many forms of disease are induced by grief, sorrow, mortification, anxiety, disappointment and kindred influences, all of which need to be taken into account by the practitioner, for they are all abnormal and discordant. In fact, there is no erroneous action of the human mind that does not, sooner or later, externalize itself in some deranged physical condition.

Effects of Fear Uncovered and Destroyed

"Science and Health" explains with much elaboration the subtle and complex action and effect of fear, which is always mental, upon the human body. This would be of little satisfaction to anyone if it did not also explain how fear can be destroyed and its effects arrested and exterminated. It shows how unnecessary fear is and how it is based on erroneous premises and false beliefs about life and health; how it is propagated and sustained by the educated supposition that pain and disease are of divine institution and that men are unable to protect themselves against them. Christian Science points out the possibility of your obtaining complete mastery over the senses of pain and disease, and just in proportion as you gain this understanding and thereby manifest the natural dominion and control over the bodily conditions, you will gradually lose all fear and escape its havoc.

Material Theories and Treatment Reversed

The changes of thought which must and will transform the world will reverse all of the purely material theories about disease and show that many of the steps that are taken to prevent and cure it but aggravate and augment it. The true understanding and scientific application of divine law will annul the spurious laws of disease, will locate mental causation and remove the consequences of fear.

Fable of the Traveler and the Plague

I think there is a fable which represents a conversation between the plague and a traveler on the road to Bagdad.

The traveler berated the plague for having caused the death of ten thousand men at Bagdad, when the plague exclaimed, "You are wrong; I killed only one man in Bagdad and fear killed all the rest." "Science and Health" goes farther and shows you that fear killed them all.

Reform of Sinners Fundamental Aim of Science

I have spoken thus on the effects of sin because the paramount work of Christian Science is to turn the people from the evil which is destroying them. The healing of the sick is an incidental accompaniment of this work, but primarily the great aim is to reform the wicked, and one way is to show them the unavoidable consequences of sin.

Science Casts Out Fear

In referring to the influence of fear I have not done it to alarm you. You need not be disturbed thereby, for not understanding the wretched and widespread havoc that results therefrom. Christian Science reveals the way to cast out fear, even unto the uttermost, and I make bold to say that there is no other revelation of the way by which to accomplish it. "There is none other name given under heaven among men whereby we must be saved," than the Mind which was in Christ, and which healeth all our diseases and casts out fear.

Fear Only to Commit Sin

If you would save yourself unspeakable sorrow and pain, stop hating your brother. Strive at all hazards to banish from your mind and character resentment, wrath and bitterness; learn to love, be kind, merciful and forgiving. Love will transform you, beautify you, ennoble you, and place upon your existence the seal of a royal, a splendid manhood. Mortals seem not to be afraid to commit sin, although this cannot possibly be done with impunity. On the other hand they cherish thousands of unnecessary and baseless fears about diseases, and these fears themselves engender the very disorders they would avoid

Mothers' Fears Baseless, and Harmful to Children

Mothers, in rearing their children, load them down with fear and penalties and thereby plant the seeds of disease and suffering. The majority of a mother's fears have no more foundation than the ghost stories which frighten the children and disturb their bodily condition. These fears are of man-made origin and act as disastrously on the health of the children as slow poison, impure air or foul water.

The Less So-called Health-laws, the Healthier Children

The mothers who, through fear of disease, bestow the most anxious care upon their children and educate them so elaborately concerning so-called health-laws and the fear of material conditions, confer upon them incalculable damage and shut out the control that they should exercise over their bodily health. All other things being equal, it is certain that the mother of a large family of children will raise more healthy progeny than in the case of a single child, who is constantly mesmerized by its mother's anxiety and excessive obedience to the most superstitious so-called laws.

Children of Science Parents Will Improve Race

Mothers who are Christian Scientists will greatly improve the race during coming generations. Already they find, as a rule, that from the very day of the birth of their children they are able to guide them among the pitfalls of infancy and childhood with very little sickness, and to avoid largely the prostrating fear which is the unfortunate heritage of nearly all other children. When mothers learn all the possibilities of motherhood, as they are disclosed in Christian Science, the race will enter upon a changed existence.

Harmful Effects of Talk About Disease

Evil thought concerning disease has an offspring in evil conversation about it, and today the race is inflicting the most appalling consequences upon itself as the result of insufferable and limitless talk about sickness. I doubt if there is any other subject known to men in whose behalf the nimble tongue wags itself with such mischievous industry.

People Expose Themselves to Mental Contagion

People who fear and avoid contagion and infection will actually submerge themselves in the introspection of self and the inspection and comments of everyone else, not knowing that those things are harmful and do vastly more damage than the others. There are countless thousands who are constantly going down to premature graves that would have lived on if they had kept their ills to themselves, instead of making the fatal mistake of exciting the fears and the alarming speeches of almost everyone that would listen. Medical records indicate innumerable instances where illness has terminated fatally simply because of the fright and discouragement that was projected upon the patient by other people who, through narrative, prediction or expressed fears, prostrated the hope and courage and expectation of the sick man who, if undisturbed, would have recovered spontaneously.

Mental Sanitation Needed More than Physical

People are intent upon sanitary improvements, ventilation and pure water, and yet they heed not the contamination of the mental fount, which is more important than all the rest. Christian Scientists urge the avoidance of the world-wide habit of over-much talking about diseased conditions of the body, because as a theme for conversation it is or should be unattractive and offensive to people of wholesome sensibilities. Secondly, because nearly all such conversation is among people who know really nothing about disease, its cause, the real signification of symptoms, or the means of cure, and whose utterances are the distressing offspring of ignorance; and lastly, because such conversations propagate fear and plant the seeds of disorder and disease, which unconsciously lodge, germinate and consume.

World Must Discover that Hope Is in God Only

This world has for ages turned in vain to matter and a materialistic philosophy for deliverance from its woes, and in disregard of its own declaration that God, Spirit, or Omniscience is all power, and regardless, too, of the fact that the divine Mind alone can govern man satisfactorily and aright, can alone wipe away tears and heal all of the diseases of the nation. The profundity of Mrs. Eddy's announcement, made thirty years ago, that the only hope of humanity lies in the direction of Mind has been recognized slowly, but, in spite of all reluctance and dimness of spiritual discernment, the world must awaken to that discovery. In the future the only march of actual progress will be in the mental realm, and this progress will not be in the way of human speculation and theorizing, but in the actual understanding and demonstration of the Mind that is infinite God, Good.

A More Correct Sense of God

I have just spoken of "the divine Mind." This phrase is very urgently objected to by some people who regard it as a serious error. When Mrs. Eddy first wrote "Science and Health with Key to the Scriptures," she saw that the world had a minimized and finitized sense of God, who is infinite, and in order to assist mankind to gain the correct concept of infinity, she gave certain technical definitions of Deity, which she explained at great length. In addition to such definitions as Life, Truth and Love, she declared that God is infinite Intelligence, Substance, infinite Mind, and divine Principle, and the person who by this means gains the grander and more perfect sense of God learns that he has been worshipping a finite mental image and calling it God. Men have opened the textbook of Christian Science, turned its pages and read that God is divine Principle, infinite Mind, and then closed the book in wrath, to exclaim: "What monstrous sacrilege! What blasphemy! The idea of calling God nothing but Mind, of reducing Him to a cold iceberg of Principle." And they have gone forth to declare that Christian Science is damnable heresy and that Christian Scientists are infidels.

Objections Considered

Let us turn a little of the sunshine of Intelligence on this objection, this precipitate frenzy, from which standpoint we are so industriously advertised as infidels. Let us see if a grain of divine logic will not allay this tumult. Let us ask a few questions to test the merit of this impeachment.

God Is Mind

Do you believe that God is infinite? Yes! Do you believe that He is infinite Wisdom, Intelligence, Truth and Knowledge? Yes! And yet you believe that God is mindless, do you? Oh, no, no! Ah! But you must believe that He is mindless if you consider it infidelity to affirm that He is divine Mind. There is no alternative for you. God is either Mind or mindless. Choose ye whom you will serve, but before you decide that He is mindless, let me tell you that a mindless God is a nonentity, for mindless knowledge and mindless wisdom is simply inconceivable.

God Is Principle

Next let us examine this riot about Principle. What does Principle mean? It means primary basis, fundamental law, government, causation. Principle is that by reason of which all exists that does exist. Now, if God is not the divine Principle of the universe and of all being, who is? If He is not the

Principle, then He is neither primary nor is He causation; and, if not these, then He is not infinite, and if your God is not infinite, then He is no God at all. All of the ill-considered objections to Christian Science have no more substance to them than this one has, and, when subjected to a scientific analysis, they become as dust and disappear. In Christian Science the allness of one God includes the allness of one infinite Mind, and one Intelligence, and shows that the true function of man is to manifest or express this Mind, which was also in Christ.

Mortal Man, Human Belief, versus Man, Divine Consciousness

The human being speaks of his mind, his soul, spirit, intellect and mentality as though he possessed all of these things. He is never able to tell the difference between them or to know one from the other. No one ever saw any of them, or is able to recognize their abode or presence, and still he talks and writes and even sings about them incessantly. The science of Mind shows that there is not the slightest evidence that mortal man has anything whatever of the kind, except a capacity to believe and accept physical sense-testimony. Consciousness, the aggregation of Mind's thoughts or ideas, constitutes all there is to individual man—the "image and likeness of God." Divine Mind is forever governing this consciousness, God's man.

Proper Government of Consciousness

If men are governed by error, by sin and the love of it, by superstition and an ignorant sense of being, then they will externalize the law and the doom of the carnal mind in sorrow, pain and sickness; for as the Bible says: "To be carnally minded is death." But if they learn of God, and are governed by the divine Mind, if the consciousness of the Truth abides in them, and the understanding of Life is manifesting man's dominion, then they will experience an entirely different existence, for "to be spiritually minded is life and peace."

"Choose Ye"

Every human being stands hourly at "the parting of the ways." Each moment he is called upon to choose whom he will serve. The understanding of the Truth and obedience thereto will lead him through the channels of health and holiness, and bestow upon him the countless benefits of intelligence; but if an evil and perverted sense of life governs appetite, affection, motive and obedience, then they will lead him into the mire of suffering and gloom and death.

"Mind, Not Matter"

The world has already entered upon an era of intellectual and spiritual advancement which was prophetically indicated in the motto adopted by the "World's Columbian Exposition," "Mind, not matter." People have languished in the supposition that matter alone was practical, and that the Mind or Spirit was vague and intangible. Today, owing to the glorious revelations of Christian Science, the world stands within the vestibule of the vast dome of divine Intelligence, wherein is found the transcendant, practical power and action of Mind over all things.

Criticisms of "Science and Health" Baseless and Futile

The textbook of Christian Science is "Science and Health with Key to the Scriptures," by Mary Baker Eddy. This book, which has passed many editions, contains a complete exposition of this Science, and its application to the healing of the sick. The frantic efforts to discredit this book by means of shallow denunciation, ignorant criticism and unfair analysis have utterly failed. No opposition or ridicule has served to suppress the sale or prevent the perusal of this book by the public. Why? Because the people who are most deeply interested in the subject, the sick and unhappy who have taken the pains to examine it in sincerity and with an honest desire to recognize its merits, have learned that it is true, and have become its beneficiaries in abundant degree by proving the verity of the Science which it discloses. If a lecturer on this subject were required to explain just what Christian Science is, he could not do better than to read to an audience this book of over six hundred pages. For the reason that this is not possible, he is necessarily confined to a limited exposition of what it accomplishes, in the hope of interesting the listener in a further and more complete investigation. To narrate, specifically, all of the works which are being performed through its influence would be simply impossible, for they have been multiplied to a point that baffles estimate and computation.

Application of Science Results in Moral Reform

We can, however, summarize the great good that is being accomplished, leaving the details to be disclosed to anyone who will inquire more definitely. I will first say that the man who feels its touch begins and continues a moral reform by means of a willing and satisfying destruction of temptation and evil desire. I know that there is no influence exerted upon the sinner that will so rationally and effectively turn him from sin.

Liquor and Drug Habits Healed

It has reformed drunkards and the victims of the morphine and other habits. Confirmed or chronic inebriety is among the infirmities of men which have been considered well-nigh hopeless. Material remedies cannot cope with inherited or acquired desire; neither have they any substance or reinforcement for the loss of will power, which, it is improperly alleged, ensues in the case of the drunkard. The entire treatment of drunkenness has been based on incorrect premises and governed by erroneous conclusions. Christian Science treatment adequately reaches both cause and effect, and has restored a multitude of drunkards to a state of sobriety and usefulness.

All Manner of Disease Healed

It heals all kinds of people of all manner of diseases. At the "World's Congress of Religions" it was authoritatively stated that more than one million cases of disease had been healed by it up to that time, and that many of them had been considered incurable. It has cured diseases that have never been known to be healed by any other means. Indeed, I doubt if there are any diseases that have not been mastered by it.

The Infidel and Agnostic Converted

It has instructed the infidel and agnostic, who, unable to adopt any of the misconceived substitutes for Deity which have disfigured human thought, has been glad to acquaint himself with the understanding of God which unfolds the very substance and the science of Being, instead of involving the believer in a labyrinth of mystery which gives no promise of yielding to anything but death.

All Human Powers Purified and Strengthened

Christian Science has purified and exalted the motives, desires and aims of mankind, increased their wisdom, their executive and business capacity, arrested the havoc of vice, refined character and elevated manhood and citizenship. These are indisputable facts, and they are indelibly engraved on the annals of humanity. To dispute them now would be folly. I leave them with you without even entreating you to give heed, being persuaded that the wise man will in due time discern that a happier destiny waits adoption by humanity, and with the confidence that toward that destiny the weary sufferer will at last turn his footsteps, to realize that the deliverance which has been the hope of ages and which is already the partial fruition of the prophecy uttered by Benjamin Franklin a century ago in these words:

Franklin's Prophecy

"The rapid progress of true science now makes occasion for regretting sometimes that I was born so soon. It is impossible to imagine the height to which may be carried in a thousand years the power of man over matter. All disease may by sure means be prevented or cured, not excepting even that of old age, and our lives lengthened at pleasure, even beyond the antediluvian standard. Oh, that mortal sense were in as fair a way of improvement, that men would cease to be wolves to one another, and that human beings would at length learn what they now improperly call humanity.''

"WHAT THINK YE OF CHRIST?"

Lecture Delivered in Dayton, Ohio, December 2, 1906

Ladies and Gentlemen: I do not know what may be before me in the future, but I do know that I would have died eighteen or nineteen years ago but for Christian Science; had it not been that Christian Science is available to a man who is dying. Now, there are a million people, almost, who might—if it were feasible—come before you and tell just such a story as mine and give you opportunity to believe that some mighty influence is at work transforming men and women. And yet, we come not to boast. We are not here to advertise, not here for converts, but simply for testimony, to tell you a little about what Christian Science means and then leave it to you to do with as you please. You need not be afraid of me, because you do not have to believe anything I say. I simply ask you to put your thought in the way of analysis, simply to investigate, simply to examine, that is all.

A Keynote Incident

I can tell you only a very little about this vast subject in an hour. I could not tell you very much about it in a week; and so what I say today must necessarily be fragmentary and incomplete. But as I was wondering what I should talk to you about, an incident that occurred a few days ago came to my thought, and it was after this fashion: I was riding in a railway train and noticed that a man and woman entered the car and sat immediately in front of me. Having nothing else to do, I noticed that the man took from his pocket one of our Christian Science periodicals. He read it in a superficial or casual way, and then passed it across the aisle to the lady and said: "Here, mother, here is something that will amuse you. The idea of calling that 'Christian Science' which denies Christ!"

Sectarianism Considered

That was what I listened to, and I sat there and ruminated, and as I remembered what history declares concerning the quarrels over Christ, concerning the sectarian differences and antipathies; as I remembered that in this behalf men had wounded each other and murdered each other and inflicted every conceivable kind of agony upon each other; as I remembered that even in our day various Christian sects are in a state of antipathy, and some in a state of antagonism toward each other; as I remembered the vast array and the innumerable Christian sects, the old inquiry came to me: "What think ye of Christ?"

Christian Science Not a Denial of Christ

Now, I do not believe that the English language, or any other language, could be so enlarged as to more completely misrepresent a people or misrepresent a religious movement or misrepresent any declaration of a religious body, than do these words of the man in the car misrepresent Christian Science, and they are employed in our midst every day. People who present the semblance of respectability, people whose business it should be to preach the gospel of love and loving-kindness, rise up day after day to utter that absolutely false statement that Christian Science is a denial of Christ.

Peter's Perception of Christ

Jesus himself once made a memorable inquiry. He asked of Peter, "Whom say ye that I am?" Do you think for a moment he wanted Peter to say: "Why, you are a tall gentleman with brown hair, engaging manners, and gentleness of speech?" Think you for a moment that he wanted someone to describe his body, his corporeal presence? No. What he yearned for, and what he got, was an evidence of a penetrating perception, which announced itself thus: "Thou art the Christ, the Son of the living God."

Christian Science Reconciles Reason to God

Now, let us inquire before we go on,—in order to get something practical out of all this, in order to get something that some day will cure you, will wipe away your tears, will bind up the broken heart, in order to arrive at some conclusion that will better our lives,—let us inquire: What is the living God? You might go to a million men and get a million answers, for no two people have the same opinion about God; and go to very many people, and possibly some in this audience, and they will tell you: "I do not believe in God at all. I do not believe there is any God." Now Christian Science promises to reconcile reason, and that means the reason of every man, to God. Now I am going to reconcile the reason of what is called the non-believer to God, in five minutes, logically and clearly and irresistibly, so that no man that leaves me will say again that he does not believe in God. What they do not believe is in somebody's opinion of God. They do not believe in the various graven images of stone or brass or wood, and they do not believe in the mental graven images that have been declared to be God. Now let us see.

What the Sceptic Must Concede

I believe that any one who knows enough to go to a lecture, knows enough to know that he did not create himself. There is no one in this room who does not know that some animating force, some impulsion of power or energy or intelligence, induced his existence; no one in all this room but knows that the universe—with all of its organized things—stands at the standpoint of effect, and knows that something has been the cause, something the origin, something the foundation, the basis and principle of this effect. Now, there is not any one in this room who does not believe that, nor any one who does not know enough to know that that which induced the universe is spiritual, above every other power, above every other force or activity. Now here comes the next contention. What was it, an intelligent or a non-intelligent cause?

The Creator Must Be Intelligent

Many philosophers will tell you that the cause of the universe is nothing but a blind force; and if that is not the manifestation of the densest ignorance, I would like to know what is. Are you intelligent men and women? Yes. Well then, is your intelligence the offspring of non-intelligence? Is the cause of your intelligence a non-intelligent cause? Who can possibly think such a thing as that? Why, it ought to have gone without a moment's debate years ago that that which created the intelligence of man is itself intelligent. So then, we ask every one to see this, that the origin of man and his intelligence is itself intelligent.

Deity Is the One Conscious Intelligent Cause

Christian Science comes to declare that the first and primary and everlasting cause of the universe is **itself** an intelligent cause. Now, there is **no such thing as unconscious intelligence;** therefore, it follows that that cause is a consciously intelligent cause. Inasmuch as, including its manifestation, it was and is All, inasmuch as it has adequately been declared to be infinite, then it is ONE; so there is but **one cause,** one conscious, infinite, intelligent source of the universe which is its will, government, law, its maintenance and sustenance. Now, is there any one in this room who does not believe that? No. Well, Christian Science declares that this is the only thing that is entitled to be called God or deity. So, if you believe in that you believe in Deity, for there is no other deity.

God Described

So Christian Science declares this: There is one God—**one conscious, individual, spiritually self-existent being; and that** being, as the Scriptures declare, is Life, Truth, Love, all-knowledge, all-wisdom, all-science, all-power, all-presence, the only creator of all that actually is. Now then, dear friends, Christian Science declares that this is the living God and the only one. This is our God.

God Is Unadulterated Good

Now, then, comes the question: Is the living God, the only true God, good or evil? It must be one or the other, for the simple reason that God is infinite. It cannot be infinite good and infinite evil at the same time. It must be one or the other. Which one? Christian Science declares that we never will know God aright, and never will know the living God, until we know that our God is Good, and mean—when we know it—that good is absolutely apart from evil, uncontaminated; that God, Good, is not involved in evil in any way, does not make use of it; that God, good, is not the author of disease, has not procured it for any purpose whatsoever, but is altogether contrary thereto. As I pass by this statement, I want to tell you what Christian Science declares, because the world's contrary belief of God has involved it in the unspeakable agony of the ages, and every man and woman pays the awful and destructive penalty for the blasphemous assumption that God does evil and inflicts evil on the world.

Fear of God Exposed

Educate mankind as we have been educated, to believe that God sends the earthquake and the fire and the pestilence and famine and disease and woe and disaster to men, and you will educate them all to be afraid of God, afraid of what He has done or may do or will do. I know just about what some of you will say to that statement. I have known people to get up and go out because I have said it. I will ask you: Are you afraid of insanity? Would you be afraid if you saw it rushing in upon you? Yes. Are you afraid of unbearable anguish?

Yes. Are you afraid of the ravages of disease? Yes. Are you afraid, instinctively or actively, of death? Yes. And if you believe God causes all these things, are you afraid of God? Yes.

Fear and the Devil Largely Synonymous

That is not all. This universal fear on the part of the universal race constitutes the primary cause of nearly all the havoc and tragedy of mankind; nearly all of it springs therefrom. This universal fear on the part of mankind is the cause of nearly all sin, nearly all disease, all poverty and all the rancor among nations. It comes about as nearly being all of the devil as anything you can think of. "Thou shalt have no other gods before me." Thou shalt have no other God than the one that is Good. Christ Jesus was the Son of the God that is infinite Good, who hath done all things well, and hath done no evil at all.

God's Law Is the Law of Perfection

Again, what is the meaning of God? What is God's law? We hear much about the law of God. According to Christian Science, God's law is the law of perfection, of health, of Life, of infinite good. Thou shalt have no other law than the law of Life, and let me say incidentally that Christian Science teaches that God has ordained no law for your discomfort, no law of disease for you. On the contrary, all the law that is necessary for your recovery from sickness, all the power necessary, all the action necessary, are in this room now, are in any room you have ever been in, are with you always, a very present law of Life and good, and you do not need to procrastinate your recovery. You do not need to wait; you do not need to implore God to do something He has not done for you. All you need to do is to stop being afraid and learn that in our God and His law and His power we have an ever-present help that is the healer of all diseases. Thou shalt have no other law to govern you than the law of health and Life.

Lay Hold Upon Your God-Given Dominion

Well, what else about the living God? What has God ever done for you? You have been educated to believe that God created you and then furnished you with the sting of pain and the blight of disease, burned down your houses, and all that sort of thing. What must we know in order to get right? We must know that God, good, gave man—provided for man—dominion over all the earth, and that surely means dominion over your body and over your own business and over your household affairs and over your surroundings and environments and conditions. It means that you should be master of your foe instead of its victim. It means that you are to learn that your dominion is essentially, divinely prescribed and divinely operative, and that the only thing for you to do is to lay hold upon it, to manifest it.

Right Knowledge of God Includes Knowledge of Dominion

Well, what is the situation? Who believes he has any such God? Who believes that this is a divine provision? Who manifests dominion over all the earth? Not one. Not one left on earth to tell the tale of divine benevolence; not one. And Christian Science teaches that we will never know God aright, never know heaven, never know Life, never know felicity, until we know enough to know that God provided for us the means of destroying evil.

Should Not Absolute Good Be Attributed to God?

What say you of the ever-living God? Am I degrading your estimate of our Heavenly Father? Does it in any way impair your confidence in God to have me plead in His name, that you shall learn that God is good, and that Good has done nothing for you but provide life and prosperity and welfare and heaven and joy and peace? Is that too good, or is it too bad, to believe about God?

The Claim That Jesus Was God

"Thou art Christ, the Son of the living God." And what is the Son of God? Again you ask the question and you get a million answers, because no two people believe alike concerning Christ and the Christian mission and the real import of Jesus' effort. You will find some people who will tell you that the bodily presence of Jesus was God. They will tell you that his historic corporeality was the deity, and that you should understand that there is no distinction whatever between the man Jesus who was on the Sea of Galilee and Deity Himself.

Jesus Denied Any Claim of Being God

And so, poor dear people, we have been trying to believe that because we are told to, and there are people who will denounce Christian Science as being non-Christian because we deny that the bodily Jesus is God. Now, if a denial is to be in question, let us deny that Jesus is Deity because he specifically denied that he was God. He said that he was the Son of God, and that his Father was greater than he was; and he said that he was going to his Father; and he said there was no good in him, that his Father did the work, and that his Father worked in him, and so on. If any statement can be explicit and to the point, he certainly used clear language to indicate that he was not God.

Supposition That Jesus Was Deity Refuted

Now what are you supposed to do, according to current theology, in order to believe, in order to be rational, in order not to be insane? First of all, you are supposed to believe that Infinity created the universe; then you have got to believe that infinite power or impulsion created the Virgin Mary; then that God or Infinity, the divine law or Principle of being, was given birth by Mary; that God was dead for three days after the crucifixion, and so there was no God during that time; and a lot of things of that kind you have to believe.

And would you find yourself a little bit tired, if you ever realized that your mind was as much of a maelstrom of havoc and chaos as it could be? There is not one who can believe it any more than we can believe that black is white. It is an impossibility for the human mind to conceive. Now, on the other hand, of all the people in the world, I believe Christian Scientists are pre-eminently distinguished for the intelligent acceptance of the declaration that Christ is the Son of God. Not one living more thoroughly, more without reserve, accepts, declares, and lives in established conviction as to the divinity of Christ. How then, are we to reconcile these two things I am saying?

The Christ Defined

Paul says: "Let this Mind be in you which was in Christ." Why? What is the object? Because that Mind which was in Christ overcame temptation and sin, healed the sick, raised the dead, raised Jesus from the dead, moved mountains, overcame obstacles, cast out devils, and demonstrated the power of something to overcome every form of evil. What Mind was it? It was the Mind which people called omniscient for so many ages, intelligent God, which can never be described in any better way, no matter how many names you use, than as the original Foundation or Mind or Intelligence of the universe. We say that it was the Mind that was in Christ which constituted his divinity, which constituted him as Saviour, enabled him to heal the sick and do mighty works. It is the manifestation of God, of Spirit, of spiritual activity; that is the Christ.

Christ Distinguished from Jesus

Now, the body of Jesus is something that you contemplate as having been murdered. Christ was never murdered. **Christ raised Jesus from the dead.** Christ demonstrated the power of God, and the unity of God and man, that raised the dead. So there is the distinction between the bodily Jesus and the divine

Christ. What does the word "Christ" mean? It means Immanuel—"God with us." It would be as though you saw Jesus endowed with extraordinary spiritual understanding, Jesus anointed by the divine Spirit, spiritual-mindedness; and in that spiritual-mindedness we have the Christ. Now, what think ye of Christ, the manifestation of God, the ambassador of God, the Word and will of God manifested to the world? What think ye of Christ?

From What Do Men Need Salvation?

It has been declared that Christ is the Saviour of the world. What does the world need to be saved from? Why, go the rounds of humanity, and one will tell you that he wants to be saved from a broken heart, another from poverty, another from a terrible weight of afflictions; and long before you had seen them all, you would learn that they need to be saved from multifarious forms of evil.

Christ a Saviour from Sin

Now comes the question: What think ye of the Saviour? Have we an irresistible, competent and adequate Saviour, or not? You have been told that the sinner has a Saviour, that the sinner has an adequate salvation through Christ from sin, but you never were told that the insane man has a Saviour, never that the poor man also has. No. Theology bids the sinner hope; it tells the sinner to rejoice, for Christ is his Saviour. It says: "I care not how rotten you are with iniquity; I care not if you are Nero, Judas, if you are the incarnation of hell and damnation, you may be hopeful unto the extreme, any time before you die, because Christ is your Saviour."

But Not a Saviour from Sickness, Says Theology

But to all these sick people, all those who are heavy-laden and disappointed, false theology says: "Why, there is nothing for you to do but weep on, nothing but the intensity of pain, nothing but more gloom and depression. Christian salvation is for bad men, not for sick ones." What think ye of a Saviour? Is he one to save, or not?

Vain Philosophy

What do you need to be saved from? Well, from the mystery of evil. Philosophy has wrestled with this subject for ages and has practically given up its own admitted solution, but this is one thing it declares to you: It says that the fear of today and the sin of tomorrow bind insanity on the sinner. All these miserable things that infest you exist because they have a right to, and they can of their own will make you sick or kill you and you have no adequate resistance; and there is nothing for you to do but to go down and die under them, and be as amiable as possible about it.

Disease Is an Abnormity, and Curable

Now, Christian Science comes with an entirely new tongue. Forty years ago Mrs. Eddy came out from the old form of thought and declared that disease and sin and fear and insanity and all kindred fears are illegitimate, disorders of the carnal mind and not of the divine Mind. She entreated the world to learn this; that evil is destructible and that disease is curable. She declared these things to be abnormities, having no basis, no God, no Truth or Science, and she was stoned. Every discoverer is always stoned. The first one to learn anything true is always stoned. But she continued to publish and to demonstrate and to teach, and this knowledge has multiplied and it has absolutely been a heaven. The physicians are now declaring that if humanity had never departed from the normal, there never would have been any sickness. What do you think of that? Go on another ten years and you will live to see the day when that will be universally declared; namely, that disease is an abnormity.

The Woman with Belief of Feathers

I used to know a woman in an insane hospital who believed that she was all covered with feathers. If you had gone to this woman and said, "Why, Mrs. Lawrence, dear woman, don't you know that you haven't any feathers? This is simply an illusion"; she would have said: "Why, my dear child, feel of my arm; feel all these feathers, how soft and silky they are. Why, dear, of course I have feathers." Now, suppose that lady came to you for treatment. What would you treat her for? Feathers? If not, why not? She says she has them; every time she sees you she says: "I am covered with feathers." Suppose that you were to begin by declaring that this woman had feathers according to divine law. Oh, no, no. You would not do that. Would you have said God furnished her with the feathers? No. Well, suppose the next person said: "I have the smallpox." Would you say God furnished him with the smallpox?

Disease Illegitimate

And so on ad infinitum. Has she got feathers according to divine law and purpose, or not? Are these feathers legitimate, or is the whole thing an abnormity? If it is legitimate, why would you try to cure her? For if it is all rational, you would be irrational to try to cure her. Indeed, a person would be insane if he tried to cure her, unless he did so on the assumption of an abnormity. Suppose she is cured; then you would simply have changed the belief. Now, do you not see what we have to overcome in all forms of disease? I do not think you see it because of my exposition, because I have not said enough about it to warrant a conclusion; but I will tell you that the conclusion is warranted by Christian Science teaching, that all disease is illegitimate. Its origin, its cause, its modus, and its law is illegitimate. That being the case, we advance against disease in the crusade with the understanding that it is unnatural and ought to be abolished.

Christ Jesus Enforced Law

What think ye of Christ Jesus? He knew more than all men combined about God, man, the universe, and law. Everything he did, he did in the wisest way, the natural way, and the lawful way. He healed the sick without a failure, spontaneously; he manifested beyond all cavil that it can be done. He declared that he did it according to the will of God, and that he did it in fulfillment of law, meaning in demonstration of divine law. He did it without any premeditation, without any process whatever. He absolutely attested the adequate capacity of something to heal sickness; and when he overcame it, did he overcome something that God had ordained, or did he overcome a disorder, an illegitimate monstrosity that had frightened the people? Christian Science says that that is what he did when he healed the sick. Now, Paul says that Christ abolished the law of sin and death. What think ye about it? What think ye about Christ? Do **you** think he abolished the law of sin and death? And that means the law of sin and disease, because death is but the culmination of disease, induced by sin, false belief, fear. Did Christ come to abolish divine law? No, no. What does it mean to abolish law? It means to extinguish, to annul, exterminate. What kind of law was it, then, that Christ abolished? Christian Science teaches that it was a spurious sense of law, a spurious pretense of law, admitted by humanity, feared by humanity, and one that has governed humanity, and according to which humanity has sickened and died.

Man Sick with Fever

I will give you an instance of how the spurious law of mortal belief will kill a man. I was visiting several months ago, out West, a lady and gentleman, and found that the man had been sick several weeks with fever. He became very much emaciated and terribly frightened because of loss of weight. His wife told me the doctor had despaired of curing him because he was so frightened. The fear paralyzed his bodily activity and the result was he could not break the fever. She said: "I wish you would go in and see him," and I said: "Well, I will." And I went in, knowing that he did not understand my Science and that I must speak to him on a very simple plane. I addressed him thus: "Do you know that the human body consists of about eighty-five per cent of water?" "Why, no." "Well, it does. You let a man who weighs two hundred pounds lose a hundred, and what he really loses is about ninety pounds of water. That is all. You are in a state of terror and dismay because you think you have lost a lot of nice blood and bones, skin and muscles and stuff of that sort, and the only thing that has happened to you is that you have leaked out a lot of water. Now all you need is to get that water back and you will be all right."

Fever Cured by Eliminating Fear

Then I said: "I will tell you how to get it back. The first thing is for you to stop thinking of all you think you have lost; then to know you do not need to be afraid simply because you think you have lost it; and lastly, that, just as soon as you stop being afraid, because you do not have to be afraid—nobody has to be afraid, the whole thing is gratuitous, absolutely— just as soon as you stop being afraid, your body will resume its normal activity and you will be well." Now, I stayed with him until the corners of his mouth had turned up and the terrified look had all gone, and shortly after his wife wrote me that the fever broke that day. Fear was gone and her husband was getting well, and by way of a little merriment she said: "He is getting that water back, too."

Death Not by Divine Law

Now, that seems like an uncommon incident, but we are doing that all the time. Suppose the man had died in three or four days, as he would, if the fever had gone on—suppose he had died, would he have died because of the law of God?

No. Would he have died because of a law of matter? No. Would he have died because of a law of Life, or death, or because of the law of Science, or anything else? No; he would not. Suppose he had died, and his friends had gotten together and written some resolutions: "Whereas, God, in His inscrutable wisdom has taken our beloved brother from our midst," and so on—you know how they go; you have seen them thousands of times. That is what would have happened if he had died in three days.

Blasphemous Mortuary Resolutions

Now, my dear friends, remembering that we profess to worship a God that is divine Love, one more tender than the tenderest mother—knowing, as we do, that He is consummate benevolence itself, knowing that Christ Jesus pleaded, "Come unto me all ye that labor and are heavy laden"—am I too rough when I say that every such resolution that was ever penned was blasphemous? Do you know a more gentle word whereby to describe this interminable impeachment of our God, which declares He is afflicting a babe while at its mother's breast, making widows of our women by taking their husbands to His bosom? Alas, how long shall we go down to the hell of mental torment for this terrible mistake? What think ye of Christ? Resist satan; "it hath bound the woman." Jesus did not say that God had bound her, and Christ instantly cured her. Satan is the word for evil.

The Carnal Mind, Spurious Law, Satan, Kills

What think ye of Christ? What would have killed the man with the fever if he had died? You do not need to plunge into philosophy or religion or theology. If he had died it would have been simply because he did not know enough to live, that is all. What would have killed him? Carnal mind, enmity against God, enmity against Life, enmity against man, operating through fear, superstition and ignorance and vice and wickedness and everything else. That is the stuff that would have killed him, and kills everybody else, unless Christ comes. Unless a man gets an intelligent understanding of his own Life, God, it will kill every last one. It is the carnal mind, so-called, that means fear; it is the mind that means disease; it is the mind that means hell and damnation; and that is what was killing that man. And do you not see that it was according to a spurious law that he was dying? Just as fast as he could, he was dying under a spurious law, an abomination supposed to be law.

Christ Abolishes the Law, So-called, of Evil

Christ hath abolished the law of sin and death. The whole Christian mission is the enforcement of the law of Life; and all that Christian Science practice is, is the enforcement of the law of Life and health, and the annulment of the spurious law of sickness and death, which is scaring everybody to death. What think ye of Christ Jesus? It is said that he came to seek and save that which was lost, and in doing so reformed the sinner and healed the sick. What did he do that for? Is that a natural purpose, a natural modus? Is that the business of Christ, to heal the sick? Then is it the business of Christ in saving humanity to overcome disease, or not? If so, how did he do it, and what did he have to know, in order to do it?

Christian Science Versus Materia Medica

Let us see about these sick people—whether or not they have a right to be healed, whether they are doing their best to be healed. I do not suppose that there are more than three or four million people in the world who, in the hour of sickness, turn to God instead of to pills. The rest of the thirteen hundred millions all turn to drugs or to material means. You know that. Do you know that, of this thirteen hundred million people, fifty million die every year? Do you know, you who are members of an organization that sanctions the drugging system, that it has practically a monopoly of the whole curative field? The government supports it by means of legislation, gives heed to it upon every occasion, and yields to a demand on the part of the drugging system that all other systems shall be excluded. Do you know that this drugging system has fifty million dead people upon its hands every year? You do not deny it, do you? The statistics compiled by our government, not at all in consonance with Christian Science, declare that fifty million people die every year. And, moreover, one of the celebrated London surgeons declared that more than twenty-five million die prematurely. Even upon this plane, half of them have no business to die; and the drugging system comes to the front with fifty million dead people, half of whom have no business to be dead, and asks the legislature of your state, and of every other state, to exclude Christian Science, which has cured every disease which the drugging system says cannot be cured. Now, Christ Jesus knew all about the healing of the sick, and he knew just what Benjamin Franklin knew, when he declared that, when the science of healing is understood and practiced, it will either prevent or cure all manner of disease. He knew he was at work with that which is omnipotent to abolish disease.

The Attitude of Christian Science

Now, what does Christian Science do? It asks the people who are not dead whether or not they are doing the best they can to live. And it answers its question and says: You are not doing the best that can be done, by employing the drugging system. Your system is inadequate and has in itself no promise that it will ever eradicate disease.

Materia Medica Not a Science

First of all, materia medica is not a science. It does not declare itself to be; it admits that it is not. Its theory and practice change every day. It is advancing or receding constantly. Why, some of you here remember the time when they used to bleed everybody who was sick. The physicians now say that George Washington was bled to death by the doctor who attended him. I remember, if a man stubbed his toe they bled him. Then they began putting leeches on everybody. Then they began giving calomel until people's teeth loosened and fell out. Then they took up first one, and then another theory, until they came to the blue-glass theory, and so on indefinitely, until we have ever so many fads and fancies.

Medical Guess-Work

Take, for example, the appendicitis habit. How common! How popular! I heard a story the other day, down in New Haven, Connecticut. It appears that there was a trolley accident in which a lot of people were injured, and they summoned some physicians and surgeons who examined the people and finally found one man who was unconscious. They could not tell what was the matter. There were no dislocations or bruises, and yet he was unconscious. Not knowing what to do, one spoke up and said: "Well, what do you think of operating on him for appendicitis?" "Well, all right, let's do it; we have to do something." So they took him off preparatory to operating on him, and in taking off some of his clothing, they found about his neck a string, and attached to the string was a tablet. On the tablet these words were inscribed: "In case of accident, please do not operate for appendicitis; my appendix has been cut off twice already." So, then, we object to what is called the theory and practice of medicine, because it is not a science at all. It proceeds after the manner of expediency, is experimental and accidental; and there is no one in the wide, wide world who will more freely admit this than the physician himself.

Materia Medica Does Not Cognize Primary Cause of Disease

Again, we declare it is unscientific, because it does not take cognizance of the primary cause of disease. On the contrary, until recent date, certainly until the hour of the homeopathic physician, the drugging system insisted upon it that matter was the whole cause of disease, and the system treated everybody as though they were just so much matter, so much stuff; and they treated the stuff without any reference to the mental, moral, or spiritual element in mankind. They would put pills into the body, run electricity into the body, bathe the body, and if this did not cure a man, they said that he was incurable. In no instance does Christian Science admit that what the physician says to be cause is cause. You go to a doctor, or let him come to you, and you say: "I want to be cured." "What is the matter with you?" "Stomach is out of order." "What is the matter with your stomach?" "Well, they tell me that the lining of my stomach is irritated." (There is the effect, isn't it?) "Have you any idea why your stomach is irritated?" "Well, I have, I must confess." "Well, what is it?" "Well, whiskey has irritated it." There, according to the matter interpretation of disease, is your cause and effect—whiskey and inflammation. Now, according to Christian Science, neither one of these is the cause, and you have to go way back of that whole business. Perhaps that man drinks whiskey because he inherited the so-called appetite. What are you going to do with that?

Cause of Illness Is Mental

In such a case, that would be the cause of the man's trouble. An inordinate appetite is always abnormal; that is the cause. You may find one person who has indigestion. He is so hateful and full of wrath and anger that he absolutely congests his stomach, and so on. The system that does not take cognizance of fear, which is the chief cause of disease, is utterly unscientific. So Christian Science is a better way because it searches out the false belief which is the mental cause; and it declares that, when you learn what is the cause of disease, you will learn why disease is healable. When you abolish the cause, then the human body resumes its normal activity. The drugging system is unscientific, because it has not shown any ability whatever to cope with disease, but is now about to abandon its own theory. You know, the physicians are abandoning the use of drugs and are admitting their inadequacy; and it will not be very long before the people who use drugs will simply be read about in books as among the barbarians and ignorant people of past ages.

Christian Science the Better Way

Christian Science would be of small value, if it could not conversely declare what is the better way. "There is a better way?" you ask. "What is it?" And before I answer what is the better way, according to Christian Science, I must tell you, alas, that the people who most industriously stone us because of our way are Christian people, inscribing upon their banners that they are followers of Christ and worshipers of God. What is the better way in Christian Science? It is the way ordained of our God, provided by God, fundamentally correct: To know God according to the law of God, according to divine purpose, which was before Abraham was, according to all that means God.

The Way Through Christ

We declare that God is the natural and everlasting healer of all diseases. It is the way through Christ, the way through the Saviour, and the way through him who said that his way was the only way. It is the way demonstrated. What he was trying to teach, and what he brought to mankind, is the way of Christ, scientifically and rationally understood. It is the practical way. It is the way which overcomes the world, the flesh, and the devil; it is the way that overcomes fear and sin and ignorance and superstition and all these things that have involved humanity. What was his way? Why, we declare that Christ Jesus invoked and showed forth the supreme power of the universe, the supreme law, when he healed the sick; and he did it, not by way of mystery or unnatural interference with law, but under the application and benevolent manifestation or demonstration of divine law   And he declared, on the basis of pure knowledge—he did not do it by way of mental suggestion—he declared: "These things shall ye know." "Go and do likewise." "Ye shall know the Truth, and the Truth shall make you free."

Scientists Have Faith in God

Now, we Christian Scientists are derided and scorned and thought to be weak because we have faith in God, because we trust in Him, and because we have faith in the promise: "Thou wilt keep him in perfect peace whose mind is stayed on Thee." Stayed on what? On the assumption that God wants you to be killed—has ordained your diseases and pains? Will they keep him "in perfect peace"? "Thou wilt keep him in perfect peace, because he trusted in Thee." Now, what do Christian Scientists do? What is the law of God to man? We begin, first of all, to stop being afraid—of what? We stop being afraid of devil, hell; we stop being afraid of disease and pain; we stop being afraid, indeed, of the whole philosophy of doom that is carrying mankind down into its own hell; and the consequence is that we Christian Science people are not one-half as much afraid as we used to be, not so often, not so much afraid.

Education in Fear Denounced

I remember how they scared me about my food when I was lying in a sanitarium. You take the people of the world, and they are all taught to be afraid of their bodies, to be afraid of the sun that shines on them, to be afraid of the air they breathe, of the food they eat, and of everything they do or do not do. So universal is the cry of alarm, so insistent is it, that the mother tells the child that it will have to suffer whether it does, or does not do, something. It does not seem to make much difference what the child does; it does not matter, there are more fears told the child than can be put in a book. And when I realize how the world is scaring itself to death, I am reminded of the conclusion of the man who, having studied the subject of damnation, came to the conclusion that you will be damned if you do and damned if you don't.

The Fear of Food

Now, when I was in a sanitarium, supposed to be dying, one would come along and say: "Now, look here, Kimball, cheer up, cheer up. I used to know a man who was sick just as you are, and he got better." "How did he get better?" "Oh, simple enough, simple enough. The man found out beefsteak didn't agree with him, and he just stopped eating beefsteak and got well." No more beefsteak for Kimball. The next day another got well. "How?" "Oh, he gave up eating bread and butter." All right, no more bread and butter for me. Next day another got well. "How?" "Well, he found out that clam soup agreed with him, and he ate enough clam soup to cure him." I sent off to New York and got a barrel of clams, and before I had eaten a peck they made me sick. And they kept on at me until they got me down to baby's food, and then I couldn't digest that. Why? Because I was scared. They scared me out of my digestive apparatus, and from that hour on I could not digest food until Christian Science broke that fear.

Scientists Gradually Cease from Fear

Now I will eat anything and everything, and mix it up indiscriminately as to the hour and time, and if they want to, let them fight it out on the inside. I am no longer afraid of my food, and that is one thing that happens to Christian Scientists—they stop being afraid of first one thing and then another, until it comes to about a thousand; and just as fast as we drop off this insane fear, because we don't have to be afraid, we lose the penalty of it, and you may do the same. No, you do not have to be afraid. Go home tonight and stop it, and tomorrow you will have a new circulation in your blood, a new nervous system; you will digest your food better, you will sleep better, you will do your business better, because you are not afraid.

Christian Science Prolongs Human Life

Fear is utterly illegitimate, altogether disorderly and improper, and the whole of it is simply because you do not know that you are entitled to dominion over every last thing that harasses. Learn this, and that will be the end of fear and the beginning of health. You as an audience will live longer for having heard this lecture than you would otherwise, simply because, henceforward, you will not be so much afraid. I care not if you came here instinctively to reject everything I say, you will live longer, because you will not be so much afraid.

Scientists Learn to Overcome Hatred with Love

We are learning not to hate so much, not to get so angry. We are learning that the most insane thing, the most irrational, suicidal thing for a man to do is to make a hater of himself, for—if there were no other reason—he would hate himself to death. Likewise, we are learning to stop the irrational and foolish bad habits of being envious and jealous and malicious and vicious, and it is because of all this that we do not fight back when all these people are pelting us. I noticed in a paper, today, that somebody, who evidently likes to fight, is going to give a lecture about shams, one of the asserted shams being Christian Science. Now you might think that we would recriminate. But no; we Christian Scientists are taught that it is an abomination before God and a decent community for one religionist to lampoon and assail and malign another who differs from him in belief. I care not what you believe; not one atom do I care. The one important thing for me to do is to know this: that you are entitled to my compassionate consideration; you are entitled to my respect; you are entitled to my applause for all that you do that is in the right direction; you are entitled to my kindest wishes, to my deepest encouragement; and you are entitled to nothing from me but that which means love, charity, loving-kindness, and you must not get anything else from me. I have not even a rebuke or a reproof to one whose light is so dark that he sees nothing in it but the impulsion to strife and bitterness and wrath.

Christian Science Proves Its Worth

Christian Scientists and their religion will stand upon their merits, be judged by their works, be commended because of their beneficent influence, or—they and it will fall. The tongues of men, the ingenuity of slander and defamation and assault, can never overthrow that which justifies its existence, and Christian Science, today, is before the world in justification of itself. Go to the home that has been debauched by a drunkard. See the woman, the mother, the wounded affections, and the unwholesome, starved brood, all in the depths of degradation because of this man. And then reform the man. And, my dear friends, have you not then a practical manifestation of that which justifies itself? And as in the case of the man who was dying, as I saw, have you not done something practical for him, if for no one else? And so on. Follow along the highway of Christian Science practice and find the sinner reformed, and you will find that which justifies itself.

Mrs. Eddy's Answer to Slander

So it is with the defamation of our Leader, who is traduced and lied about and subjected to every abomination and every pusillanimous thing that humanity can try; but it matters not. Every reformer has been stoned; every one of them has been lied about or murdered. And in answer to it all, this dignified woman has no answer to the world other than the innocent rectitude of her purpose, uncompromising honesty, her faithfulness to her mission, and the declaration that it has not been in vain. There are one million people who declare that by means of that mission they have been extricated from the very depths, and brought to all that means health.

"I Know That My Redeemer Liveth"

I wish—I would wish, if I felt it proper to intrude a wish on you—I wish that you might sometime know why it is that so many people declare that they have been cured of incurable diseases and so unspeakably benefited. I do not ask you to believe anything today. I wish you might some day want to know, because whenever you want to know, you can learn; and what you learn the first day will produce a dividend in happiness; the next day another dividend; and before long, possibly to your surprise, you will find heaven opening to you; you will find a balm that heals the wounds; you will find that which casts off the fetters of disease, casts aside alarm and consternation, and begins to reflect God and law and dominion. All that means the right man and the rights of men will reveal it unto you, and you will then say in answer to the question: "What think ye of Christ?"—you will say: "I know that my Redeemer liveth."

HUMANITY'S NORMAL RIGHTS AND POWERS

Lecture at Second Church, Chicago, March 12, 1908

One man is troubled because he cannot have faith in God. He regards Christian Science as a mere vague, intangible, impalpable theory. There is nothing in sight, nothing he can comprehend, touch, taste, hear, or see. When it comes to something you cannot rub on him or stick on him, he thinks nothing is being done. We who are in trouble must learn our way out, and get out in consequence of what we know and can do or accomplish in our own behalf. Moreover, Christian Science comes to tell you that you can do this, that you can both learn and gain dominion. And it also comes to tell you that you can gain nothing in the race by getting sick and dying.

The Universe as Effect Implies Cause

Now, take what we regard as material dependence—consider what the world calls materialism for a moment, and the point I urge upon you is this: If you will contemplate all that is called matter or the material universe, you will come to the conclusion that something has made it, that it exists at the standpoint of effect. Something has produced it; something has been the animating creator of it all. Now, what was it? What is the creator of the universe?

Even Materialism Presents But a Hypothetical, and Therefore a Mental Cause

Go to the materialist and he will tell you that that which lies back of the material universe, including men, is atomic substance, atomic dust. Then he will tell you that the existence of this atomic dust is altogether a matter of theory, that it cannot possibly be observed or cognized by any power that mankind has. Then, when he has told you this, he has given you the only possible basis for a materialistic philosophy; namely, an invisible, imponderable, theoretical, atomic substance which, in the ultimate, is unobservable.

Materialism, if True, Means Extinction of Life

Now, there is one thing which every one in this room has to know. Not one person in this audience or upon this earth can ever reach that which he calls heaven until he learns, appropriates, and applies as law unto himself what I am going to say in the next few minutes. It is this: If the origin and source and foundation of human life is atomic substance, or is in any way procured by atomic aggregation, then every man is doomed to utter annihilation and death. If the atomic theory of creation, or the matter theory of creation, is correct, every man and woman in this room is doomed to extinction.

Proof That Materialism Implies Extinction

Now, why? Because, as a matter of science, as a matter of sheer philosophy, as an irresistible postulate, this is true:— that no phenomenon can possibly rise superior to its noumenon; no effect can rise superior to its cause; and so, if you were caused primarily by atomic substance, you are doomed—you will return to it absolutely. This is what the Bible means when it speaks of "dust to dust." There is not a shred of possible hope for this race in materialism. Every one is damned, not to eternal hell, but to speedy extinction, if it is true. Then the man who, today, works side by side with that philosophy is absolutely sure to sicken and to die; and if his philosophy were correct, he would be extinct. The very law of materialism, the very rule of materialism, demands the disintegration, the disorganization, the decay, the decrepitude and the decomposition of every one of its phenomena; and so mankind will go down under it unless it is rescued by something competent to do it.

Christian Science the Only Sure Antidote for Materialism

Speaking in this behalf, I come to declare unto you that Christian Science alone, of all in the world, promises with assurance to overcome materialism. Not all the theory and all the philosophy and science of all times includes the slightest intimation that you may ever, in any other way, overcome it.

Evolution Fallacy Exposed

Moreover, here is another thing that you will have to learn. We have been fascinated more or less by the modern theory of evolution, which means that an inferior basis or initiative can evolve itself into a state of superiority; and that is utterly impossible. It is amazing that a man so studied, so profound, in what might be called learning, as was Mr. Darwin, did not know enough to know this; did not know enough to know that no fountain can rise higher than its source, no effect can be superior to its cause. It is impossible for nothing to evolve itself into something, for non-intelligence to evolve intelligence. Impossible! You might as well expect a barrel of lime to evolve itself into an angel with wings and sky-blue eyes and a harp and such things, as to expect atomic dust to evolve itself into an intelligent man. Can you think of any more intangible basis for theory than that, one that is so confessedly theoretical, one that declares that there is no possible way whereby you can grasp that which is the basis of being?

Mind, God, Is the Basis of Being

What is the basis of being, according to Christian Science? It is Mind—Mind that does not need to be evolved; Mind that does not need to be improved, does not need to improve its offspring; Mind which is self-existent, which changes not; Mind which is forever perfect, intact; Mind which is its own self-sufficiency, its own law, its own government.

"Choose Ye"

Now, at this point, in this belief in materialism that means sickness, that means pain and inferiority—at this point is where the parting comes, and the question comes to every man: Am I to be governed by the carnal mind which means death, or am I to be governed by the divine Mind which is in Christ; for "to be carnally minded is death, but to be spiritually minded is life and peace?"

Both Power and Law Are Invisible

There are certain important things for every man to consider. One is law. Without law you would have no manifested existence. Law means the enforcement of power, and without power you would have no manifested existence. And I want to call your attention to the fact that both power and law are invisible. You cannot see either one. You may rely upon law and power, and yet none of you ever saw either one of them. None of you were ever able to see or feel or touch either power or law. You have seen power exhibited in action, in concrete form, but you never saw anything except the concrete manifestation of either power or law. Then do you not recognize that you are always depending upon something which is invisible, so far as the senses go?

Power Exhibited in Christian Science Treatment

Now, what is relied upon in Christian Science practice? It is law and power, law and power. And the law and power in Christian Science practice exhibits itself always in concrete form. I have known a person with an invisible and inaccessible tumor to resort to all medical means known to the world; I have known everything that is called material skill and material power to be invoked; and known that person to go on day by day along a tragic course towards the end; and then, I have known that person to be delivered of that tumor in thirty-six hours, because of Christian Science treatment. Think you that it was done without power? Power! Do you not suppose that there was some power manifested in such an exhibition, the concrete exhibit of that power?

The Power Relied Upon to Run a Locomotive Is Just as Invisible as That Relied Upon by Christian Science

Do you demur because the power is invisible? Then you do not know that power is always invisible. Do you demur because the law, likewise, is invisible? Do you demur because the *modus operandi* is not in sight? Do you? Why, my friends, you would be in perpetual demurring if you did, because you have never seen an act which presented the visibility of the power which induced it. Never.

Christian Science Is Working Wonders

Now, the work of healing that is being done in and through Christian Science, through invisible law and power, exceeds that which is being accomplished by all other means. There is nothing known by way of impulsion, by way of initiative, that is accomplishing what Christian Science is doing today. Mountains are being moved, rocks are being rent; things are being done in Christian Science called wonderful and miraculous that have really no parallel except in the days of primitive Christianity. Moreover, let me say to you that the world at large knows very little about it.

The Real Significance of Law

Now, here is another important thing that every one has to know. I will put it more agreeably, that every one may know, and that as soon as he does know it, he will find himself a happier man. It is this upon the subject of law—that all that means primary law, all that means divine law, all that means divine provision for you, all that is included in potentiality by way of law and privilege and provision for you, means for you life, means health for you; it means harmony; it means the overcoming of evil; it means the domination over all that would beset you and torment or molest or hinder you. There is no law against you.

Law Is All in Your Favor

Now, if you mourn, if you have been cast down because of disease, know this: There is positively no **law** against you. And, moreover, know this still further: You are entitled to enforce **law** in your own behalf; you are entitled to enforce the **law** of your own health, of your own prosperity. You may do it; you may learn to do it. It is within the divine provision concerning your very life, your daily needs. Be not afraid. You may be a law unto yourself, a law to your recovery from disease, a law to your business, a law of harmony to your welfare and your household and all the things of your life, because God gave man dominion and you are entitled to it. In this very hour you are entitled to be a law of recovery to your own self.

The Enforcement of Law Illustrated

In Wood's Museum, several years ago, were three little men, each weighing about forty-five or fifty pounds. A man weighing 150 pounds would climb on the shoulders of another man weighing 200 pounds, and one of the little men would clasp his arms about the legs of the man weighing 200 pounds and lift them both. How did he do it? And why? He did it simply because he was a law unto himself, that is all. I saw him do it. He positively did it. He did it because of a human belief of law, controlled in that direction.

Another Illustration of Law-Enforcement

Again, there was a party of men. One agreed that he would wake up at four minutes after five the next morning, and he did it; the next morning that he would wake up at twenty-seven minutes after six, and he did it; the next morning at eighteen minutes after eight, and he did it. And this last was an hour beyond his ordinary waking hour.

Limitation Is Abnormal

You have heard of Blind Tom. He would listen to a piece of music and then go to a piano and play it. He was called phenomenal; but instead of his being abnormal, as compared with him we are abnormal. You have heard of phenomenal lightning calculators, even little boys, who could with spontaneity give you an instant answer to a long problem. They are more normal than we are. Every one ought to be able to do it. Why can't we? It is a mere matter of belief. I have myself lifted one thousand pounds of cold iron, absolutely lifted a thousand pounds of iron. I never could do it until I became a law unto myself, to the accomplishment of it.

Spurious Mortal Law (Belief) Limits

These lightning calculators are able to do wonderful things because they are not bound by so-called laws of limitation and become a law unto themselves. In their ability to do these things spontaneously, they are really more normal than the rest of us, because men should spontaneously know everything that it is right for them to know, since man reflects infinite Intelligence.

The Law of Success

Now, these are a few of the instances, showing the capacity of what we call the human mind to be a law unto itself. Why is it that some business men never fail; or, if they fail, always come out on top? Because they become a law to the belief of their own success; because they put into the scale of being that which is efficacious.

How Employment Is Often Secured

Take, for example, a man who is out of work and wants a situation. What is situation? Why, it is, first of all, the conviction on the part of somebody that he needs a worker and wants to employ some one; next, it is his conclusion that he will do so; and lastly, it is his decision that he will employ you, if you please. Now that is the situation—all mental. The whole matter of situation exists at the standpoint of supply and demand, which, scientifically understood, are one and the same in the mind of the employer and employee. Now, suppose that you spend all your time being afraid that you will not get the situation. Have you the slightest concept of what you are doing? Do you know what you do to your situation when you spend your time being afraid you will not get it? You scare it off; positively, you are doing that which will mesmerize it away from you. Now, take the man who is buoyant, expectant, whose very attitude is law. What does he do? He does not spend any time being afraid. No; he knows he will get something, and that becomes a law of success both to the employer and employee.

The Divine Law of Possession

That is all simply in the realm of limited, finite mentality. Now, let me carry it up and consider this one thing in Christian Science: That the Creator of man created with him and for him the law of his own continuity and sufficiency; the law of his dominion; the law of his control over circumstances and conditions; the law of his felicity and his heaven; and the law concerning all that means his life, all that means his health, his environment and all that this implies; did it all fundamentally, with the result that man is perfect, unhampered, unobstructed and unhindered; and all this is so available that this man is enabled to be a law unto himself. And the teaching of Christian Science is simply this: That every one of you may learn that you are entitled to unlimited power and control and welfare to yourself. There is not one here that may not be a law unto his own life; and if I had not learned that years ago, I would have died long before this.

When you understand law, you lose fear, become confident, and maintain health and success.

Of what consequence is it for you to know, or even believe

or hope, that you may be a law of life and control and welfare unto yourself? Simply this; if you know that you have righteous control, you never again will be afraid of anything in the world; and when, for that reason, you lose all fear, you will lose all that means hell, because fear is pretty much all there is to hell or devil or disease or pain. There is too much of it; and the reason we are in hell, in belief, according to this sense of insistent mental aberration, is simply because we have been discouraged by the philosophy of doom and submission to sickness and to the supposed law of sin and death. Now then, of what service is Christ to the man thus involved? Why, Christ has abolished, does abolish, is the abolition of, the extinction of, the spurious, abominable thing called "the law of sin and death."

Preaching the Gospel Heals the Sick

Never more than two or three times in my lecture work have I attempted to speak about the law of heredity. I did it Tuesday night, and I have heard since then of three people at least who were then and there healed of hereditary diseases; and I was asked in particular to speak of it again.

Depressing Effect of Belief in Hereditary Contamination

There is nothing more mischievous today than that miserable sense which declares itself over and over, asserting that men inherit diseases and evil propensities, that these are irresistibly and naturally carried on from parent to child, and that hereditary taint, impairment and contamination can be transmitted from one generation to another. Nothing is more discouraging to the patient than to be told, or to believe, or to hear, the supposition that he is sick because of hereditary contamination.

Human Heredity no Actual Law, but a Lie Posing as Law

Now, Christian Science comes to explode that outrage, to undo it, and to end all fear about it. There is positively no such law. All the so-called procurement of disease and taint by what is called hereditary disease is utterly false, gratuitous and illegitimate, and may be avoided and all of it overcome, every bit of it.

The Scientific Enforcement of the Law of God Abolishes the Effects of Seeming Hereditary Influences

The person who says he has hereditary rheumatism does not need to be treated for rheumatism at all. You might treat that person for rheumatism for a century, and you could not possibly heal him. I have known people to be healed in five or ten minutes, many of them of so-called hereditary diseases which they had had for ten to forty years, through Christian Science treatment; and the whole thing was done by the scientific abolition and extinction of the supposed law of heredity. It is not law at all, not in the realm of law, but in the realm of universal mortal belief and fear which operate as law, though spurious and false; and you who may have been cast down by the thought that you are under this law, you may take heart. Tonight,—indeed, in this very hour, at this moment, by this very Word, by reason of the law and power which are a law of extermination and elimination to every such thing,— you are now emancipated, you are now redeemed, you are now free. You are no longer under the distress of the supposed hereditary law of doom. Now, this is all that needs to be done to heal any one of a supposedly hereditary disease.

Christ Jesus Did Not Destroy, but Fulfilled Law

What did Christ do? What did he come to do? He came to do the will of God, to do according to the divine Mind. He came to show the law. What law? The law of Life, the law of health. He came to seek and to save that which was lost, and to do something for the lost. And he did it. And when he did it, he expelled and abolished nothing that had a right to exist, nothing that was originated of God, nothing that was inherent in nature or according to nature's laws. He overcame mistaken and illegitimate and spurious manifestations and a spurious sense of law.

All Diseases Healed by Cancellation of Spurious Conditions

It is a fact that consumption, blindness, the worst forms of Bright's disease, epilepsy, locomotor ataxia, leprosy, tuberculosis, and so on, all have been healed. What was done? Nothing more than the cancellation, by extermination, of a spurious condition; that was all. And that will go on being done until, in the course of time, this race will be redeemed from sickness.

Dispositions Transformed

Take a man who has a temper; it is always breaking out; he is disagreeable to everybody. He will tell you that he inherited it from his mother, perhaps. Some men claim that they inherit it from their mothers-in-law. We will suppose that he inherited it from his great-great-grandfather. What are you going to do about it? You cannot go and fight it out with his great-great-grandfather. He may put mustard plasters on himself and take mud baths, with no effect. The only thing that will transform that man in one minute, is to relieve him of that blight of hereditary law; and the same thing is true of the drunkard. Most drunkards are healed by, and because of, the abolition of that so-called law, which is not law, but lawlessness.

"Climbing Up Some Other Way" for Healing

Here is a distinct proposition in Christian Science: Christ, doing the will of God according to the divine purpose, in the fulfillment of law, healed the sick without a failure, healed the multitude of all manner of diseases, and he did it spontaneously. He healed the sick in the only right way; there is no other way of doing it. Take these propositions and they can be proved. God, divine Mind, is the healer of all diseases. That means that that which is God is equal to the healing of them all, and Jesus Christ demonstrated that. He did it in the only right way to do it. And every one on earth, pretty much, is trying to get well some other way, and they keep on trying and trying, and they keep on dying at the rate of fifty millions every year. One would almost think they would try the Christ way. Wouldn't you?

Dominion Is Yours for the Learning of It

Is this a race which is essentially and irrevocably doomed, irretrievably doomed, or not? Have you an inherent or continued right to exist, to exist in a state of health and self-containment and sufficiency? Are you under the stress of tragedy, disaster and disease, or not? Is there hope, or not? Are you in the grasp of an unavoidable doom, or not? It is an important question. And the answer has always been that you are a child of fate, that you are a bubble on the sea of capricious existence, and that you are liable to be stricken and to die at any time. The answer of Christian Science is: No; you are not doomed. You may learn to live; you may learn to exercise dominion over all the earth. But you will never learn until you learn the right way, the Christ way.

The Right Way to Dominion

Now, what is the right way? The right way is that way which employs the supreme power of the universe, the power which is equal to the overcoming of every semblance of power, that is equal to every emergency, that can silence every opposition, and undo everything that even tries to pretend to be something. The supreme power of the universe affords the only right way. Where is it? It is where you are, any time and every time, and is always available to you. To what extent is it available to you? It is always all that is needed; and if you will stop being afraid, you will win.

Unlimited Ability and Possession Is Normal

What is it that will break down the only mischief-maker of humanity? What is the right way? It is the way that will abolish fear. Fear is the chief curse and torment of this race. The only thing that will break it is the Mind that is in Christ, Truth, the Mind that will be in you just as soon as you begin to learn the way. How much mental dominion have you? Precious little. How much ought you to have? Unlimited dominion. That is the difference between Blind Tom and me. He could do something that I could not, and he is more natural than I. The difference between the little men that we now seem to be and the man who is our real self is apparent because we have not yet risen to the supersensible perception of the vastness of the possibilities of our own one Mind.

Your Real Hereditary Endowment, Transmitted by Your Father, God

You do not need to regard Christian Science as complex at all, nor far off, nor unattainable. It simply means this: that the only Creator of the universe, long before the material sense of universe appeared, by law, by design and purpose, decreed and provided that you, as man in the divine likeness, were, and should be entitled, first to life, then to health, then to activity, then to faculty, to joy, to heaven, and to dominion over everything. You are entitled to felicity, to control, and you, as a human, are not to gain this by miraculous and mysterious interposition, but because you by your very fundamental, spiritual nature have the right to exercise all by way of control.

The Power to Remove Mountains of Obstacles Is Normal

Now try it. Did you ever move a mountain? I have done things that were equivalent to moving mountains by being a law unto the case, and Christian Scientists are doing these things every day. There are people in this room, possibly a hundred, that have moved mountains, that have done things that were absolutely as miraculous as that; and they have done them by that which is their normal birthright, the consciousness of divine Mind. I do not mean any power and merit of their human selves, but the demonstration of power, the manifestation of power, to which they have a normal, spiritual right.

Expectancy without Measures Is Rational

There is not one here who may not go from this building tonight having lost fear, and having assumed hope. There is no limit placed upon what you may reasonably expect. Limitation is a spurious, illegitimate belief that may be abolished. When it is abolished, you spontaneously recover from the so-called law of trouble. Every one in this room is entitled to spontaneous recovery, not because of some tremendous upheaval or reconstructive process, but because it is God's law unto you as **man**, the consciousness of divine Mind.

Victory Is Your Normal Right

You are bound to win. Be not afraid. It makes no difference what the trouble is, keep at the winning. You are bound to win. It may not be speedy; you may not get rid of the ghost of trouble at once. I did not; the belief with me was that my inherited temperament interfered. Some people are healed quickly; some are not. I was of the latter class. If I had been healed quickly, I would probably have given up Science, or, at any rate, would not have gained in the measure that I have the understanding of Christian Science. I have known people to be discouraged even unto death. Be not afraid. When evil besets you, turn at once. Resist the fear. Do not give up; do not yield. You are entitled to win, for all that means power and law are on your side.

KIMBALL REPLIES TO CHAPMAN

Lecture Delivered at Fifth Church, Chicago,
September 28, 1906

In the month of August, an Associated Press despatch was sent broadcast to the newspapers of the United States and was generally published by them. It was stated as follows:

Chapman, the Evangelist, Scores Christian Science

Warsaw, Ind., Aug. 20.—Speaking at the opening of the eleventh annual Bible conference at Winona Lake, this morning, the Rev. Mr. Chapman arraigned Christian Science, saying:

"False doctrines have arisen, and chiefest of those is Christian Science. The Christian Scientists dishonor our Lord. Anything which covers or hides the purpose for which Christ came is false and ought to be rebuked."

Mr. Kimball Replies to Mr. Chapman

It is my purpose to give some attention to this statement because it is utterly false and utterly unjustifiable.

Sectarianism

The history of religious sects and activity declares that sectarian antipathies and rancor have shamefully disfigured humanity. Men have instinctively been searchers after God, and in their search have stopped to formulate innumerable conceptions of Deity, most of which have been absurd, fantastic, impossible, but being good, bad or indifferent, as the case may have been, they have all fallen in line with the inveterate propensity of sectarian intolerance to waylay and to obstruct or destroy everything unlike themselves and particularly to make common cause against every new phase of religious thought.

Ecclesiasticism, Crimes of

History declares that in this behalf sectarian strife has done every foul and ruthless thing that the human mind could discover or invent, and impeaches it as having been the monster assassin of the race. It also records the fact that the Christian sects have afforded no exception to the rule, but, on the contrary, have conspicuously stained themselves with the blood of unrighteous conflict and the poison of falsehood. Alas that the Christian church, whose glory has added luster to the centuries, has not yet learned to "put up the sword."

The Conflict of Creeds

A half a century ago there were more than one hundred Christian sects on earth claiming to be representative of the Christianity of Christ and each one justified its separate existence and aloofness on the ground that it was different from all the others, and in many instances so vastly different that reconciliation was impossible, yea inconceivable.

Christian Science Appears

Upon this scene a generation ago, when every Christian sect admitted that it was different from all the rest, the religious sect which is designated as Christian Science made its entrance and declared itself to be likewise different from all the rest. In that hour when scores of Christian sects were in confessed disagreement as to what Christianity is, which one, if any, was qualified to define with unerring amplification the substance, vesture and activity of pure Christianity? It is doubtful if any of them would have admitted that any other one was thus qualified, and yet, ignoring the incongruity of the act, they, with characteristic unanimity, stoned the newcomer and declared it un-Christian, simply because it was different from them, which were also different from each other.

TEACHING AND ADDRESSES

Scientists Too Wise to Repine

I believe that we are too wise to repine much because the Christian Science movement has been so pitilessly maligned, so stung by misrepresentation and libel; too wise not to expect that history will repeat itself and that enmity will continue to smite Christian Science until Christ reigns on earth absolutely. It would be folly to yoke ourselves in unprofitable contest with every one who chooses to misrepresent or defame. We ought to be too dignified to contend with each self-appointed marauder whose challenge is couched in a falsehood, which should not be dignified by means of a denial.

Falsehood Exposed

Ten years ago, the opponents of Christian Science were industriously announcing that we do not believe in God. By means of its Lecture Board and the other agencies at the disposal of the denomination, this falsehood has, within these ten years, been so thoroughly exposed and refuted, that, by this time, the one who would utter it well knows that he would instantly be accounted grossly ignorant or grossly dishonest. Recently, as if by concert of action, these same opponents, intent on bringing Christian Science into disrepute and upon obstructing its influence, are declaring that it is in denial of the mission of Christ.

Sectarian Differences

Among religious people of today, many say that God foreordained the damnation of some of His creatures. Many others say He did not. Many claim that He has ordained the damnation of unbaptized infants, and others say He has not. Some say that He has provided for the damnation of the heathen, and others say not. Millions believe in the confessional and in absolution as being essentials of Christianity, and other millions believe they are not. Some believe in probation after death; others deny it. Many believe in eternal punishment in hell, and others reject such belief.

Unity Lacking in Doctrines of Churches

I might go on indefinitely in the mention of such antipodes as these, all of which make conspicuous the fact that the Christian sects hold widely different views as to what constitutes Christianity, and, in doing so, I would disclose the fact that there is no unity of Christian beliefs, and no universal, faultless standard among them from which to sit in judgment on Christian Science. Moreover, we freely admit that the one whose estimate of God includes the belief that our infinitely good heavenly Father requires the damnation of a little irresponsible baby, because some one has neglected to baptize it, will hardly approve of Christian Science, which insists that Jesus was right in declaring, "for of such is the Kingdom of Heaven."

Reprisals Not Made by Scientists

Although other people license themselves to indulge in indiscriminate and offensive references to Christian Science and its exponents, we are taught never to make any reprisals nor to retort in kind. Nevertheless, there is no intention to endure without protest or correction such statements as the one I am to consider at this time. I would be glad if we might regard it as being simply an innocent mistake, but, on the contrary, it is a gratuitous, inexcusable wrong. The one who utters it, with intent to discredit a people who claim to be Christians, assumes a grave responsibility.

Teaching of Christian Science Concerning Christ

In refutation of this wrong, I shall make a brief statement, not merely of my views, but of the teaching of Christian Science concerning the divine Christ and the nature of his mission. In the text-book of Christian Science, "Science and Health, with Key to the Scriptures," by Mrs. Eddy, she has done this far better than I can do it, and with greater amplification than this limited hour affords me. To anyone who will investigate the subject, this book is urgently commended, and the promise is made that whoever may study it with an hospitable willingness to learn the real meaning of the author, rather than with a predetermined intention to mangle and pervert her meaning, will learn that Christian Science is pre-eminently Christian, honoring God and Christ in its every word. Although not attempting to use her phraseology or to republish any part of her book, it is proper to say that no Christian Scientist does more in making such an explanation than to reproduce in part or to reiterate what she has already written and taught on the subject.

What Is God?

In order to consider properly the mission of Christ, it is essential to know what was the cause, animus and inducement of that mission. By common consent the Christian sects will all concede that the one infinite God was the author thereof, and that it was in accord with His nature, purpose and law, and this admission compels the inquiry, What is God? Millions of opinions obtrude themselves upon the attention of the world in reply to this question. Contemplating the vast network of finite conjecture concerning the Infinite One, some one has aptly said, "Every man is the creator of his own god." Paul, who understood that God is Spirit, declared that He must be spiritually discerned and this great truth upsets and annuls all human, anthropomorphic conceptions and abolishes all manlike and man-made gods.

God Described

It is impossible for human terminology adequately to depict infinite Spirit, but to the extent that recourse is had to a form of words, thereby to exalt human conception, they must at least declare that God is one supreme, infinite, self-existent, all-inclusive, spiritual, individual, self-conscious Being; that He is the sole creator of all that has actual, legitimate existence, and is therefore the origin, cause, source, basis, foundation, and Principle of all actual things, and the government and law which control all things.

God Is Life, Truth, Love

The definition must declare that God is Life, meaning thereby that He not only is Life, but has ordained all that manifests Life, and is the positive, changeless, ever-active law of life to all that He has created. God is Truth, meaning thereby that He is Omniscience, all science, all wisdom, intelligence, all Mind. God is Love, meaning that He is Good, wholly, always, necessarily, and that He hath done all things well.

God Is Omnipresence and Omnipotence

God is Omnipresence, meaning that the only real, eternal presence, substance and continuance is and will be spiritual. God is Omnipotence, must mean that Good, Spirit, is the only, actual and supreme power. The omnipotent God is indivisible as power, is adequate and irresistible, without an equal or a competitor.

The Relation of God to Men

The realm of God, Spirit, is the spiritual, and "to be spiritually minded is life and peace." The relation of God toward His children indicates that God is more benevolent than the fondest parent, more tender than the tenderest mother, more watchful than the most faithful shepherd.

Another Definition of God

This is a diluted abridgement of Mrs. Eddy's definition of God. Thus she has presented the pure, spiritual science of Being. By way of a correlated analysis or definition, Christian Science teaches that God is incorporeal,—"without body, parts or passions"—that He is inorganic, non-structural, imponderable, and that He cannot be discerned by what are called the material senses of mortals, which senses promise nothing but the annihilation of men.

God versus Evil

Christian Science teaches that God's immaculate nature and allness does not include evil, that He does no evil and does not co-operate with evil, and does not need to have recourse to it in order to accomplish good.

God Transcends Description

The unspeakable glory of God, the supreme sovereignty of His spiritual perfection and completeness, His limitless beauty, holiness and volition,—all that means our adorable God,—surpass immeasurably in majesty and sublimity the poor words of mortals, who, as yet, see through a glass darkly. Nevertheless, in this transitional hour, when words lend wings to ideas and serve as heavenward guides, I venture to ask you to sit in judgment on this inexcusable insinuation, and declare to yourselves whether or not the words of Christian Science dishonor God.

God Is Changeless Good

Is it dangerous to plead that God is changless Good? Is there mischief in the entreaty that mortals will turn from the fatal philosophy of materialism and become acquainted with God as Spirit and find heaven as the result? Are we a menace to the race in reiterating the words of the apostle: "To be carnally minded is death, but to be spiritually minded is life and peace"? Ought we to be stoned because we expect too much in the hour of peril and are taught to obey His every mandate and to live without reproach before Him?

Theology of Christian Science

The theology of Christian Science is based on the foregoing postulates. All the derivatives and correlatives of this theology are in consistent and exact accord therewith. They constitute the basis of all correct reasoning and conclusions. Everything unlike this primary statement concerning God is rejected as being unsound and unlike God. Mrs. Eddy contends that the mission of Christ was in exact accord therewith and that any theory concerning that mission which does not parallel this asserted divine nature, will and law, is erroneous. In her text-book she has grandly explained the application of this divine Science, this spiritual theology, as to the uplifting of a fallen race, and I am obliged to use almost her exact words in order to do any justice to the idea.

Mission of Christ

It is this: that the divine will and power, God's law, which is the law of immortal harmony and perfection to His own,—the things of His creating,—is conversely "the law of annihilation to all that is unlike God,"—the law of extinction to sin, vice, and all that defiles and distresses humanity. This divine law of annihilation to evil indicates the motive, the initiative of Christ's mission,—the manifestation of God for salvation through Christ.

The Divinity of Christ

What is the Messiah? What is the truth about Christ Jesus? What does the name mean? It means Jesus, the anointed. As one wise person has expressed it, it means "Jesus possessed of spiritual understanding and power without measure." The historical Jesus was born of a woman; his body, his bodily presence or corporeality, was not God. He knew it was not God nor a part of divinity. Speaking of the human sense of himself he said, "Of myself I can do nothing." "Why callest thou me good?" The chemical elements that constituted the body that was born of Mary do not constitute immortal, indestructible Spirit, and are no part of God. What and wherein then is the divinity of Christ? What was it that was the son, the offspring of the living God? Paul said, "Let this Mind be in you which was also in Christ Jesus." Why? Because it is the Mind that overcame sin and reformed the sinner; it healed the sick; it raised the dead, raised Jesus from the dead and overcame every law of evil and of matter that was inimical to the welfare of mankind.

The Mind of Christ

What mind was it which was in Christ Jesus? The Bible refers to the Mind that is Spirit, "to be spiritually minded is life and peace"; and it also refers to "the carnal mind which is enmity against God." Which mind was in Christ Jesus? He himself explicitly declared the answer. He said, "My Father doeth the work." "My Father worketh in me." Is his Father Omniscience, all knowledge, all truth? Was it not this all-knowledge, this divine Mind, that worked in Christ Jesus? Was it less than the divine Mind? Could it be more? Is there any rationally conceivable explanation of the words of Jesus other than that the Mind which was in Christ Jesus is the Mind that is God? Did not this Immanuel constitute the divine sonship, the divine Christ who was the manifestation of God, begotten only and wholly of God, and expressing the unity of God and Christ which was declared in the words, "I and my Father are one?" This explanation alone is unmysterious, fathomable, convincing, satisfying. What then was the Saviour, the Messiah? It was the Mind which was in Christ Jesus and which antedated Abraham.

The Saviour's Mission

Why did the Saviour come? The Scriptures state that he came to do the will of God. What God? The God that is good and that has already done all things well. The spiritual understanding of Good manifested by Jesus came as the representative of God, to do wholly according to the divine nature, and it ought to be concluded that all the acts of Christ Jesus were in such accord. The Scriptures also state that Christ came to fulfill law. What law? The law of God, the law of Life, of perfection, completeness, harmony,—the law of health. This simple statement that Christ came to demonstrate law ought to have sufficed to withhold men from the utterly untenable supposition that Christ Jesus acted in contravention of law in healing the sick, and thereby upset the order of nature and of the universe.

Humanity's Need of a Saviour

What was his mission? The Bible says he came "to seek and to save that which was lost." What did he find that was lost? He found a world that was involved in sin, ignorance, vice, disease, woe, oppression, tears; it was in every way insufferably disturbed by the hard attrition of evil.

Saved from What?

How much of this evil which defiles and tortures humanity does Christ come to save men from? What does the world need to be saved from? Go ask each one of the people of earth, "What would you be saved from?" and you will get by way of answer, "Oh, from these bitter tears," or, "from this breaking heart," or, "from the agony of disease," "from insanity," "from the bondage and penalty of sin and fear and from the law of sin and death." Ask the question and get the answer, and you will learn that a fallen, lost race needs to be saved from everything that is evil.

Salvation to Be Complete

Was it and is it the mission of Christ to save from all evil and to abolish the law of sin and death? Christian Science declares that such is Christ's mission, and insists that that mission is adequate, unlimited, ample. Does it dishonor our Lord Jesus Christ to declare that his work was to "overcome the world, the flesh and the devil," meaning thereby all evil? The Bible states explicitly that his mission was to destroy the works of the devil. In pursuit of his mission, what did he do? He reformed the sinner, healed the sick, raised the dead, and did other mighty works for the relief of humanity. Inasmuch as Jesus indicated his sense of disease by saying, "Satan hath bound the woman," and in consideration of other similar statements in the Bible, can it be said, in defiance or ignorance thereof, that Christian Science dishonors Christ in declaring that sickness is one of the kinds of evil which he came to destroy and did destroy.

The Nature of Sin

Christ came to deliver the world from sin. What is sin? Did God create it? Is it like Him or unlike Him? Is it a part of the reality of being which He made and pronounced good? Does God co-operate with sin? does He give it deliberate sanction or permission; does it possess, in spite of God, all the elements of self-continuance and immortality?

Christian Science Teaching Concerning Sin

What is the discovery or revelation of Christian Science concerning this mystery of evil? Considered as a phenomenon of human experience, sin is a form of moral insanity, the intoxication and delirium of wickedness. Compared with the Mind which was in Christ, sin is the paraphernalia of the so-called carnal, fleshly, mind, an utter abomination, destructive, inexcusable, intolerable, awful.

Sin Is All that Is Unlike God

With undeviating discrimination, Christian Science pronounces as sin all that is unlike or contrary to the pure Mind which was in Christ Jesus, and points out the inevitable punishment which sin imposes on its victim. From the standpoint of Christian Science, sin is abhorrent and fatal, and from this standpoint it entreats the sinner to absolutely abandon sin. The word of Christ Jesus is a warning to mortals that they must forsake sin in order to escape the hell (mental torment) which sin kindles within its victims. Considered as a phenomenon of the carnal or mortal mind, all of which is "enmity against God," sin in its all phases, including its consequences, sickness and death, is found to be a monstrous abnormality, a disorder, an illegitimate impropriety, having no basis in God or Truth, no inherent power of continuance, no immortality. It is the very opposite of the reality which constitutes divine Spirit and God's actual creation, and is the antipode of spiritual righteousness. Jesus clearly indicated the nature of sin by designating it a lie.

Mrs. Eddy's Teaching About Sin

I do not believe that any one living more fully understands the nature of sin than does Mrs. Eddy. No one more fully sees the necessity of exterminating it. No one more radically denounces it or deplores it, and yet she knows and says concerning this offspring of ignorance and degradation that it is in the realm of awful unreality, the riot of a false sense of life. She says that mortals are making a reality of that which is scientifically unreal; that which is a fraud and imposition, the impure invention of evil,—false belief.

Unreality of Sin No Excuse for License

No one makes a poorer use of that which he calls his mind than he who rushes precipitately and prematurely to the conclusion, that this scientific, Christlike analysis gives license to sin, or ignores it. No sane person can intelligently read Mrs. Eddy's works on this subject with honest purpose, and arrive at any other conclusion than the one which I have stated; but in order that there may be no uncertainty about this refutation, I will say that because of the practical application of Christian Science to humanity, the Christian Scientist recognizes and contends against all the phenomena of sin. He knows that, to all intents and purposes, all mortals are sinners and are under condemnation.

Need and Means of Salvation From Sin

He realizes that they are as disastrously involved in sin as though it were a legitimate entity and a part of God's kingdom. He knows that it is unpermissible and in violation of divine law, and he knows that mortals must turn from it in order to be saved, and that they will suffer for it until they are redeemed.

He knows that there is but one Saviour and one way, and that Christ, spiritual understanding of Truth, is that Saviour and Way. He knows, moreover, that Christ Jesus, as the Son of God, afforded a mediatorial intercession, and pointed the way to at-one-ment, through which mortals may be delivered from sin and its hell of punishment.

Sin, Differing Views of Its Nature

The distinctive difference between Christian Science and other phases of religious belief is that they hold that sin is a part of reality, is natural and is as indestructible as good itself, whereas we hold that it is wholly temporal and destructible, the spawn of an evil philosophy, and is no more a part of the naturalness of real being than hysteria and delirium are among the normal concomitants of human existence.

Christian Science Does Not Deny Atonement of Christ

The condition of belief which seeks to crucify Christian Science has, with indecorous violence to its teaching, forced the erroneous conclusion that, because Christian Science denies the reality of sin, it necessarily denies the atonement of Christ. After erecting this man of straw, it proceeds to revile and stone it, and to continue in ignoble service its own unwarranted conclusion. If this wrong thing were true, it would indicate a perversion on the part of Christian Science that would be equivalent to the denial of the services of a physician who had healed an insane patient, but whose work was repudiated on the ground that insanity is abnormal.

Christ the Only Way

The ordinary layman protests against the numberless creeds, dogmas, doctrines, beliefs, and theories which encumber human thought with their confusion. Therefore, in correcting this false conclusion, I will avoid all technicalities and say that Christian Science teaches that the human being who is to be saved can only be saved because of God and through Christ. It teaches that every step of the way from the mire of his sinful living to the glory of a pure heaven, every footstep of reform, every touch of truth that is to purify and exalt him and to procure his redemption and deliverance from evil—all this must be and may be accomplished because of what Christ is, what Christ has done and will do. There is no other way; and this way demands more than morality, more than mere ethical probity; it demands spiritual regeneration.

Christ's Commands

According to Christian Science, Christ Jesus was the voice of God, and therefore the voice of pure Christianity to all men throughout all time. The supposition that he spoke to but one particular age or for a limited personnel is far below the grandeur of his ministry. As the voice of universal Truth he said, "Go, preach," "Heal the sick," "I am the way," "Follow thou me," "The works that I do shall ye do also," "Ye shall know the truth, and the truth shall make you free."

Should Christians Heal the Sick

Did he mean what he said, or was the utterance a mockery? Did he mean that men needed to obey this divine mandate? Did he mean that Christians must preach the gospel according to his way, or not? Has any one divine authority for declaring that he meant one and did not mean the other? Is it reasonable to regard his works as correct interpreters of his words? If so, is it legitimate to believe that his work of healing the sick indicated that, according to his word, it ought to be done and can be done? Is it sacrilegious to heal according to his command and way? If so, is it also sacrilegious to be pure in heart according to his command and way? Do the Christian Scientists dishonor Christ in seeking to obey every mandate, to heed every rule, and to follow in his way without evasion or rebellion?

Immaculate Conception

Christian Scientists believe in the immaculate conception. They believe that there is but one divine Christ and that there will be no other. They believe that no mortal is equal to Christ and that there will be no equal. They believe that Christ Jesus' entire work was of divine impulsion. They believe that the Messiahship of Christ affords the only possible forgiveness of sin and that Christ alone can effect the reconciliation of mankind to God.

Proofs Given by Christ Jesus

Christ Jesus gave proof of the supremacy of Spirit and manifested to mortals, in every word and act, the power of God, Good, over all evil. He confirmed the Scriptural declaration that God, Mind, is the natural healer of the sick.

Instead of hiding or covering the purpose for which Christ Jesus came, Christian Science is dispelling the mystery that has enveloped the human sense of that purpose, and is lifting the veil which has largely obscured the full import of his mission and of its promise and possibilities for mankind. The human estimate of Christ Jesus and his salvation has been dwarfed, minimized, and limited. By reason of an amazing mutilation of the teachings of Christ Jesus, it has set aside the healing of the sick as being a manifestation of mystery instead of utility and of local rather than of universal import.

Forty years ago Mrs. Eddy began her plea for the acceptance of a more spiritual interpretation of this mission and for a larger and more explicit obedience. She sounded a recall to the purity and ampleness of primitive Christianity and to the original healing work which history declares marked the first three Christian centuries. She still makes the same plea and urges the world to consider the subject and to learn that the healing of the sick according to the way of Christ Jesus is not only an essential of Christian progress, but is a privilege of unspeakable benefit to a stricken people.

The theology of Christ was based on a pure theism; on one infinite, spiritual Good, unsullied by any taint of evil, because God is of "purer eyes than to behold evil."

Evil Destroyed Through Christ

The crusade of Christ Jesus against evil shows clearly that he regarded it as something to overcome and to destroy. By destroying evil he exhibited its destructibility. He certainly did not come to destroy that which was indestructible.

His Christianity reveals the divine rule whereby sin and disease and kindred evils are to be exterminated rather than avoided. The amplitude of his adequate way was indicated by his words: "Come unto me all ye that labor and are heavy laden." Is this an invitation for the wicked man whose burden is the sting of sin? Is it also for the good man whose burden is the sting of pain? Yes!

How did Christ Jesus heal the sick? He knew more about God, man—the universe—than all the people that have ever lived. Indeed, he was possessed of accurate, definite knowledge without measure. He was therefore qualified to act from the standpoint of pure knowledge or science. In healing the multitude of all manner of diseases did he act according to wisdom and science, or not? If possessed of absolute knowledge and science, would it not have been consummate folly to resort to ignorance, mystery, and disorder?

In healing the sick, was he sensible, practical, natural, and lawful? Did he do this practical thing in the best, wisest, and right way? If it could be shown that he did not, then Christianity would collapse in the showing. There is no alternative; the answer must be that he healed the sick in the best and right way, according to infinite Science and divine or primal law. Any other conclusion would degrade the mission of Christ to the level of inferiority. In coming to show the way of salvation and in entreating the world to do likewise, did he mean that they should heal the sick and do it in the right way, or after thus exhibiting the right way did he think that Christians could follow him and do the same things by adopting a contrary and inferior way? Finally, if Jesus healed the sick according to knowledge or Science, and did it lawfully, is it possible for a Christian Scientist to "go and do likewise"? Yes, it is; and if he can do it, then the kingdom of heaven is at hand. If it were true that he cannot do it, the utterances of Christ Jesus would be valueless.

Jesus, the Christ, and the disciples healed the sick by invoking and relying upon the supreme power of God. He knew that the law of divine Love is the law of Life and health to men and the law of extermination to sin and fear and disease, and he knew that all that is necessary to accomplish the cure of disease is available to mankind now.

Theology and Practice

The theology and practice of Christian Science are in exact unity with the words and works of Christ Jesus. They constitute precept, example, and goal for the Christian Scientist. By them he is incited to aspire to holier living and to overcome everything that defileth. Remembering that Christ is the overcoming of the world, the flesh, and the devil, he who is a genuine, sincere Christian Scientist is striving to go and do likewise.

I know that words cannot be made adequate to set forth the unspeakable glory of our divine Christ, nor indicate the consummate blessedness of his mission, nor measure the gratitude and adoration which responsively flow from those who have felt the touch of his divine afflatus and who yield willing obedience to Christ's rule and way. I do not urge that these simple words furnish more than feeble tribute to our Lord, but I am reminded that since the day when Mrs. Eddy first published Christian Science to the world and consecrated her all to his ministry, hundreds of thousands of men and women have been delivered from the depths of sin and vice and disease and woe, and as these people come with penitential tears and chastened hearts and song of rejoicing and grateful praise, I know that these things eloquently do honor to our Christ who promised that "these signs shall follow them that believe."

VICTORY OVER FEAR

Extract from Lecture Delivered in Third Church, Chicago, November 15, 1907

What is it that we need to be saved from, and can we be saved from it? Theology would tell you that it is sin we need to be saved from. Sin is not the initiative of humanity's disaster, unless sin in embryo is recognized as fear. Sin is a phenomenon, pure and simple; something is its cause. So man must be saved from something that is anterior to sin. What is it? Why, it is **fear**. Fear is the chief torment and foe of this race. It induces nearly every bit of sin. I speak of fear in a broad sense. Fear means anxiety, worry, trepidation, alarm—the opposite of confidence and reliance or self-containment. It is the opposite of that which means rule and dominion and courage and capacity, and sin is the result, almost invariably, of fear. For example, do you think that anybody would ever sin if he could get what he wanted without it? Think you that anybody would be so discomfited and so uncomfortable as to sin if he were able to find supreme enjoyment and satisfaction and variety of experience without it?

Fear the Result of False Education

The reason that everybody is afraid is that they have all been educated to be afraid. Religion has educated us to be afraid of the Almighty. We are afraid of God, afraid of heaven, afraid to go to heaven. There are people here who may say: "I am not afraid to go to heaven." Suppose all the people in Illinois were to be invited to die tonight at eleven o'clock and go to heaven? What would they do? They would all put for the woods. Not one would accept the invitation. And it is to the glory of God, Intelligence, and to the glory of the people of Illinois that they reject the proposition that our infinitely good God needs to prostrate them with disease and crush life out of them in order to introduce them to the felicities of heaven.

Fear Falsely Regarded as Good

What is the matter with this race that makes every last man and woman a coward? Go to the philosopher, go to the man called a scientist, and he will tell you that fear is a natural concomitant of existence, a very salutary feature; that it acts as a warning, breeds caution; and it is literally instilled into the thoughts of men that fear is an essential to be expected and respected.

Fear Is Wholly an Abomination and a Monstrosity

Forty years ago, had you attended any of our great colleges and entered a scientific course, you would have been told that possibly, some time in the future, electricity might be used for illuminating purposes, but as a motive power—never. Impossible! Somebody has had to change his mind since then. The first thing this race must do in order to be saved is to learn that fear is un-Godlike, unnatural, absolutely without divine ordination, a gratuitous, fabulous abomination, without one solitary shred of reason or rationality or excuse or propriety or tenure; that it is without any basis in Truth or Science, in law or intelligence.

Fear the Result of Ignorance of Humanity's Normal Rights

In order to be saved, we must rationally understand whence cometh fear, and we shall learn that we have come to be victims through ignorance and superstition; through ignorance, first, of what lies at the very basis of existence—what there is by way of nature, provision, ordination and routine; through ignorance of the foundation and basis upon which all things rest and according to which all things must pursue their way. In other words, what is the Science of the beginning? What is the Science of creation, of Life, of man's destiny? What was he created for? What has he a right to do? What may he express by way of power and capacity? How much dominion over the earth is he entitled to and may he set forth and exhibit?

Fear Cast Out by Gaining Dominion

In order to be saved from fear we must come into the possession of that which will cast it out. Dominion will cast it out. That is, the conscious realization of power on your part to resist and overcome it will cast it out. Moreover, just to the extent that you get any realization of that power, it will cast out an equivalent of fear, and consequently of fear's havoc. I speak as an expert on fear, because in my day I was the most frightened person on this planet. I do not think you could crowd any more fear into a being than there was in me, and I have learned whereof I speak to such an extent that I do not believe I am more than forty per cent as much afraid as I used to be, possibly not more than twenty-five per cent. In other words, I have gotten rid of about seventy-five per cent of hell, mental torment.

Fear Springs from a False Sense of God

Why is it that, instead of existing as a sovereign in the realm of mental equipment, showing forth the Mind that is equal to the removal of mountains, to all intents and purposes there is a creeping, cringing, frightened world? It is because we have been educated to believe that our own God is against us; because we have been taught to believe that for some inscrutable reason (and it is always apologized for by the word "inscrutable") infinite Wisdom has seen fit to make everybody sick and to arrange tragedy and death. So that, at the outset, we start with the proposition that we were born to die; that we were born under the law and rule and provision of pain, sickness.

insufficiency, and sin; and so, with that start, there is no other ultimate than sorrow and suffering.

Fear Cast Out by Knowledge of God's Nature and Purpose

What must we do in order to be saved from fear? We must learn, and we can learn it tonight, that all that means God, all that means source, origin, foundation, and power, all that means creative force, all that is entitled to exercise any influence, to sustain the universe, to hold it in its grasp—that all of it is good, infinitely good, surpassing all possibility of human comprehension. We must learn that, in spite of appearances, the foundation of being is Good. Our God hath done all things well. Be not afraid of God. That is the last thing to be afraid of, and the Christian Scientist is learning that God is his dearest friend, his Life. No babe ever nestled its head upon the breast of a more loving mother; none ever had mother so intent upon the felicity of her child; none ever had father so bound up in the protection and guidance and maintenance of his child. So we are to learn, just as fast as we will, that God means life and health and welfare and prosperity for us.

Fear Arises from a Wrong Sense of That Which Is Right

If we may be assured that the foundation of being is Good, and we find that we may stop being afraid at this point, then what? You may say: "There is no more delight in trouble or pain if it isn't of God than if it is, and how can I be saved from fear so long as the consequences are in sight? Suppose you do shift the burden of responsibility from God, where is it to be placed so I need not be afraid of it?" Christian Science answers this question by declaring that all that means sorrow, disappointment, poverty, sickness, and death, all of it is but an illegitimate sense of Life, a perversion of the facts of Being; it is pure aberration; it is a wrong sense of Life, a wrong sense of that which is fundamentally all right. People are all wrong because they have got a wrong sense of that which is primarily all right. What they need to do is to get a right sense of that which is right and lose a wrong sense of that which is right, and then they will be all right. That which causes all this mis-estimate about the origin of disease, and is the procurer of pain and disaster, that which is to be dislodged, and from which we are to be saved, is a wrong sense of that which is all right. It is nothing more than that.

Fear Vanishes as You Oppose It with Understanding

I once knew a woman in an insane asylum who believed that she had turned into an animal and was all covered with feathers. Had you or anyone else gone to her and said, "Do not allow yourself to be deluded; you haven't got any feathers," she would have said, "Why, look at me, feel of them, put your hand on them; why, of course I have feathers." She had a wrong sense of that which was all right. What did she need to get rid of, feathers or a wrong sense? Salvation means transformation of mind. You have no contention against some mighty enemy. You do not have to wrestle and be tossed about by something that is powerful, that is natural and ordained. You have got to contend against something that will flee just as you oppose it and to the extent that you oppose it.

Fear Shown to Result from Man-made Standards

If Christ were to come on earth in India today and look around for sinners to be saved, and those who were ready to confess, he would find that, according to the moral code of that country, ever so many people would say: "I need to be forgiven and saved because I have lately been killing chickens and lambs and eating them." A man in India who had thus transgressed would be afraid, would he not? Over here we find people asking God to bless the chickens and lambs for our use. The Buddhists who were here at the World's Fair were much shocked to find us killing and eating about every animal we could lay our hands on. I have too much reverence for our

God, I am too deep in my affection for the splendor and beauty of Spirit, I have learned my lesson concerning Deity too well to supplicate God to bless to my use any animal that I have killed and eaten.

Fear Vanishes When We Understand Our Rights

One needs something vastly more accurate than the human standard of morality in order to steer his way, in order not to be afraid. In order to be saved from fear we are to learn that everything that induced it can be mastered, can be controlled, set aside, exterminated and annulled. What will do it? That which will induce us, first, to know that we have a right to overcome it; and then that will induce us to try to exercise the right. The great service of Christian Science, today, is that it is redeeming mankind and setting forth man's dominion over all evil and exhibiting the rule whereby it may be accomplished, whereby we may work out our own salvation and accomplish for ourselves the sufficiency of deliverance.

Fear, Penalty, Suffering and God Are Polar Opposites

Why are we afraid? It is because we have a sort of an idea that there is a God that has been watching us all the time and has seen every funny little thing we have done, and all the rest of the things; that he has them all marked down, and in the background is retribution, vengeance, punishment, and sometimes hell, more or less damnation, etc. In other words, we are educated to believe that God is an executioner, and that He Himself is going to settle the account with us to the extent of our everlasting agony. Every bit of that sort of thing is untrue. There is no God involved in it. It isn't the business of God. Now, what is it that punishes a mortal? It is sin itself; it is error itself; God doesn't punish anybody; He doesn't have to. Sin invariably brings its own sense of punishment, its own suffering, its own hell; and it is all evil. There isn't any God in it at all.

Fear Victimizes, God Saves, Humanity

When we come to understand this it will be a relief, because we will then be able to view men—not as original sinners—but as victims. They have been outrageously defrauded, and only when you come to know that concerning men can you heal them. The reason Christian Science is able to reform sinners is that it differentiates between the reality of the man and the fraud that imposes itself upon him by way of a false sense of desire or pleasure or satisfaction or need. Would you condemn the woman who thought she had feathers? No; you would remove the blight of outrageous mesmerism, and when that is done she gets well. And so we have got to stop charging God with any form of evil in order to get ourselves right, in order to be in the proper mood for our own deliverance.

Fear Breeds Self-condemnation, Remorse. They Are Useless

It will not do you a particle of good to enter upon a career of self-condemnation. Remorse never got anybody into heaven. A sense of regret and self-condemnation is not the right application. That is reform; it is change; it is correction. The man who is today under the imposition of an evil sense of being does not need to be whipped and scourged and punished; he needs to be educated. In other words, it's a case of feathers. Does the woman who has this sense of feathers need to be whipped? How about the sinner? There is no merit whatever in suffering. The only merit there is is in transformation. I have found people carrying along their agony because they thought it was entirely proper to be everlastingly berating and condemning themselves. You will never get into heaven, or heaven into you, in that way.

Fear Resisted and Cancelled, Healing Follows

When we find that God is not responsible for evil; that it has no real, scientific, or natural basis; that, at best, it is nothing but a fraudulent, perverted sense of being; when we find that there has been manifested to humanity an absolute, adequate way whereby to overcome the whole thing, that way having been demonstrated through Christ; when we begin to learn that a man has a right to stand up and overcome, what does a man who has learned that do? He **resists**, and one thing he begins to resist is fear. "Resist the devil and it will flee from you." In every instance of disease there is latent or immediate fear, and it is the business of the practitioner to reach and cancel that fear; and just to the extent he does it will his patient begin to improve.

Fear Eliminated by Seriously Taking God as Omnipotent Good

I can remember when it came to me that I did not have to be afraid. I did not expect to be healed; I couldn't see how I was ever going to pull out, until one morning, about three o'clock, when things seemed pretty near the edge, it absolutely dawned on me that the things people had been saying for centuries were true, that God—meaning Good, right thinking, right knowing —is Omnipotent, that that means all power and the only power. And when that came to me, then followed this, that if God—Good—is the only power, then there isn't any other power that I need to be afraid of; and because there isn't, I won't be afraid; and just as soon as I stopped being afraid, because I did **not** have to be afraid, I knew that I was going to get well. And let me say to some of you who perhaps are patients, that you do not need so very much treatment; what you need to do is to take God at His word. "Be not afraid," because you do not have to be afraid.

Fear Is Never Your Fear. Don't Claim It

To keep fear at arm's length, never admit that it is yours, because if it is yours you had better keep it. Never admit that it has a right to continue in business at the old stand. As soon as possible, you want to put up an advertisement mentally that this place has changed hands. Resist fear upon the ground that it has no right to be, and that it does not help the situation at any rate. Think for a moment of the mighty transactions that occurred when Jesus came on earth and entreated humanity to be not afraid. He could not tell them why, because they would not understand it. He simply said: "Be not afraid," "Fear not."

Fear Destroyed by the Demonstration of Truth

Think of the other mighty transactions that have occurred since Mrs. Eddy, discoverer of the essence of Christ's teachings and works, came and entreated humanity to be not afraid, and told the reason why we need not be afraid—explained the modus of deliverance, explained what Jesus meant when he told the people that he had much to say to them but they were not spiritually strong enough to bear it. But he did say prophetically: "Ye shall know the Truth, and the Truth shall make you free." And now this Truth has been discovered, uncovered, revealed, and it is making people free.

The Imposition of Fear Cast Out

Not one person in this room will ever again be so much afraid, not because of me, surely, but because of the Truth, that which was before Adam or planet or sun or stars, that which meant joy to the earth, because that which cometh in the name of the Lord cometh in the name of Life and health; because the very splendid Truth about our God and about the right man, and the right of the right man to live—because it has declared itself to the consciousness of every one in this room and cannot return unto itself void. So blessed is the blessedness of that which saves, that it will transform to some measure every one in this room, for "God hath not given us the spirit of fear, but of power and of Love and of a sound mind."

THE CAUSE AND SCIENTIFIC CURE OF DISEASE

Lecture Delivered in Kansas City, Sept. 30, 1900

By way of justification for assembling this vast audience, I declare to you that Christian Science, in its nature and influence, includes nothing but supreme good for all mankind.

Appearing to a race and generation that is hard pressed by the tumult and vicissitudes of its existence, Christian Science comes like a dove of peace, bearing upon its wings a ministry of healing and of deliverance for suffering humanity in this hour of its pitiful need. Standing here in testimony and witness of its sublime blessedness, I seek to engage your attention because Christian Science is demonstrably true and because its natural and inevitable influence on human behalf is being manifested to thousands whose lives were being desolated by sin, disease and despair.

Mrs. Eddy's Great Work

For thirty years a brave, loving woman has, with holy impulse, been presenting the Christian propaganda to the world. During this time the Principle and Science thereof have been set forth in a text-book and elaborated by teachers, practitioners and lecturers. Many misconceptions and misstatements have been corrected, and gradually the public has been led to relinquish a false estimate and to realize that it is a subject which is justly engaging the attention of earnest, sensible people and bestowing upon them greater happiness, better health and better morals.

The Nature of Christian Science

Christian Science is primarily and essentially a religion. As a religious denomination which is manifesting its right of existence by destroying sin and sickness, it is proper that we should present it to our fellow men and justify it before this generation; nevertheless we have no need nor disposition to quarrel over religion or engage in unseemly controversy. On the contrary, we deprecate the evil of religious strife and assault, and deplore the facility with which sectarianism denounces everything unlike itself.

The Board of Lectureship

Our Board of Lectureship was instituted for the purpose largely of establishing a complete offset to, and refutation of, the misrepresentations that have been bestowed upon Christian Science and Christian Scientists, and in this behalf these lecturers have stood forth throughout the land, and have told you much of what we believe and what we are doing.

Doctrines and Works of Christian Science

They have told you that we believe in God; that we are learning to know His will and are glad to obey it. They have told you that Christian Science rests upon and is fully sanctioned by the Bible, and that we accept the Scriptures as containing the inspired word of God. You have been told that we accept the Messiahship of the divine Christ and are endeavoring to follow literally in the way which he established by precept and example.

It has been stated that Christian Science purports to present the actual truth or science of Jesus' mission, and that its aim is the re-establishment of the primitive Christianity which was governed by his teaching and works. You have been told that we are striving to turn from and obliterate evil; to live according to a high moral and ethical standard, and that the primary office of Christian Science is to effect a moral reform

It has been explained that we believe in prayer without ceasing, in the highest social and individual purity, and that the demands of Christian Science are in strict accord with the Ten Commandments and the "Sermon on the Mount."

You have been told that through the influence of Christian Science, many thousands have been healed of all manner of diseases, and that these people are insistently bearing testimony as to these facts and impressing the world with the conviction that a transforming influence is exerting itself in behalf of men. In this very city all of the prevalent misrepresentations have been categorically denied and refuted, and the opposite facts have been so amply stated that there is no longer a semblance to justification for false and misleading statements.

The Right to Freedom in Religion

Men and women are struggling with the enigma of human existence. Many noble people have exhibited splendid devotion to the cause of human welfare. They have been disciples of numberless phases of philosophy, religion and non-religion. As Christian Scientists, we glory in every good thing they have ever done or thought. We respect their right to exercise independent moral and mental integrity and to worship God as seems best to them, without molestation. On the other hand, we know that we should be lovingly accorded the same right, conscious as we are that the substance and animus of Christian Science is Godlike, Christlike, moral, and spiritual. We stand on its platform and demonstrations, confident that it will redeem mortals from all evil, and we are unmoved by ridicule, defamation, or falsehood.

The Way in Which Benefits Are Derived

I do not need to reiterate the statements which have heretofore been presented by my predecessors, but shall devote this hour to the endeavor to make some explanation to you concerning the way in which we derive benefit through Christian Science, and the way in which you can benefit yourselves today and ever afterwards. The subject is vast and I shall only attempt to bring to your attention one or two simple phases thereof, but if you will appropriate them and put them into practice, they will be of incalculable value to you.

Bishop Morrison's Opinion

Bishop Morrison of Iowa, in a public address, uttered substantially these words: "I do not wish to be understood as indorsing Christian Science, but I am persuaded that the rapid growth of this movement is in consequence of their insistent recognition of God."

We do seek to recognize and acknowledge God in all His ways, because we have a far better and larger sense of Him than ever before. Indeed, if it would not give offense, I would venture to say that we have a larger sense than most other people have, because we think specifically that He is the healer of the sick as the Scriptures declare, and we are proving that this is true.

Why May One Expect to Be Healed?

The question then arises, "What is God and what has He done that any one may, in consequence, expect to be healed of disease?" According to Christian Science, God is the Principle and animus of Christian Science Mind healing.

The Agnostic and Infidel

If there is any one here who is an agnostic or infidel, who has not been able to comprehend or believe in any of the many conceptions called God, and who instinctively rebels against my statement, I ask him to wait. I do not mean any such god or any of the gods that he has repudiated and rejected.

Misconceptions of God

If there are any here who have feared or idolized a god of wrath and vengeance, or one that has ordained sickness and death, and who in consequence are incredulous as to the willingness of God to heal, I say to them, I do not mean any such god as they refer to. Indeed, I do not mean that any one of the numerous misconceived mental substitutes for Deity is the Principle of Christian Science healing or of anything else.

All men differ and always have differed as to what Deity is. It is not my purpose to compare or comment on these wide and confusing differences, but will give you some idea of what we mean by God as the healer of the sick and the Principle of such healing.

Nature of God Described

According to divine Science or the Science of God, the man who confesses himself finite cannot with a sweep of mere words adequately describe infinity, but this science declares that infinity necessarily means ONE—one God, one supreme, all-inclusive entity or individuality.

God is infinite intelligence and wisdom. He is omniscience, all science, all knowledge. He is the one infinite consciousness of Being or conscious Being; the one infinite Mind.

This infinite Mind includes all consciousness and continuity of life, and therefore is Life. Infinite God or Mind or Spirit is the sole Creator, source, cause, origin, basis, and foundation of all that really exists.

He is primal and is therefore the divine Principle of the universe, and is its law and government. He is good and is the power of Good, and He has already done all things well.

He is not only Life, but hath ordained eternal life, and is the law of life and health to man. He is omnipresent, not as a corporeal being or personality, but is present as Truth, Intelligence, Good, and the law of harmony and life, and all of this is available to mankind—not by way of miraculous intervention, but because of the everpresence of everything and every power necessary to the permanent welfare of men.

God the Redeemer

The God we worship is good, and He is able, willing and ready to redeem mankind from the evils imposed upon them by an utterly perverted sense of existence.

What the Sick Should Comprehend

Mankind will never emerge from the area of disease until they comprehend the scientific fact that all that means God —all that means the natural law of God—all that means basis, source, and cause, law, government, and power, is contrary to the inception and continuity of sickness.

Difference Between Christian Science and Other Religions

At this point is seen one of the chief differences between Christian Science and all other schools of religious belief. We know that all evil is finite, unlawful and unnecessary, and that it has no immortality or inherent power of continuity. We know that through a knowledge of the Truth which Jesus said would make us free, we may in time dominate and abolish every form of evil in accordance with His command and example.

False Philosophy

Now what I have said is true, and it follows that nearly the entire philosophy of life which has governed men for ages is false and destructive. Certain it is that people regard sickness as natural and according to law, and are submitting to it and living and dying in accord with a philosophy of death which Christian Science declares to be absolutely wrong.

The Causes of Disease

A discussion of this subject of healing hinges on the question: "What are the primary and intermediate causes of disease?" Physiology, which takes no cognizance of the mental, moral and spiritual nature of men, answers that sickness and death are caused by matter and by material laws, and the prevalent human belief is that matter includes in its nature and law the power and disposition to make a man sick and finally to assert a fatal mastery over his existence

Matter Falsely Regarded as a Cause

This theory of causation naturally creates a universal and individual state of dread, alarm, and fear. In fact it is absolutely indisputable that the whole human family is in a state of conscious and unconscious fear of pain, disease, and death which it supposes are caused by matter.

Disease of Mental Origin

Here Christian Science differs from materia medica, physiology, and all other material theories and beliefs. It declares that nearly all disease is caused primarily by ignorance, superstition, false beliefs, sin, and fear, and locates causation in the mental realm instead of in material belief.

I do not intend to try to consider all of this subject now, but will refer to evil and sinful conditions of belief, and to fear and its effects, in order to indicate the way in which Christian Science becomes available in such cases.

Men Can Successfully Cope with Disease

One of the first things that a student of this science grasps is that the fundamental nature of the Science of Life and its law includes no law of sickness and death; that these twin evils are abnormal and that matter has no actual power to make him sick. Then, regardless of all theories and practice to the contrary, he changes his entire standpoint of thought and action and is governed by an entirely different philosophy,— the Science of Life. He is relieved to find that God has not made him sick and that matter cannot keep him sick. The tension of fear which has been lifelong begins to relax as he learns that disease is something that he can cope with.

Overcoming Fear Heals

As this fear, which has insidiously disturbed the bodily conditions, begins to subside, the human organism resumes a more normal condition, and he establishes in his own experience the fact that an understanding of this science of healing is breaking down the cause of his trouble and annulling the effect.

The Cause and the Prevalence of Fear

The ordinary human being is educated to fear from his very babyhood. He is taught to fear what he eats and drinks; to fear the heat and cold, the atmosphere, moisture, and climate: He fears to exercise and he fears to be inactive. He is afraid of germs and microbes that never used to disturb any one, and he is afraid of nearly everything else under the sun, moon and stars. Not only this, but he feels the mesmeric influence of the universal fear on the part of the race. And all this is in consequence of the supposition that matter holds at its disposal the issues of life and death.

What It Is to Take Cold

The common belief that if a person gets his feet wet with his shoes on, he will take cold, is erroneous and unlawful. It is the universal false belief and concurrent fear relative thereto, rather than matter, that brings to pass that which is termed the cold. The human body very largely consists of water. Now, I ask you, is there any good reason why water should take cold when it gets wet? Is there any good reason, in scientific cause and effect, why the matter in a man's foot should take cold when it gets wet any more than the matter in a duck's foot or in the tail of a fish?

Body in Absence of Mentality Does Not Take Cold

Take all the substances that are said to compose the body, such as water, lime, starch, iron, phosphorus, etc., and aggregate them in a mass or body minus the so-called human mind, and that body will not take cold or congest. If matter knows enough to take cold when it gets wet, it would always take cold under similar circumstances, and all bodies would do the same thing.

It is not material causation, but mental, that governs the

case, and such mental influence and procurement is not a necessity under natural divine law, but is the unnatural and abnormal consequence of erroneous human belief and fear on the subject.

Disease the Effect of Mesmerism

One difficulty in understanding this, is that people are not aware of the mesmeric influence which universal, fundamental false belief has on individuals, including infants, who manifest prevalent evil conditions before they acquire any conscious belief or fear. Metaphysical science, which diagnoses or analyzes disease from the basis of mental causation, reveals the fact that many kinds of bodily ailments and organic derangements are the direct consequence of the belief that matter governs rather than mind.

Up to the time that Mrs. Eddy discovered the Science of Mind or divine metaphysics, the world had a very defective knowledge of what mesmerism is and the extent and nature of its influence. After years of study, observation, and scientific investigation in the light of Christian Science, she announced in her text-book the nature of mesmerism and its action as the procurator of disease.

People had believed, and most of them now believe, that the word mesmerism refers to some mysterious influence or power which a few people as individuals have over the minds of some others, who are susceptible thereto, and whose consent is necessary before any results can be manifested. The world has been densely in ignorance on this subject. It needs to understand this phenomenon of the human will in order to escape from the evils which it entails on every one.

The Range of Mesmerism

Mrs. Eddy has explained it at great length in "Science and Health," and shows that it is not the man that is mesmeric, but universal false belief, animal magnetism. It is a well ascertained fact, that all mortal, human thought, so-called, is more or less mesmeric in its action and influence, and that every one, without exception, is subject to it who does not know how to resist and overcome it. This discovery has made it possible to account for many diseases and occurrences that have seemed mysterious and baffling, and has also made it possible to effect a remedy.

Christian Science Healing Not Mesmeric

It is well to say here that the superficial antagonist, who is intent on discrediting the healing work of Christian Science, which is so palpable, rushes into print or to the rostrum to declare that this healing is accomplished by means of mesmeric or hypnotic suggestion. He does not know what hypnotism really is, and has no real knowledge whatever as to the *modus operandi* of Christian Science healing, but these things are easy to say, and it is particularly easy to repeat what some one else has said.

Hypnotism Opposite to Christian Science

Now let me tell you that the Christian Scientist understands the nature of both of these influences, and I declare to you that in every solitary case of healing we have to meet and remove the effects of some form of mesmerism, and never make use of what is called hypnotic suggestion, which is the very opposite of Christian Science.

Stomach Trouble

One of the most common errors is the belief that, when there is stomach trouble, it is in consequence of food, and we frequently hear the remark, "My food does not agree with me," or that some particular article of food does not agree.

In perhaps four cases out of five the stomach trouble is the result of continued fear, anger, grief, anxiety, malice, or some other form of known sin or ignorant belief. In such cases the only scientific and adequate remedy is to cancel the cause and thus abate the effects.

Wrong Method Employed for Cure

I know from experience and observation that people who are afflicted with stomach trouble gradually abandon first one article of food and then another, because it does not agree with them. They are under the supposition that this is necessary and this practice is often continued until the diet is reduced to a crust of toast and a little hot water. Even after this fearful concession is made, the patient finds there has been no relief, simply because he has been augmenting the cause while doctoring effects.

No Incurable Disease

One of the most prostrating evils, incidental to sickness, is the assumption or declaration that one has an incurable disease. *Materia medica* admits that there are very many diseases that cannot be cured by material means, and in consequence the world has come to regard such diseases as necessarily fatal. All that this really means is that the physicians cannot cure them. The Principle of Christian Science does not include the admission that any disease is incurable, and its practice has always resulted in the healing of all the supposedly incurable types of disease.

This unnecessary supposition that one has an incurable disease is mischievous in the extreme, and often insures the speedy decline or collapse of a patient. If, according to Christian Science, the deplorable fear about fatal diseases should subside, the improved mental state which would ensue would instantly improve health and prolong life.

Clouds of Fear Lifted

This form of fear is largely projected by the patent medicine advertisements, and their alarming display of what are called fatal symptoms, and the ordinary conversation of people is equally bad, as well as the hopeless diagnosis of the physician and its death sentence. Imagine the vast relief that mankind will experience when they learn that all diseases are curable.

Beliefs in Decrepitude and Decadence Exposed

Another pernicious mental habit is the universal expectation of decrepitude and decadence. There is a common fear of overdoing, of getting tired, of exhausting one's strength, of too much study; there is an incessant admonition to be careful, and there are penalties without number that are prophesied and pronounced.

The Old Age Bugaboo

No sooner do people reach a state of manhood and usefulness than they begin to talk about growing old and to settle into the grooves of incapacity, failure, and imbecility.

This entire area of evil expectations, and of submission, based upon the assumption that people cannot perform or endure, is the principal cause of most of the nervous prostration, mental impairment, breaking down, premature age, and helplessness. All of this is the havoc of evil so-called mind and its beliefs and laws, rather than the product of the laws of God, nature, or necessity, and Christian Science is destined to destroy this evil.

Influence of Fear on the Body

I might go on indefinitely and indicate hundreds of ways in which general fear, and even the fear of pain and disease, affects the body disastrously. I might cite countless instances, well known and acknowledged by all, which would illustrate or give emphasis to what I have said. Many of you would admit that fear has some influence on the body, but until the day of Christian Science the obscure and yet far-reaching influence of this evil mental action was practically unknown and unresisted.

Assurance of Needlessness of Fear

The important service that I desire to render you at this moment and at this part of my address is this:

You do not need to be afraid of thousands of things that you have been afraid of.

You do not need to be afraid of matter or of any so-called material law of disease, or that the symptoms of disease can dominate you.

You do not need to be afraid of what you eat; of overwork; of draughts of air or loss of sleep.

You do not need to be afraid of insanity or nervous prostration, or of a broken constitution, simply because you have an active mentality and think much and constantly about business or the affairs of your life. These and many other calamities are inflicted upon people, not because of law or necessity, but contrary to it, and are the result of the action of human beliefs and fears.

"The Law of the Spirit of Life" Sets Free

I have stated to you that Christian Science declares that all that is included in the divine nature and phenomena means health and life as the normal state of man, and that all of the actual law of Being supports this scientific postulate.

You may say that this seems very strange, and that you do not know whether it is true or not, and I understand very well that you do not know, but I will say to you that nearly two millions of instances of healing through Christian Science have been based on this scientific fact and attest its verity, and these instances include the healing of diseases that have never been known to be healed by any other means since the world began.

Mr. Kimball's Experience with Science

When first presented to me, I had no faith in any of these things; but, as a last resort, I was obliged to venture upon a test, and when I did venture persistently and in good faith, I found that the demonstration verified the Science and its promise. It saved me from the grave.

As You Understand Science, Fear Disappears

A study of Christian Science logically and rationally induces one to abandon many false beliefs and fears, and you will find, if you will likewise investigate, that you will gradually enter upon a transformed existence. You will find that the pains and symptoms will begin to abate and disappear. You will learn that this new understanding of Life and its laws enables you to dissipate fear and its consequences, and that you are gaining a lawful and God-given dominion over sickness.

Personal Application

Go to your homes and test this statement thoroughly. Try to realize that God never made or procured sickness, and that it is simply a monstrosity of human misconception.

Begin to act as though you had dominion, and as though the fear was a baseless fraud; and for the sole reason that Good is omnipotent, and that a knowledge of the Truth does make free from error, you will find, to your joy, and perhaps surprise, that men, governed by Intelligence, can triumph over evil.

Teachings of the Bible Against Fear

Throughout the Bible, there appears, on one hand, the repeated outcry of men for deliverance from fear, and, on the other hand, we find that the words of Jesus and other men of God entreat mankind to "fear not" and bid them wipe away their tears and hope that God will destroy fear. Certainly we should have no such teaching if fear was not destructible and contrary to the naturalness of existence.

Christian Science Compasses Destruction of Fear

If you were to question Christian Scientists on the subject, they would tell you that a great blessing had been conferred on them through the ability to mitigate or destroy fear, and I make bold to utter the statement that there has never, before the day of Christian Science, been a complete exposition of a scientific method by which this could be accomplished.

Continuing our discussion of the cause of disease, I refer again to the statement that sin is a cause.

Sin Responsible for All Disease

The Bible says, "Through sin came death into the world, and death by sin," and this, of course, should be understood to mean that through sin came sickness, of which death is the ultimate. We do not understand this to mean that the word sin refers only to crime, vice, or immorality, but that through all kinds of ignorant and destructive beliefs, and an evil and fatal misconception of life and what pertains to it, the world has involved itself in mortality.

Careful observation is demonstrating absolutely the verity of the disclosure made in the light of Christian Science, which is that hatred, grief, remorse, envy, and kindred evils, as well as fear, will—if persisted in—inevitably cause bodily disorder and suffering. It shows that the Bible statement that, "whatsoever a man soweth, that shall he also reap," is positively true.

Such evil and inflaming mental conditions quickly disturb the nervous system, the circulation of the blood, and the integrity of organic action. Very many instances of sickness have no other cause, and yet how much attention is paid to the moral or immoral element in the patient in the ordinary diagnosis of disease? None. In such instances the drugging system is absolutely oblivious to the actual cause. No wonder that it does not dominate disease.

People have been urged for hundreds of reasons to abandon sin. Christian Science joins in this entreaty, and while it pleads this cause because righteousness is far better, it also warns men to flee from sin because of the penalty which sin inflicts upon its victims.

Good and Bad Characters

Picture to yourself some man or woman who is kind, loving, and upright; one whose fair life is marked by the milestones of benevolence and good deeds. Notice the effect that such a mental condition has produced on the face of this person with the softened expression and pleasing lines.

On the other hand, witness the man whose mind is evil; who for years has been animated by hatred and other brutal propensities that distort and debauch mankind. Witness his face, hard, repellent, and twisted. Its very offensiveness of outline and shape is itself an evidence of the incarnation of evil. You know that this disfigured and twisted face has been caused by a wicked and sinful mind.

Evil Thought, Distorting Face, Can Distort Liver

Now, I ask you, if such evil thought can twist and distort his face, don't you suppose that it can twist and distort his liver? Suppose that such a man, who was suffering in consequence of his evil thoughts, should resort to the prevalent theory and practice of medicine for relief. Can you conceive it possible that there would be any scientific procedure in administering liver pills to him, or in changing his diet? Such a patient does not suffer because he has eaten ice cream or mince pie, but because his very being is wrenched and torn by evil beliefs and motives. He does not need a change of diet, but the transformation of mind, for "to be carnally minded is death, but to be spiritually minded is life and peace."

Christian Science Leaves Nothing Unexplained

I am not attempting to explain fully all of the causes of disease, although Christian Science leaves nothing of this kind unexplained. I know that the thought may come to you that I am not satisfying you concerning hereditary diseases and such types of diseases as locomotor ataxia, abnormal growths, failing eyesight, and many other difficulties, but this is not because of inability, but a lack of time, and so—anticipating criticism in this direction—I shall simply try to impress upon you the declaration of Christian Science—that evil feelings and practices, which may be briefly classified as sin, fear, and erroneous and fatal beliefs, are the cause, immediately or remotely, of the sickness which afflicts mankind.

Science Heals by Removing Mental Cause

Knowing this to be true, the practice of the Christian Scientist is directed to the removal or destruction of the mental cause, and he proceeds in accord with the knowledge that neither fear, sin, superstition, nor ignorance are indestructible. He knows that you cannot remove ignorant fear by means of a plaster, nor transform the moral and temperamental status by means of mud baths. He knows also that these discordant mental causes are abnormal, unlawful, and unreal, and that he can master them because of divinely ordained and divinely bestowed intelligence or science.

The declaration of Mrs. Eddy that sin or evil is unreal greatly disturbs many who do not understand what is meant by it, and who assume that acceptance of such a belief would be the license of sin.

Why Sin Is Unreal

Let me say that no one knows more thoroughly than does Mrs. Eddy that mortals are manifestly sinful, and that sin is evil, destructive, and indefensible. No one knows better than she does that sin entails upon its victim its own suffering and damnation, and that the only possible escape from punishment is through reform and regeneration. And yet she rightly declares that sin is in consequence of an unreal sense of existence, and that mortals are making a reality of that which is unreal.

It will be admitted by all right-minded people that men ought to stop sinning. It will also be conceded without argument that all men could stop sinning if they wanted to and knew enough. Now suppose that every one should stop sinning tonight and never sin again, what would become of sin? Men would continue to exist and be far happier than now. Do you suppose that if sin was an entity and had all the inherent elements of immortality, it could be thus silenced and become obsolete forever? Would it not appear that, if sin could be thus abolished, it is at most but a temporary and false sense of that which is real? Would it not appear that sin is a mental and moral derangement and an unreal state, just as the vagaries of the insane are unreal?

Sickness and Suffering Unreal

Again, suppose that sin did cease to prevail, and to improperly animate mortals. Do you not see that it would cease also to act as the cause of disease, and that, to a corresponding extent, sickness and suffering would likewise cease?

Think for a moment of the effect on the ordinary mortal if he should be informed of an occurrence that caused him the most acute distress, grief, or alarm. If continued, he would manifest physical disturbance and finally be sick. Now let it be known to him that the report which had caused all this havoc was utterly false and unreal, what would happen? Why, the tension of fear or distress would immediately relax and he would gain peace of mind and peace of body.

Racial Bondage

Now, my friends, Christian Science shows that the entire human race is in very much this same condition. It is in a state of active or latent alarm and dread, because it supposes itself to be at the mercy of material causes, subject to a law of sickness and death, and liable at any time to fall, helpless and hopeless, under its dire and offensive operation.

Enlightened Sense Destroys Bondage

Let us suppose that an enlightened sense of life should touch the consciousness of humanity and show that all these beliefs are false and unreal. What would then happen? In such an event, the whole area of universal as well as individual fear would relax, evil and ignorant beliefs would give place to a normal sense of life, and as these procurators of sickness were disarmed and abolished, the sickness which they caused would also be abolished.

The Mystery of Evil Cleared

Such enlightenment concerning this mystery of evil is just what Christian Science bestows on those who understand it, and it is this Christ-Science or Christ-knowledge of Life and its naturalness which destroys sin and fear and ignorant beliefs and heals the sick.

God the Principle of Healing

You will readily understand that, if these evils were thus destroyed, it would be because of the action and power of Intelligence, or Truth, or God; and it would thus be seen that God or divine influence produces the result or healing, and is, therefore, the basis or Principle of the transformation.

First Step with an Invalid

The suffering invalid, who has contended in vain against what he has supposed to be the cause of his trouble, is first told that he has been working in the wrong direction. Then he learns what it is that needs to be met and mastered and the necessity for a radical change in endeavor.

Mind the Remedy for Sin and Disease

It would be of little satisfaction to any one to be told that his sickness was caused by fear or sin or some other evil mental influence, if there was no remedy; but Christian Science reveals an adequate way whereby all evil can be lessened and dispelled.

How all this can be accomplished is explained in the textbook of Christian Science, ''Science and Health with Key to the Scriptures, by Mrs. Eddy. I would be glad if we had time in which to explain the application of divine law now, but I will say that all these evil influences, such as fear, the desire to sin, depraved appetites and their evil consequences, are mitigated and removed through the power of Mind; and when I say Mind, I mean that Mind which was also in Christ; and when I refer to this influence, I mean it is divine Intelligence bestowed upon man.

Knowledge of Science Confers Power

Describing it more specifically, it means that a man or woman who has gained a demonstrable understanding of Christian Science, and who has imbibed the spirit of it and is honestly living in compliance with its holy teachings and in imitation of the life of Christ Jesus, can for himself and others remove fear and its effects, destroy temptation and evil desire, and heal disease.

In doing this they illustrate the supremacy of Good and of spiritual law and righteousness, and they do it in accord with the Scriptural promises, a few of which I quote:

Scriptural Proof

Ezekiel 18:21, 32: "But if the wicked will turn from all his sins that he hath committed, and keep all my statutes, and do that which is lawful and right, he shall surely live, he shall not die. For I have no pleasure in the death of him that dieth, saith the Lord God; wherefore, turn yourselves and live ye."

Luke 20:38: "For He is not a God of the dead, but of the living."

Jeremiah 33:6: "Behold, I will bring in health and a cure and I will cure them, and will reveal unto them the abundance of peace and truth."

. Throughout the Bible there are many definite declarations and intimations that if a man is righteous he will escape from evil. I quote one from Exodus 23:25:

"And ye shall serve the Lord your God, and He shall bless thy bread and thy water; and I will take sickness away from the midst of thee."

Righteousness More Than Morality

According to Christian Science, to be righteous means more than to be moral. It means to be right in every way. But the man who is moral and religious, and yet believes that God has ordained sickness, is not right. If he fears any inherent power of disease to kill him he is not right. If he is even afraid to get his feet wet, he is not right.

Why Do the Good Suffer?

One of the questions which perplex mankind is this: "Why do people who have been good all their lives suffer so much? Why are they sick so much, when sinful people seem to prosper?" It is for the reason that, while they are good in some directions, they are wrong, and fatally wrong, in others. One of the most difficult patients to heal is the one who believes that God has brought sickness upon him for some good purpose, and has entered upon a sort of suicidal reconciliation to sickness and death, on the supposition that this is God's way of getting men into the joys of heaven.

It seems to be a common habit for clergymen to think that they have got to break down, or give out, or to suffer in some way, because of their occupation or form of life. But this is not from any law of Being which naturally afflicts them because they read the Bible, pray, study, think, or do anything else that is right to do, but it is because of the individual and collective fear and belief on this subject, which they can destroy when they learn how to do it.

Bible Teaching on Life and Destiny

The Holy Bible, which millions regard as containing the word of God to men, or at least a certain perception of the truth on the part of sacred writers, indicates that God ordained that man shall have dominion over all the earth. It declares that the human race has brought evil upon itself. It prophetically indicates that evil can and will be destroyed, and that the time will come when there shall be no more death, pain, sorrow, or crying.

God the Only Helper

It will be impossible for this millennial state to occur until all of these evils which now withhold it are abolished. Now can you in reason conceive of any influence that can possibly effect the needed change, except the government of God, of Intelligence, Truth, Good? Is there anything really available to men except the right knowledge of God and obedience to Him, whom to know aright is life eternal? Shall we look for any other panacea than that uttered by him whom all Christians have denominated as the "Saviour of the world," and who said, "Ye shall know the truth and the truth shall make you free."

The promises and prophecies are not a mockery, but they point to the salvation which this saving knowledge of the Truth will procure; and moreover, they do not point the sufferer to mindless drugs nor to a far-off and unavailing God, but to the resource, which, like the kingdom of heaven, is always within.

Our Saviour Is Within

My friends, Christian Science teaches that God has already done everything for man that he requires, and that we need only to lay hold upon the possibilities of life and find that in the Mind which was in Christ is health, life, prosperity, and dominion over evil, and to find that this Mind, this Saviour, is within consciousness. The Christian Scientist is gaining understanding which is power and an ever-present help. Under all circumstances he finds that it equips him the better to withstand evil and to manifest good, and to fulfill the utterance, "I can do all things through Christ which strengtheneth me."

Science Helps in All Affairs of Life

The practical influence of Christian Science does not stop at the reformation and healing of the sick and sinful, but extends itself into the every-day life and into all the affairs of busy men and women. It accomplishes for such people benefits that are as marked and as much needed as the cure of disease. The lives, efforts, pursuits, and achievements of them all, including artisan, farmer, teacher, merchant, clerk, housewife, and professional man are all hampered with fear, anxiety, and lack of confidence as well as by very many other evil influences which they do not understand. They often find that their best plans and wisest endeavors go amiss; unseen obstacles thwart them; inadequate results, disappointments, and failures prevail.

False Belief in Destiny

What is the matter with these people? You will find some who believe that all of the bitterness, trials, and failures of their careers are according to an inevitable or prearranged destiny.

The "Law" of Competition a Lie

You will find that professors of a speculative philosophy have formulated an ungodly theory that these people are engaged in a fratricidal and competitive struggle for the survival of the fittest, and that at the bottom of the entire social fabric is a law which provides that success is wholly contingent on the caprice of fortune, and that only those who can outdo or overwhelm others can succeed or have the right to exist. You will find, indeed, that nearly all men are joined in a monotonous reconciliation to evil and to a belief that its fierce despotism and procurements are resistless.

Science Available in Business

I would speak to those whose problems, day by day, seem as perplexing and urgent as though they were sick; to the people whose lot is already hard and who seem to be the prey of circumstances and difficult conditions. It may seem to you to be an unavailable declaration, but nevertheless, I am here to tell you that these evil conditions are not lawful, but are the results of abnormal causes which can be controlled. The same evil sense of life and the same defective philosophy of evil which have entailed sickness upon men, have likewise entailed discord upon all their affairs, and the same Science of Life which controls and corrects a man's body will also control his business.

Again I ask, "What is the difficulty?" It is that people do not understand what the trouble is, how to master it, or that they can master it through the power of Mind rightly directed. The dominion which was God-bestowed is the dominion of Mind over evil, and Christian Science is revealing this Mind to men. It is explaining the Science of Life. It is educating men to use the power of Good, and for good purposes, and, as a result, business men find that they have a larger control over their affairs. They can do business on a more satisfactory basis and with better results. They can do it without fear and anxiety. They can better learn how to deal with others, how to detect evil mental conditions, and how to better accomplish anything that it is right for them to do. The same is true with people in all other spheres of occupation. The teacher can do better; the farmer can do better; every one can do better.

Mrs. Eddy's Mission

Thirty years ago, Mrs. Eddy, whose entire previous life had especially fitted her for such a ministry, appeared in the very front of this religio-scientific age to fulfill a mission and declare a message which we consider was of divine impulsion, simply because we know that it is true, and because we know that, if true, it must have proceeded from God, who is all Truth.

The world, which is finally recognizing the great value of her mission and the beauty of her life, is acknowledging her service and fitness as the leader of a great religious movement, and bringing to pass a new truism—that in this day a prophet is with honor and respect in his own country.

More than thirty years ago, after being rescued at the last

moment from impending death, she knew that she had been healed by the revelation to her of what she afterwards proved to be Christian Science. Leaving all the old moorings in philosophy, materia medica, and scholastic theology, she stood absolutely alone as the only Christian Scientist on earth. Surmounting obstacles and opposition that were appalling, she has so impressed the truth of Christian Science on the world that there are now well toward two million believers who are witnesses to the cure of two million instances of disease.

Words of mine fail utterly to scale the lofty summit of her moral and spiritual culture, or indicate the exalted nature of her purpose and the wide range of its philanthropy.

God No Longer Unknown

In conclusion I say unto you that in Christian Science there is no longer an unknown God. No longer do the distorted graven images of human thought mask or hide from us the real God, who is altogether lovely, who is our Life, whose help is ever available, whose grace is sufficient, and who creates mar as the very manifestation of life and peace.

Promises of Christian Science

Christian Science promises to lead mankind to God through the highways of health and life, instead of death. It promises to naturally and willingly incline men to a more spiritual life which will satisfy them, and it promises that, as they wend their way to a sure heaven, this Christ-truth will be the Christ way-shower through all the mazes and besetments of evil sense and an evil age, until they shall, with undeviating trust and confidence, abide under the shadow of Him who has said, in the words of David:

"Because He hath set His love upon Me, therefore will I deliver him; I will set him on high, because he hath known My name. He shall call upon Me and I will answer him: I will be with him in trouble. I will deliver him and honor him. With long life will I satisfy him and show him My salvation."

WOULD YOU LIKE TO KNOW MORE ABOUT CHRISTIAN SCIENCE?

There exists today a vast treasury of works on Christian Science that is virtually unknown to the world. These writings have been accumulating since 1866, when Christian Science was first discovered by Mary Baker Eddy.

The Bookmark was established in 1980 to offer outstanding books and papers on Christian Science from the early days of the movement up through the present time. This literature includes works by Mrs. Eddy, the Discoverer and Founder of Christian Science, and those of her students. It also offers writings by contemporary Christian Scientists who are advancing scientifically in the same line of light. These writings adhere strictly to the teachings of Mrs. Eddy.

To learn more about Christian Science, send for a free Bookmark Price List which offers you a large selection of excellent papers and books on this Science -- many of them available only through The Bookmark.

You will find in these timeless writings spiritual enlightenment, inspiration and understanding. They explain how to heal through prayer alone, how to understand God, and how this closeness to Him brings health and happiness.

For your free Bookmark Price List write:

The Bookmark
Post Office Box 801143A
Santa Clarita, California 91380
United States of America

We look forward to hearing from you.

TOPICAL INDEX

A.

	PAGE
Ability and possession normally unlimited	310
Absolute good should be attributed to God	280
Acclimated, belief about being, handled	113
Activity	177
" and glorious progress	244
" in the truth	241
" of body normal and necessary	90
" of right ideas saves	123
" of spiritual understanding required	41
Affirm God and man	177
" perfect man	177
Affirmation not sufficient; denial necessary	52
Affirmations of Christian Science	25
Affirmative condition of thought	79
Advent of Christian Science	252
Adverse thought, handling	191
Advising others discouraged	76
Age	155
Aggregate of mortal thought acts as law	257
Agnostic and infidel	342
" and infidel converted	272
Ailments of mankind healed by spiritual conception of man	37
Alert scientist meets arguments	59
Alertness	242
All unlike God is harmful	261
Animal magnetism	154
" " annulled .106,	209
" " defined and explained	61
" " described	211
" " discussed	124
" " evil seen as, enables us to cope with it.	42
" " forms of	189
" " handled and destroyed .. 109, 184, 221, 224	

	PAGE
Animal magnetism, handling	118
" " how it reaches us	185
" " malicious	214
" " protection from	127
Animality classified	183
Annihilation does not occur	182
Antagonism, handling of	132
Antidote for argument of reversal	122
Anxiety	158
Apathy, treatment for	107
Appearance of error must disappear	38
Application, erroneous	176
" of science results in moral reform	271
Appreciation	179
Armor of God	143
Ascension	146, 177
Association, beneficial	204
Astrology	167, 172
Atheist, see Skeptic.	
Atonement of Christ, Christian Science does not deny	325
At-one-ment	130
Attacks not needed are not experienced	167, 172
Awake and working, let us be	241
"Awake to righteousness and sin not"	246

B.

	PAGE
Bacilli	141
Banish apathy	246
Basis of being is Mind, God	301
" of healing	189
Belief general, not personal	56
" in matter hinders treatment	72
" versus understanding	22
Beliefs, better	177
" not fundamentally personal	56
Better beliefs	146

365

TOPICAL INDEX

	PAGE
Benefits, the way in which they are derived	341
Beneficial association	204
Bible	135
" concessions	178
" interpretation	150, 179
" teaching on life and destiny	359
Bishop Morrison's opinion	342
Blame not others	245
Blasphemous mortuary resolutions	288
Blood, treatment to demonstrate perfect	111
Bodies many	148
Bodily activity normal and necessary	90
Body	139, 145, 146, 149, 151, 174
" and perfection	109
" as sacred as Mind	87
" consists of right ideas	88
" declare for eternal	89
" despising	177
" do not hate or deny any part of	88
" eternal	111
" in absence of mentality does not take cold	346
" is spiritual, knowledge of this overcomes the flesh	81
" learn and declare the truth about	87
" not to be condemned, but improved	86
" only one	88
" overcome material sense of by living, not by dying	89
" parts and functions of spiritual	180
" perfect	177
" spiritual	87
" the human, is a false belief about real body	86
" the real	132
" there is but one	44, 110
" treatment to demonstrate a perfect	110
Boils	174
Bondage destroyed by enlightened sense	350
Bravado	157
Burglar, how he should be treated	141
Business	138, 186

	PAGE
Business demonstration	155
" mesmerizing one's	63
" problem solved	62
" science available in	361
" success, treatment for	104
" treatment for	155
Busy, false argument of being	41

C.

Carnal mind, spurious law, satan, kills	288
Calm dominion	93
Cancer	138
Case, helping on	160
Cause and scientific cure of disease	339
" of Christian Science	49
" proof of an intelligent	231
Causation	153
" wholly mental	299
Caution with the Truth	98
Censoriousness condemned	118
"Chance" a misnomer	55
Changeless ethics	21
Chapman, the evangelist, scores Christian Science	313
Characters, good and bad	354
Charity in judgment commended	131
Chemicalization	141
Chief work of Christian Scientists	67
Child born, definition of	139
Children harmed by mothers' fears	265
" of Christian Science parents will improve the race	265
" treatment of	174
"Choose ye"	61, 242, 270, 302
Christ a saviour from sin	283
" abolishes the law of evil	289
" Christian Science not a denial of	275
" defined	282
" distinguished from Jesus	282
" evil destroyed through	328
" is your consciousness which heals	30
" Jesus enforced law	286
" mission of	320
" Peter's perception of	275
" teaching of Christian Science concerning	316
" the divinity of	320
" the mind of	321

TOPICAL INDEX

	PAGE
Christ, the only way	325
" the practical	71
" what think ye of?	274
" commands	326
Christian Science, affirmations of	25
" " appears	314
" " as a movement	49
" " attitude of	290
" " compasses destruction of fear	352
" " defined	19
" " demonstrably true	24
" " Difference between and other religions	344
" " discloses deliverance	260
" " discovers Truth and uncovers error	42
" " doctrines and works of	340
" " does not treat matter, but error	131
" " healing not mesmeric	348
" " infinite	254
" " in the world depends on Scientists	117
" " is the Christ-salvation	40
" " is working wonders	303
" " leaves nothing unexplained	354
" " misunderstood	21
" " not a denial of Christ	275
" " operative	40, 47
" " practice	43, 156
" " practice of defined	51, 57
" " prolongs human life	296
" " promises of	363
" " proves its worth	297
" " reconciles reason to God	276
" " significance of	27

	PAGE
Christian Science, spurious counterfeit of	51
" " sublimest of discoveries	252
" " the better way	293
" " the only sure antidote for materialism	301
" " the nature of	340
" " uncovers sin and its consequences	261
" " versus materia medica	289
" " what it is doing	69
" " why the name?	18
Christian Scientist, what constitutes a?	51
Christian Scientists, chief work of	67
" " duty of	49
" " genuine and spurious	182
" " not getting what they should	28
" " object of	241
" " unscientific	176
Christianity scientific	20
" what is it?	23
Christians, should they heal the sick?	326
Church quarrels	207
Churches, unity lacking in doctrines of	316
Claims not met	187
Claim of sickness, elements of a	56
Class instruction	175
" teaching	175
"Climbing up some other way" for healing	309
Clouds of fear lifted	349
" what causes mental, to disappear?	127
Coffee	146, 177
Cold, what is it to take?	346
Commission from God to you to heal	29
Compensation, practitioners deserve	98
Competition, the law of, is a lie	361
Conception, immaculate	109, 119, 326
" mortal and immaculate	184
" my immaculate	111

	PAGE
Concessions	146
" in Bible and Science and Health	178
Condemnation	159
" cannot argue....	110
" don't practice...	68
" is from the devil; salvation from God. Don't imitate the devil....	84
" mortal ordinance of must be met..	81
" of sinner to be avoided	84
Condemnations, Scriptural.....	135
Confidences	175
Confidence plus understanding equals mastery	33
" requisite	191
" versus discouragement	46
Conflict of creeds.............	314
Consciousness	147
" one	147
" of God is your own self	35
" proper government of	269
" which heals is Christ	30
Consequences, belief of, dealt with	128
Contagious disease............	157
Contamination, **depressing effect** of believing in hereditary	307
Continuity not in evil..........	106
Conversion of infidel and agnostic	272
Cosmic nature of error.........	61
Courageous, be...............	121
Courtship period, diseases peculiar to....................	167
Creator, see God.	
" must be intelligent....	277
Creeds	151, 155
" conflict of............	314
Crimes of ecclesiasticism.......	314
Criticism condemned...........	118
" repress	69
Criticisms of "Science and Health" baseless and futile..	270
Crucifixion, lesson of..........	126
Culture	102
Curability of all disease........	284
Curtain lecture...............	27

D.

	PAGE
Darkened consciousness........	139
Dead man, what constitutes a...	151
Death, cause of...............	189
" handling of...........	136
" not by divine law.......	287
" of a Scientist, what shall we think about it?......	217
" prevention of..........	189
" there is none..........	102
Declare truth specifically and actively	128
Declaration	177
" an important.......	129
Declarations for truth..........	104
" of truth are the enforcement of law..	108
" useful	115
Decrepitude and decadence exposed	350
Defamation and slander annulled	249
Definition of Christian Science.	19
" of Christian Science practice	51
Deity is the one conscious intelligent cause..............	277
" of Jesus denied..........	281
" See God.	
Delay unnecessary.............	175
Deliverer, The only is love......	117
Demonstrable character of Christian Science......	24
" understanding yours	27
Demonstration	138
" defined	128
Denial......................	114
" and affirmation both necessary	52
Denominational beliefs.........	23
Deny not your Saviour.........	33
Depression handled............	113
" is sin..............	121
" treatment for......	186
Desire, right.................	130
Despise not your youth in Science	35
Destiny, Bible teaching on.....	359
" false belief in.........	361
Destroying beliefs is correct treatment	37
Devil and fear largely synonymous	279
" condemns; God saves. Don't imitate the devil..	84
" how regarded...........	58

TOPICAL INDEX

	PAGE
Devil, the arch-hypnotist	120
" wiles of	59
Diagnosis	157
Directions for mental work	103
" for Scientists	106
" for treating	207
" for working	205
Disease, a general treatment for	112
" and sin not, fundamentally, personal beliefs	45
" all manner of, healed	271
" brought about by wrong thought	256
" healed by the removal of sin	262
" illegitimate	285
" is an abnormity	284
" is but belief	44
" men can successfully cope with	345
" mental origin of not incredible	256
" needful to know name of?	157
" not incurable	349
" not fundamentally a personal belief	56
" of mental origin	345
" primary cause of not cognized by materia medica	291
" See illness.	
" seat of	183
" the cause and scientific cure of	339
" the causes of	344
" the effect of mesmerism	347
Diseases all healed by cancellation of spurious conditions	309
Discouragement dealt with...46, 130,	185
" source of	59
Discovery, the great	62
Displacement, there can be none	111
Dispositions transformed	309
Divided primal cause is impossible	232
Divine Love is the only power	73
Divinity of Christ	320
Doctrines of churches, unity lacking in	316
Dominion, calm	93
" how gained	183
" is yours for the learning of it	310

	PAGE
Dominion is your right, your ability	237
" lay hold upon your God-given	280
" no limit to your	101
" our God-given	234
" right knowledge of God includes	280
" the right way to	310
" the source of	243
" through Mind	235
Door of receptivity closed by evil in ourselves	66
Doubt, how it is dispelled	55
" of the efficacy of treatment, occasion of.....36,	57
Dream, unfavorable	147
Dreamer, awaken the	125
Drug and liquor habits healed	271
Drugs	159
Duality 135,	151
Duty of Christian Scientists	49
Dwell in highest thought and feeling	100
Dying man, recovery of	180
" student healed	65

E.

Ecclesiasticism, crimes of	314
Eddy (Mrs.) solves cases with love	144
Eddy's (Mrs.), answer to slander	297
" " discovery of Christian Science is established	253
" " great work	339
" " mission	362
" " practice consistent	254
Education 102,	178
" gain, the demand of Science	78
Effect of false doctrine	24
Efficacy of treatment, why doubted?	36
Efficiency, treatment for	120
Effort, no good is lost	101
Elements of a claim of sickness	56
Elimination, belief of faulty, handled	127
" of impurity and discord	112

	PAGE
Elimination proper, the secret of health	90
" treatment for	90
Embodiment	177
Emmanuel	51
Emotionalism	135
Employment, how it is often secured	305
Encourage and stimulate good in others	68
Enforcement and protection of treatment	105
" of law	234
" of treatment	126
Enlightenment is the right of the sinner	83
Error	154
" analyzed	162
" appears but to disappear	38
" cannot give itself up	79
" clinging to truth saves from	118
" cosmic, general, not personal	61
" destroyed by love	117
" do not listen to pleas of	66
" how handled?	53
" impersonalize	165
" keep ahead of	106
" let not thought be engaged with unnecessarily	121
" nature of	58
" not overlooked	117
" overcome by truth	80
" recognition of necessary	52
" segregations of handled	190
" separate from person	74
" uncovered	95
" uncovered by Christian Science	42
" varieties of	186
Essentials for good work	44
Eternal body	111
" life, attaining	178
Eternity	136
Ethics changeless, when right	21
Etiquette, professional	175
Evasion of life's problem is impossible	244
Evil acts as though intelligent	58
" Christ abolishes the law of	289
" destroyed through Christ	328
" do not claim it as yours	64
" in false belief, not in matter	57

	PAGE
Evil in ourselves closes the door of receptivity	66
" nature and action of uncovered	124
" no continuity to	106
" not known to God	232
" origin of	150
" resistance to, important	60
" seen as animal magnetism more readily destroyed	42
" thought, distorting face, can distort liver	354
" the mystery of cleared	357
" treatment a law of destruction to	56
" unity of	139
Eve, the mistake of	184
Everlasting punishment	151
Evolution, fallacy of exposed	301
Excuses made by Scientists	29
Executive, you are an	119
Exercise	170, 177
" normal and necessary	90, 170, 177
Existence, mystery of, solved	57
" of God proven	231
Expectancy without measure is rational	312
Expectation	136, 178
" of good	188
Experience, words spoken from	18
Externalizing of thought	126
Extinction the fact, if materialism were true	300
Eye lost	146
" troubles, treatment for	130, 181

F.

	PAGE
Fable of the traveler and the plague	263
Faith	199
" is active, not passive	129
" necessary	53
Failures	152, 155
False doctrine, effect of	24
" practice	180
" security	248
" sense of what heals	29
" theology	146
" views	35
Falsehood exposed	315
Falsehoods denied	127
" scientifically handled	248

Fear 130, 173	Fear shown to result from man-made standards........... 334
" effects of uncovered and destroyed 262	" springs from a false sense of God................... 332
" and responsibility laid off by practitioner........... 32	" vanishes as you oppose it with knowledge.......... 334
" and the devil largely synonymous 279	" vanishes when we understand our rights.......... 335
" arises from a wrong sense of that which is right.... 333	" victimizes, God saves, humanity 336
" assurance of the needlessness of................. 350	" victory over.............. 330
" breeds self-condemnation, remorse. They are useless 336	Feathers, woman with a belief of........................71, 285
" cast out by knowledge of God's nature and purpose 333	Female trouble................ 157
" cast out by gaining dominion 332	Fever cured by eliminating fear 287
	" man sick with........... 286
" clouds of lifted........... 349	Fidelity of great religious leaders 27
" destroyed by the demonstration of Truth......... 338	Finger healed................. 141
" disappears as you understand Science............ 352	Food, fear of.................. 295
	Foolishness 158
" education in denounced.... 294	Force not what you have not demonstrated 91
" eliminated by seriously taking God as omnipotent good 337	Forgetfulness, treatment for.... 107
	Franklin's prophecy........... 272
" falsely regarded as good... 331	Freedom in religion, the right to. 341
" how to meet............. 208	Fruits of scientific living....... 246
" influence of on the body... 350	" of sectarianism.......... 23
" is never your fear. Don't claim it................. 337	" of the discovery of Christian Science............. 253
" is the chief enemy........ 234	Fully persuaded in your own integrity and rights............ 101
" is wholly an abomination and a monstrosity........ 331	
" legitimate to use medical opinions to allay.......... 181	**G.**
" teachings of the Bible against 352	Gain is your right............. 108
	Generation 148
" tension induced by, overcome 235	Germs 141, 169
" the cause and prevalence of 346	God 141
" the result of false education 330	" a more correct sense of.... 267
	" and man..........15, 110, 163
" the result of ignorance of humanity's normal rights. 331	" another definition of...... 318
	" answers prayer............ 123
" of food................. 295	" -consciousness is your only self 35
" of God exposed........... 278	" described 277, 317
" of malpractice exposed.... 95	" desire for a personal...... 71
" only to commit sin........ 264	" false sense of............. 181
" penalty, suffering and God are polar opposites....... 385	" fear of exposed........... 278
	" how known?...50, 128, 136, 177
" resisted and canceled, healing follows............... 336	" is changeless good......... 319
	" is Life, Truth, Love....... 318
" Scientists gradually cease from 295	" is Mind.................. 268
	" is omnipresence and omnipotence 318

	PAGE
God is Principle	268
" is unadulterated good	278
" manifested through idea	50
" misconceptions of	342
" nature of	50
" nature of described	343
" neither is evil, uses evil, nor knows evil	232
" no longer unknown	363
" now knowable	258
" our helper	241
" potentizes His ideas	232
" price of help from	68
" proof of the existence and nature of	231
" -reliance	203
" Scientists have faith in	294
" see Creator.	
" see Deity.	
" take your troubles to	116
" the great gift of	196
" the only Healer.....30, 73,	360
" the principle of healing	357
" the Redeemer	343
" transcends description	319
" treatment is the manifestation of	95
" versus evil	319
" what is?	317
" with us.................103,	189
" working with us	199
God's commission to you to heal.	29
" government is my government	246
" law is perfection	279
" laws infinitely natural	20
" power ours	54
Golden rule	68
Good and evil thought externalizes itself	257
" every, is yours now	99
" for you is the law of God	42
" in others, Encourage and stimulate	68
" intentions not sufficient	22
" our highest is love	118
" see and cultivate	132
" treatment for realization of.	100
" why do they suffer	359
" work, Essentials for	44
Government by law	55
" good and bad	242
Grace from God is sufficient	33
Great discovery	62
" gift of God	195

	PAGE
Greenback; wart; blood	145
Growth of a Scientist	34

H.

Handling adverse thought	191
" animal magnetism	118
" error	53
" malpractice 100,	113
" malpractice as impersonal	74
" mortal mind beliefs	147
Happiness	135
" a duty	121
Hard problems force progress	246
Harmful effects of talk about disease	266
Hatred and resentment chief obstacles	248
" how dealt with	47
" overcome with love	296
Healed, why may one expect to be?	342
"Healer," do not use term, say "practitioner"	181
Healer, God is the only	30
" is God	73
" is the Christ-consciousness	30
Healing accomplished by spiritual conception of man	37
" agent not understood by some	29
" basis of	189
" faith is active reliance upon God	129
" hindered by waywardness	245
" hindrance to	67
" how to know when it is accomplished	37
" not a person, but destroying beliefs	31
" not in but from the flesh.	80
" of Mr. Kimball	18
" power not a personal sense	32
" Requisites for	135
" the problem of is mental.	36
Health, demonstration of	104
"Heal the Sick," the command	28
Health-laws, the less, the healthier children	265
Health, the secret of, proper elimination	90
Hearing	149

TOPICAL INDEX

	PAGE
Heart	138, 139, 158
" disease	158
" treatment for	181
Help from God, Price of	68
" when entitled to	203
Helping on a case	160
Hereditary endowment really transmitted by God	311
" influences scientifically abolished	308
Heredity	140, 142, 162, 165
" belief of, scientifically dealt with	127
" no actual law, but a lie posing as law	307
" none but good	239
" the depressing effect of belief in	307
Hindrance to healing	67
" to receptivity by human will	116
Home, mental protection for	122
Hope is in God only	267
Horoscope	172
How God is known	50
Human body, a false belief about body	86
" life prolonged by Science	296
" love	132
" philosophy false	236
" powers purified and strengthened	272
" problem, A great	69
" thought not original	60
Humanity, Needs of	25
Humanity's need of a saviour	322
" normal rights and powers	299
Humans	142
" are not originators of either truth or error	41
Humility, false	94
Hunger for knowledge	250
Hypnotism	172, 185
" opposite to Christian Science	348
" the devil's method of working	120

I.

"I am God," the healer	31
Idea manifests God	50
" the spiritual	40
Ideas	172

	PAGE
Ideas and symbols, Seen and unseen	145
Ignorance must be corrected	52
" Treatment for	107
Illness, See disease.	
" Cause of is mental	292
Illustration of method of treatment	38
Immaculate conception	109, 111, 119, 326
Immaturity should be scientifically denied	248
Immortality	137
Impenetrability	149
Impersonal handling of malpractice	74
" sense gained	77
" treatment	152, 156, 157, 160, 187
Impersonalize error	165
Imposition of fear cast out	338
Improvement is your right	108
Impulsion, Divine	128
Impurity eliminated	112
Impute not sin	73
Inactivity	176
" Refrain from it	91
Incurable disease does not exist	349
Individual completeness	111
" demonstration to be respected	76
Individuality	102, 128, 138, 156, 169
Infidel, See "skeptic" and "atheist."	
" and agnostic converted	272
Insanity	173
Insomnia	164, 182
Instant denial and affirmation	38
Instant in the Truth	186
"Instant in season, out of season"	61
Insects	141
Instantaneous understanding	175
Instructive religion	50
Intentions not sufficient	22
Intuition	199
Invalid, The first step with an	357
Invariability of law	21
Invention	143
Invisible, both power and law are	302
Ivy, poison	173

J.

Jesus Christ	151
" Demonstrations of	150

TOPICAL INDEX

Jesus distinguished from Christ. 282
" The claim that he was God. 281
Judgment, Charity in, commended 131

K.

Keynote incident 274
Kimball's experience with Science 351
"   healing 18, 159
"   teaching absolute
              Science 175
Kimball replies to Chapman..... 313
Kingdom of heaven within...... 142
Knowing 138
"   evil 143
Knowledge of God, Starting
              point for, is that you
              are conscious 231
"   of Science confers
              power 358
"   that body is spiritual overcomes flesh.. 81

L.

Law 114
" 140
" 142
" 160
" 170
" and opportunity 109
" and power through right
    thought 94
" Christ enforces against spurious law 239
" enforcement, another illustration of 304
" enforcement of............ 234
" enforcement of, illustrated. 304
" fulfilled, not abolished, by
    Christ Jesus 308
" Government by 55
" invariable 21
" is all in your favor........ 303
" Nature of 19
" of God is the law of your
    good 42
" of Mind and its results.... 111
" of success 305
" suit 176
" The counterfeit of......... 238
" The real significance of.... 303
" What is 238
"Law of the spirit of life" sets
    free 351
Laws of God infinitely natural.. 20

Lay hold upon your God-given dominion 280
Leaders, Fidelity of religious.... 27
Letter, An open 203
"   to a patient............. 205
Life 149
" claim it as yours.......... 65
" defined 180
" eternal 177
" without love impossible..... 70
Life's problem, Evasion impossible 244
Lifted up 152
Limitation is abnormal 305
"   is mesmerism 115
Limited opportunity, belief in exposed 85
Liquor and drug habits healed... 271
Listen not to pleas of error...... 66
Liver distorted by evil thought... 354
Lonesomeness 188
Loss of good effort impossible... 101
Love and uncovering error...... 47
"   Human 132, 146
"   Learn to 69
"   minds its own business..... 118
"   No life without........... 70
"   the only solvent........... 117
"   Our highest good.......... 118
"   Science of, the greatest need 131
"   The great accomplishment.. 116
"   versus hatred 47

M.

Malaria 162
Malicious animal magnetism.214, 218
"   animal magnetism annulled 106
"   mental malpractice annulled 247
"   mesmerism annulled... 123
Malpractice 114, 140, 142, 158
          ..165, 171, 173, 174, 177
"   defined 176
"   Do not handle it as
        personal 210
"   Fear of exposed.... 95
"   Handled as impersonal 74
"   Handling 100, 113
"   illustrated 187
"   met 88
"   not on yourself..... 96
"   Treatment for
        ....96, 103,188

TOPICAL INDEX

	PAGE
Man	137, 148, 164, 170
" is activity	168
" Spiritual conception of, heals mankind	37
" the perfect reflection of God	110
" The real	132
" There is but one	110
Man's relation to God	15
Manifestation	177
Manifestations of mortal mind are sin and matter	82
Manifesting body	163
Manipulation	171
Mary and her conception	184
Masters, We must be	243
Mastery through understanding plus confidence	33
Material theories and treatment reversed	263
" things are false concepts of spiritual ideas	43
" remedies	159
Materialism, Christian Science the only sure antidote for	301
" if true, means extinction of life	300
" presents but a hypothetical, and therefore a mental cause	299
" Proof that it implies extinction	300
Materia medica does not cognize primary cause of disease	291
" " not a science	290
" " versus Christian Science	289
" Medica's declarations, Result of	176
Matter	139, 148, 160
" falsely regarded as a cause	345
" a manifestation of mortal mind	82
Meaning of Science	19
Meat eating	169
Medical guess work	291
" opinions, legitimate to use, to allay fear	181
Medicine	159
Meeting malpractice	88
"	18

	PAGE
Memory, Loss of, treatment for	107
Men, The relation of to God	318
Mental attack, Handled	122
" " How to meet a	60
" " on Scientists	60
" cause of disease	292
" contagion, People expose themselves to	266
" malpractice	168
" origin of disease	345
" origin of disease not incredible	256
" work, Directions for	103
" " General	188
" wickedness dealt with	218
Mesmerism, be not deceived by	242
" handled	123
" lifted	64
" The range of	347
" uncovered and handled	46
Mesmerizing one's business	63
Method of treatment illustrated	38
Microbes	141, 169
Mind all-inclusive	116
" and body	179
" and matter	180
" and thought, Science of	255
" God, is the basis of being	301
" heals disease	256
" Law of, and its results	111
"Mind, not matter"	270
Mind of Christ	321
" the remedy for sin and disease	357
Minds many	148
Ministers	155
Misconceptions of God	342
Misrepresenting	145
Mission of Christ	320
" of the Saviour	321
Misunderstandings of Christian Science	21
Moral reform results from the application of Science	271
Morality alone is not righteousness	359
Mortal man, Human belief, versus man, divine consciousness	269
" mind	147
" " A handling of	185
" " a liar	183
" " one	143

376 TOPICAL INDEX

	PAGE
Mortal law, Not personal belief, must be destroyed	74
Mortals	148
" have been resigned to misery	259
Mother-in-law	164
Mother's fears baseless and harmful to children	265
Mortuary resolutions blasphemous	288
Moses and the law	184
Movement of Christian Science	49
Mrs. Eddy's answer to slander	297
" " discovery of Christian Science is established	253
" " great work	339
" " mission	362
" " practice consistent	254
Music	149
Mystery of evil cleared	357
" of existence, How solved	57

N.

Name of disease	157
Names of patients, Necessary to know?	156
Nature of Christian Science	340
" of error	58
" of God	50
" of Law	19
Natural character of God's laws	20
Need, Every legitimate, already provided for	102
Need is salvation, not punishment	82
Needs of humanity	25
Neighbor	144
Nerves	188
Nerve troubles handled	119
No varieties of doctrine	252
Noah and the ark	184
Now, everything exists	119
" is every good yours	99

O.

Object of Christian Scientists	241
Objects of sense, Replace with spiritual ideas	92
Objections considered	268
Obstacles scientifically denied	247
Obstetrics	149
Occultism	185

	PAGE
Old age bugaboo	350
" methods, Science reverses	78
" theology, Renunciation demanded by	78
Omnipresence	138
One body	88, 110, 144
" man	110, 144, 147, 211
" Mind	138
" " is mine	180
" " is the Saviour	40
" mortal mind	143
Oneness	151
One perfect body	44
Operative Christian Science	40, 239
Operative Christian Science is the thought and feeling of Christian Scientists	47
Operative Christian Science is no better than Scientists	117
Opportunity	109
" Door of never closed	85
" Never too late	85
" Right idea of, makes for receptivity	86
Ordination, Yours	235
Organs and functions, Treatment for	189
Origin of evil	150, 168
" of Truth or error not in mankind	41
Other gods	151
Others not overzealous in instructing	98
Overcome material sense of body by living, not dying	89
Overcoming error with truth	80
" fear heals	345
Overtaxing strength not to be feared	65
Own business, Love minds its	118

P.

Pain	188
" Method of dealing with	247
" Treatment for	130
Palmistry	167
Parasites	169
"Passing Out," There is none	102
Patience	135, 142
Patient, How know when he is healed?	37
" There is no personal	93
Patients, Instruct them	181
Peace of God needed in treatment	107

TOPICAL INDEX

	PAGE
Penalty	178
" and pushishment not of God's ordering	81
" Illegitimacy of demonstrated	84
" not ordained by God	108
Perfection is the law of God	279
" Practitioner must be conscious of	37
Persistence	187
" in treatment	187
Persistency in working	120
Persistent effort commended	75
Person not treated, but beliefs destroyed	31
Personal application	352
" God, Desire for	71
" sense of healing power falacious	32
" treatment	157
Pessimism	137
Pests	141
Peter's perception of Christ	275
Philosophy, False	344
" Vain	284
Pleas of error, do not listen to	66
Plurisy	188
Pneumogastric nerve	173, 182
Poison	174
Poison Ivy	173
" Treatment for	107, 188
Poisonous secretions, Belief of handled	113
Possession and ability normally unlimited	310
" The divine law of	306
Poverty	137
" is mesmerism	115
Power	142
" and law are invisible	302
" divine Love is the only	73
" exhibited in Christian Science treatment	302
" Reality of spiritual	54
" Receptivity the condition of	66
" to heal, No personal sense of	32
" to remove mountains of obstacles is normal	311
Practical Christ	71
Practice of Christian Science	43
" of Christian Science defined	51, 57
" what you know	34

	PAGE
Practitioner	140
" Correct attitude for	32
" lays off responsibility and fear	32
" More than one?	160
" must be conscious of perfection only	37
" The progressive	77
Practitioners deserve compensation	98
Prayer	127
" God answers	123
Preaching the gospel heals the sick	307
Present salvation possible	240
Price of help from God	68
Primal cause	236
Principle	139
" unchangeable	21
Problem, A great human	69
" of healing is mental	36
Professional etiquette	175
Progress forced by hard problems	246
" Glorious	244
" in discovery	250
" in understanding and discovery expected by Mrs. Eddy	77
Progression	105
Promises of Christian Science	363
Proof by works	20
Proofs given by Christ Jesus	327
Prophets	184
Protection of treatment	105, 126
" Treatment for	100, 120
Prudery	146
Punishment	178
" and penalty not of God's ordering	81
" Everlasting	151
" Illegitimacy of demonstrated	84
" not needed, but salvation	82
Pure unaffected by impurity	183
Purity	130, 146

Q.

Quarrels in the church	207
"Quenching fiery darts of the wicked"	224
Questions	176

TOPICAL INDEX

R.

	PAGE
Race improvement	165
Racial bondage	356
Radical changes necessary	259
Rain	163
Rats	141
Reality, Vivid sense of needful	44
Realization	154
" darkened	139
" of good, Treatment for	100
Reason reconciled to God by Christian Science	276
Receptivity	178
" of good hindered by human will	116
" the condition of power	66
" Right idea of opportunity makes for	86
Recognition of need makes ready to receive Truth	251
Recovery is the only law for the sick	233
Redeemer, I know that my, liveth	298
Redemption, We should be agents of	110
Reflection	150
"	179
" of God must be kept unclouded	76
Reformation	136
Reform brought about by application of Science	271
" of sinners the fundamental aim of Science	264
Rejection and triumph of Truth	250
Rejoice in your understanding	39
Relapse, Argument against	105
" Handling argument of	191
" Mortal law of must be handled	74
Relapses	171
Relative statements in Science and Health	78
Reliance upon God	203
Religion, Instructive	50
Religious aspect of Science	22
" leaders faithful	27
Remedy for sin and disease is Mind	357
Remedies, Material	159
Remorse useless	336
Remuneration	175
Renunciation not required	108

	PAGE
"Renunciation," The demand of old theology	78
"Replace objects of sense with spiritual ideas"	92
Repetitions, No vain	108
Repose	176
Repress criticism	69
Reprisals not made by Scientists	316
Resignation to evil bad practice	259
Resistance to evil important	60
Responsibility and fear laid off by practitioner	32
Results of good and bad thought	255
Resume	173
Resurrection, Lesson of	126
Revelation	179
Revelation, The	179
Reversal	171
" Seeming law of should be met	122
" Treatment for belief of	107
Revolutionary effect of discovery	250
Right ideas	178
" " Body consists of	88
" idea destroys false belief	243
" " is our Saviour	243
" ideas, When active, save	123
" knowledge of God includes knowledge of dominion	280
" thought is law and power	94
" " must externalize itself	126
" to gain, unfoldment, improvement is yours	108
" way to dominion	310
Righteousness more than morality	359
Rise in the strength of Spirit	197

S.

	PAGE
Sabbath Day	143
Salvation	102
" by changed thought	257
" Declare the necessity and presence of	83
" From what do men need saving?	283
" is Christian Science	40
" to be complete	322
" through mental activity	190
" Where found?	26
" without knowledge of Principle impossible	258

TOPICAL INDEX

	PAGE
Sanitation, Mental, needed more than physical	266
Saved from what?	322
Saviour, A competent	237
" Do not deny	33
" Humanity's need of	322
" is the one Mind	40
" is the right idea	243
" is within	360
" What is the	51
" What is your	64
Saviour's mission	321
Scarlet fever	157
Scholastic theology	146
Science and Health, Concessions	178
"Science and Health," Criticisms of, baseless and futile	270
Science and Health, Relative statements in	78
Science	199
" Application of results in moral reform	271
" Demand of is education, Gain	78
" casts out fear	264
" called "Christian"	19
" heals by removing mental cause	355
" helps in all affairs of life	361
" Nature of	18
" of life needed	251
" Meaning of	19
" of Mind and thought	250
" Religious aspect of	22
" reverses old methods	78
Scientific Christianity	20
Scientist, Growth of a	34
Scientists and child-bearing	189
" are responsible for continuance of Christian Science in the world	117
" hinder their work	72
" learn to overcome hatred with love	296
" make excuses	29
" Mental attack on	60
" Practical directions for	106
" Shortcomings of	28
" too wise to repine	315
Scriptural condemnations	135
" proof	358
Secrecy	175

	PAGE
Secretion, Belief of faulty, handled	127
Sectarianism	313
" considered	275
Segregations of error handled	190
Self-condemnation useless	336
Self not dual	51
Self-condemnation	136
" should be avoided	131
Self-depreciation	130, 158
" bad	94
Self-righteousness exposed	75
Self-treatment	102
Self, Your real, is consciousness of God	35
Self-will	130
Sectarian differences	315
Sectarianism and its fruits	23
Sensuality, Don't charge everything to	154
Separate error from person	74
Separation, There is none	122
Serious case	136
Sex	148
" disease	163
Sexual poison	188
Shortcomings of Scientists	28
Sick, Recovery is the only law for	233
" What should be comprehended by	344
Sick yourself, Should you treat another?	30
Sickness and suffering unreal	356
" not because of law	238
" regarded as real	71
Sickness, Spiritual healing of denied by theology	283
Significance of Christian Science	27
Sin	159
" Christ a saviour from	283
" Christian Science teaching concerning	323
" Differing views of its nature	325
" Do not impute	73
" fundamentally cosmic, not personal	183
" Handling of	137
" is all that is unlike God	323
" thought before it is action	255
" legitimate wage is not death	82
" matter, manifestations of mortal mind	82
" Mrs. Eddy's teaching about	324

TOPICAL INDEX

	PAGE
Sin, must be healed to remove disease	262
" Need and means of salvation from	324
" needs not suffering but application of Truth	83
" not fundamentally personal	45
" responsible for all disease	353
" The fundamental nature of	260
" The nature of	323
" the proper sequence of is salvation, not condemnation	84
" Unreality of no excuse for license	324
" versus man	131
" Wages of, is learning right ideas	178
" Why it is unreal	355
Sinner, Best procedure for	183
" entitled, not to death, but to enlightenment	83
Skeptic, See Atheist.	
" What he must concede	276
Slander annulled	249
" Mrs. Eddy's answer to	297
Sleeplessness	164
" Treatment for	182
Solar plexus spoken of	119
Space	137
Solvent, the only is Love	117
Specific causes	153
" declaration of truth	128
Spirit, Rise in the strength of	197
Spiritual body, Parts and functions of	180
" body	87
" body unpicturable	180
" conception of man heals mankind's ailments	37
" idea	40
Spiritualism	167, 184
Spiritual power, Realty of	54
" understanding must be active	41
Spiritualization	158
Spurious Christian Science	51
" mortal law limits	305
Stagnation scientifically impossible	247
Stagnation. Spiritual activity not manifest in physical stagnation	92
Stepping stones to higher things	190
Stomach trouble	348
Strength, No fear of overtaxing	65

	PAGE
Subconsciousness	183
Sub-conscious mind	162
Success	102
" No limit to your	101
" The law of	305
" through being courageous	121
" Treatment for	104
Suffering	178
" Even for sin, not to be mentally enforced	187
" No transference of	107
" not a remedy or a saviour	80
" not from God	335
" not necessary, even for sin	83
" not required	108
" Why is it experienced?	261
" unnecessary	80
Sufficiency of grace from God	33
Suggestion	156
Sunday	143
Supersensible capacity	236
Supply	137, 138, 178
" for every legitimate need or want already exists	102
" not lacking, but understanding lacking	233
" not limited to one channel	99
" Talk on	201
" Treatment for	99
Symbols and ideas	145

T.

	PAGE
Talk about disease, Harmful effects of	266
Talking	145
" Wisdom in	175
Tea	177
Teachers, Other	175
Teach patients	181
Teaching	169
Ten Commandments	142
Tension induced by fear overcome	235
Tests	139
The Board of Lectureshi.	340
The devil, Wiles of	75
Theology	146
" and practice of Christian Science	329
" denies that Christ is a saviour from sickness	283
" of Christian Science	319
" True and false	29

TOPICAL INDEX

	PAGE
Theosophy	185
Things resolved into thoughts	43
Thought primary in all activity	255
"Thy will be done", interpreted	39
Time	137
" is a falsehood	120
Transference of suffering impossible	107
Transitional state	168
Transportation	138
Treat against mortal law, not personal belief	74
" until you annihilate fear	130
Treating 142-143-144-145-147	
" Directions for	207
Treatment 88-109-152-153-154-155-156-158-160	
" 163-164-165-169-170-172 173-177	
" against ignorance, apathy and forgetfulness	107
" A good one described	105
" Basis of	113
" Belief in matter hinders	72
" Co-operative	174
" deals with false beliefs, not persons	92
" defined	53-112
" described	128
" Directions for	104
" enforcement and protection of	126
" entitled to the power of God	45
" False sense of	72
" Faulty, described and corrected	129
" for argument of reversal	122
" " business success	104
" " efficiency and protection	120
" " eyes	181
" " eye troubles	130
" " heart	181
" " malpractice	96-103
" " nervous diseases	119
" " organs and functions	189
" " pain	130
" " poison	107-174
" " protection	100
" " realization of good	100
" " supply	99

	PAGE
Treatment, Fundamental points in	114
" General, for a claim of disease	112
" Impersonal	152-160-187
" is law	56
" " the manifestation of God	95
" law of destruction to evil	56
" Method of illustrated	38
" Most important point in	58
" must be law	94
" " know that it is God manifest	125
" Nature of	181
" necessary elements of	53
" Needful power in	73
" occasion of doubt in the efficacy of	36
" of a treatment	209
" " others by a Scientist under a claim	30
" Peace of God needed in	107
" Persistence in	187
" Point in	183-186-187-188
" Power exhibited in	302
" Protection of	105
" requisite for	103
" should be all-power	55
" to demonstrate perfect body	110
" What is a?	93
" " occasions doubt in?	57
" " you are to handle in	124
" Wrong	140
Troubles, Take them to God	116
Trust is active, not passive, reliance upon God	129
Truth, Caution with	98
" Declarations of	104
" How learned	168
" of being now knowable	258
" overcomes error	80
" Power of	137

U.

Unchangeable Principle	21
Uncovering and handling mesmerism	46
" error	42, 95, 138, 191
" of evil	124
" error through Love	47

	PAGE
Unfoldment is your right	108
Understanding bestowed upon you	27
" Do not deny or doubt your	115
" plus confidence equals mastery	33
" Rejoice in your	39
" versus belief	22
Unity lacking in doctrines of churches	316
Universe as effect implies cause	299
Universality	105
Unknown, God is no longer	363
Unlimited ability and possession is normal	310
Unreality of sickness and suffering	356
Unscientific Christian Scientists	176
Unselfishness, Result of	182
Urging	152
Useful declarations	115

V.

Vain philosophy	284
" repetitions	108
Victory is your normal right	312
Victory over fear	330
Voicing error	203

W.

Wages of Sin	142
"Wages of sin" not legitimately death	82
Wake up	242
Wash your mentality before you wash your hands	245
Wasting	141
Watching, Necessity of	67
Way through Christ	293

	PAGE
Waywardness, Banish it, to make room for healing	245
Weather	163
What to handle	62
Why do the good suffer?	359
" does the sinner suffer?	261
Wiles of the devil	59, 75, 221
Will hinders our receptivity of good	116
" power	158
" " Do not try to force results by	91
Within is our Saviour	360
Wisdom in talking	175
Words spoken from experience	18
Work, See "Treatment."	
" more for truth and good	79
Workers, An address to	98
Working, Directions for	205
Works, Proof by	20
Worth of Christian Science proven	297
Wrong method employed for cure	349
" thinking	176
" thought the procurer of disease	256

Y.

Your good is the law of God	42
Yourself, Do not malpractice on	96
" Hold correct sense of	190
" sick, should you treat another?	30
Youth in Science not to be despised	35

Z.

Zealous, Be not excessively	98